International Human Resource Management

International Human Resource Management

A case study approach

Daniel Wintersberger

KoganPage

Publisher's note
Every possible effort has been made to ensure that the information contained in this book is accurate at the time of going to press, and the publishers and author cannot accept responsibility for any errors or omissions, however caused. No responsibility for loss or damage occasioned to any person acting, or refraining from action, as a result of the material in this publication can be accepted by the editor, the publisher or the author.

First published in Great Britain and the United States in 2017 by Kogan Page Limited

2nd Floor, 45 Gee Street	c/o Martin P Hill Consulting	4737/23 Ansari Road
London	122 W 27th Street	Daryaganj
EC1V 3RS	New York, NY 10001	New Delhi 110002
United Kingdom	USA	India

© Daniel Wintersberger 2017

The right of Daniel Wintersberger to be identified as the author of this work has been asserted by him in accordance with the Copyright, Designs and Patents Act 1988.

ISBN   978 0 7494 8098 1
E-ISBN   978 0 7494 8099 8

British Library Cataloguing-in-Publication Data

A CIP record for this book is available from the British Library.

Typeset by Integra Software Services, Pondicherry
Print production managed by Jellyfish
Printed and bound in Great Britain by CPI Group (UK) Ltd, Croydon CR0 4YY

CONTENTS

Contributors x

PART ONE The context of international HRM 1

01 **Introduction and background to international HRM** 3
Daniel Wintersberger

About this book 3
The context of IHRM 4
Case study: Deregulation and the global civil aviation industry 6
The field of IHRM: approaches and level of analysis 7
Structure of this book 9
References 12

02 **The cultural context of international HRM** 13
Daniel Wintersberger

Introduction 13
Methodological underpinnings 15
Measuring cultural differences 18
Conclusions 25
References 26

03 **Leadership across cultural contexts** 29
Shing Kwan Tam

Introduction 29
What is leadership? 30
Cross-cultural leadership 35
Case study: Global leadership development in a global fashion
    retailer 41
Case study: Global leadership in the 'fast-fashion' industry: the
    case of Gap 43

Conclusions 44
References 45

04   Cross-cultural communication 52
James Baba Abugre

Introduction 52
Cross-cultural communication in international business 54
Cross-cultural training and cross-cultural communication 58
Case study: Insights from subsidiary locations in Ghana 60
Conclusions 66
References 67

05   The institutional context of international HRM 70
Daniel Wintersberger

Introduction 70
The background to institutional analysis 71
The varieties of capitalism approach 74
Case study: Transplanting Japanese models of HRM to the UK 84
Case study: The Volkswagen system of corporate governance 89
Conclusions 91
References and further reading 92

06   Global labour governance and core labour standards 97
Christina Niforou

Introduction 97
Public forms of labour governance 98
Private forms of labour governance 102
Local impact of global labour governance 104
Case study: Compliance with the Telefonica international
    framework agreement 107
Conclusions 112
References 113

PART TWO Functional areas of international
HRM 117

**07   International recruitment, selection and
talent management** 119
Peter Foss

Introduction 119
Defining talent 121
Talent management process 122
Strategy, culture and structure 124
Employer and talent brand 124
Diagnosing and planning 127
Acquiring and selecting 129
Case study: Recruitment and selection at Skullcandy 135
Managing, developing and retaining 138
Case study: Talent management at National Instruments 140
Conclusions 142
References 143

08   International staffing in multinational companies 146
James Baba Abugre

Introduction 146
Staffing composition and practices in international business/
    management 148
Cross-cultural training and development of international
    assignees 153
Cross-cultural training programmes 155
Cross-cultural adjustment successes and failures of expatriates in
    the subsidiaries 158
Case study: Cross-cultural staffing in Ghana 160
Conclusions 166
References 166

09   International reward 172
Daniel Wintersberger

Introduction 172

Managing pay 173

Case study: Market-leading compensation at a low-cost airline: the
case of Southwest 174

Determining pay levels 174

Equity in compensation 179

Reward beyond pay 182

Case study: Flexibility as a reward with mutual benefits at BT
Group PLC 187

Reward across cultural and institutional contexts 189

Case study: Home working and employee performance in
China 191

Case study: Total reward at Unilever 192

Conclusions 194

References 194

10   International training and workforce skills 199

Daniel Wintersberger

Introduction 199

Global labour market developments and their impact on
workplace-level training 200

Case study: The 'deficit' view of training at a liberal market
economy low-cost airline – Ryanair 204

Varieties of capitalism and workforce skills development 208

State-managed vocational training and the Taiwanese economic
miracle 208

Case study: National training infrastructure and competitive
advantage in biscuit manufacturing 211

Conclusions 214

References 215

11   International employee relations 218

Geraint Harvey

Introduction 218

What are the dimensions of employee relations? 219

The labour process and labour power 221

Frames of reference and structured antagonism 223
Degree of influence 224
Management style 226
Globalization and employee relations 227
Case study: International civil aviation and employee relations 228
Conclusions 234
Further reading suggestions 236
References 236

12   Work organization and job design across national contexts 243
Daniel Wintersberger and Jorge Muniz Jr

Introduction 243
Work organization over time and across continents 245
Case study: Scientific management in the global fast-food industry 249
The impact of flexible specialization on HRM 253
Case study: Job redesign and the Swedish model of production 254
Case study: Towards 'lean' thinking: the Toyota production system 256
Case study: Transferring lean management to Toyota plants in Brazil 260
Conclusions 264
References 265

13   Conclusions: change or continuance in national systems of HRM? 269
Introduction 269
Different trajectories between emerging and advanced industrial economies 271
Globalization and the future of IHRM 274
Convergence or divergence in national systems of HRM? 276
References 278

Index 281

CONTRIBUTORS

Daniel Wintersberger is a teaching fellow at Birmingham Business School, University of Birmingham. His research focuses on high-performance work systems as a means of extracting quantitative (efficiency) and qualitative (emotional labour) discretionary effort in interactive service work and the impact of such new forms of work organization at the mental (job strain, burnout) and physical (occupational health and safety) level. Daniel also has a strong interest in union and non-union forms of employee voice. Both these research interests have been covered in prior research on the impact of the low-cost model on work, employment and trade union representation in the Indian and Brazilian civil aviation industry, which was funded by the International Transport Workers' Federation. More recently he has been looking at factors facilitating tacit knowledge sharing on automotive assembly lines.

Shing Kwan Tam is currently conducting doctoral research at Warwick Business School. Her research focuses on the role of gender in cross-cultural leadership in organizations and how this is influenced by leader identity construction. Prior to academia, she worked in leadership development and talent management functions in a number of multinational fashion retailers with key responsibility for developing high-potential leaders in Australia, China, Hong Kong, Malaysia, Singapore, Germany, the Netherlands and the UK.

Geraint Harvey is a senior lecturer in Industrial Relations and HRM at Birmingham Business School, University of Birmingham. His research is primarily focused on employee relations and considers the role of trade unions in the high-performance paradigm, business ethics and corporate social responsibility, although he has also published research on aesthetic labour and green HRM. He has conducted research into employee relations in the civil aviation industry on behalf of the European Transport Workers' Federation, International Transport Workers' Federation and the International Labour Organization. He is the author of the book *Management in the Airline Industry* and his research has been published widely in a range of media.

Christina Niforou is a Lecturer in Human Resource Management at the University of Birmingham. She received her PhD from Warwick Business School, University of Warwick. Her interests include comparative employment relations, global labour governance and corporate social responsibility. She specializes in the role of labour agency in global value chains and compliance with labour standards in the Global South. Her research has been funded by the Onassis Public Benefit Foundation, the Economic and Social Research Council, Warwick Business School, Birmingham Business School and the Trade Union-related Research Institutes (a joint initiative of the European Trade Union Institute and the Hans Böckler Foundation). She has published papers in journals such as the *British Journal of Industrial Relations*, *Human Resource Management*, *Business Ethics* and *Economic and Industrial Democracy*.

Peter Foss is a teaching fellow at the University of Birmingham in the areas of Organizational Behaviour, Change Management, HRM and Leadership Development. One of the themes running throughout these courses is that of linking concepts with organizational practice alongside personal development. These teaching interests are supplemented by research interests in the areas of intimacy, team working and communication. Previously, he worked in the USA as a psychotherapist, vocational evaluator, management consultant and sailboat captain. He also undertakes dissertation supervision at undergraduate and masters level.

James Baba Abugre is a Senior Lecturer at the Department of Organization and HRM at the University of Ghana Business School. His research specialization is in international human resource management, corporate communication and cross-cultural studies and business. Dr Abugre's publications are centred on human resource issues in multinational companies and local organizations.

Jorge Muniz Jr is an Associate Professor in the Universidade Estadual Paulista (UNESP), São Paulo, where he is currently editor in chief of the *Production Journal*, as well as coordinator of the executive master programme in production engineering. He completed his doctorate in operations management at UNESP, which was awarded by the Brazilian Association of Production Engineering, and holds an MSc in operations management from the University of São Paulo. Additionally, he has worked at the Ford Motor Company as a quality manager, integrating Lean thinking to the quality operations systems. His research focuses on knowledge management in production systems, quality management and Lean thinking.

You can download extra material for this book at
koganpage.com/InternationalHRM

PART ONE
The context of international HRM

01
Introduction and background to international HRM

About this book

This book provides a comprehensive yet accessible case-based overview of international human resource management in a global context. By doing so, it makes a timely contribution by not only focusing on HRM in multinational companies, but more importantly, by also examining distinct national-level factors impacting on HRM at the local level. Beyond relevant cultural factors impacting on HRM at national level, the book also explicitly focuses on relevant institutional factors impacting on the nature of HRM across different national contexts. As Chapter 5 will show, these institutional factors, including employment legislation and the nationally distinct interplay between the three key actors (the state, trade unions and employers' associations) arguably continue to exert a strong influence at national level, hence leading to distinct HRM outcomes in different countries, often in close geographical proximity to one another.

As would naturally be expected with a textbook on international HRM, significant attention will be turned to the multinational enterprise and its role in 'diffusing' HR 'best practice' from the home country to the host countries within which it operates, either through wholly owned subsidiaries or via international joint ventures. Conventional approaches to IHRM have examined the issue of multinationals and diffusion of HRM practices mainly from the somewhat ethnocentric vantage point of western (mainly American) multinational companies and the extent to which they cascade their HRM practices 'downwards' to their subsidiaries (see for example Bjorkman and Lu, 2001). In contrast, due to changes in the tide, this book also examines the emergent phenomenon of firms from 'Eastern' as well as emerging economies transferring their HRM practices 'westwards' to subsidiaries in Europe and North America. For example, we will examine the way in which and the extent to which Japanese firms implement

Japanese systems of work organization and job design in mature (UK – see Chapter 5) and emerging (Brazil – see Chapter 12) economies.

Crucially, for a textbook on international HRM, this book contains case studies from numerous countries, including major economies such as the US, UK, China, India, Brazil, Hong Kong, Ghana and Germany.

Who is this book for?

Whether you might be studying an entire master's programme in international HRM, or just taking a module on HRM or international HRM, you are likely to find this book to be an accessible yet comprehensive companion as you engage with the international context of HRM as well as its key functional areas (such as recruitment, selection, reward, and employee engagement). Those taking an HRM or international HRM module as part of an MBA programme are likely to find the practical emphasis on real-life case studies from different countries stimulating and thought-provoking.

The remainder of this chapter provides a brief overview of the context of international HRM (IHRM).

Learning objectives

After reading this chapter, you should have an understanding of the following:

- the key forces (internationalization/transnationalization of business, globalization and free movement of capital) that have led to the development of IHRM;
- the various routes businesses may take towards internationalization and their implications for the IHRM function;
- the key challenges and opportunities emerging for practitioners of international human resource management.

The context of IHRM

Firms rarely start as truly multinational enterprises, but undergo a sometimes lengthy or sometimes brisk process of internationalization. This chapter therefore examines the processes by which firms internationalize, and the impact this has on the HRM function within the organization. In order to come to grips with the process of internationalization, we need to understand some of the contextual developments (such as globalization) which facilitate the internationalization of businesses. This chapter therefore provides an introduction to the context within which IHRM takes place by highlighting first the changing context of international business and second, the way in which firms internationalize and what impact this process of internationalization has on HRM.

Why do firms internationalize?

One of the key reasons for firms to internationalize is to become more competitive by developing beneficial networks in other countries. Such networks may incorporate production and assembly, as well as sales and distribution. Of course, not all firms internationalize, and whether they do so depends on an array of factors that are internal and external to the firm. One key external factor is the type of industry within which the firm operates; in some industries, comparably greater benefits can be derived from circuits of capital and the new international division of labour (Hymer, 1982). This new international division of labour entails a shift in industrial production from *core* to *periphery*. The core in this context is a term used to describe the old established industrialized countries, whereas the periphery refers to the emerging economies where labour costs are cheaper. For manufacturing firms, for example, the potential benefits derived from shifting labour-intensive production processes to countries with cheaper labour costs are greater than for those firms that specialize in more knowledge-intensive activities. A well-known case in point for this is Apple and their global production value chain. Knowledge activities (such as research and development) have been retained in California, while the labour-intensive activities of production have been outsourced to supplier firms in China, such as the infamous Foxconn, where exceptionally appalling working conditions have recently been documented (see for example Ngai and Chan, 2012). Knowledge-intensive activities such as research and development can be retained in tech hubs in and around the Bay area in California where skilled workers command high wages, but relatively few of them are needed for the more abstract conceptual work associated with the design of new products.

International offshoring and outsourcing are both facilitated by the fact that it is becoming increasingly easy for companies to enter foreign markets. Globalization is viewed by many as an inevitable trajectory resulting from increasing functional integration of economic activities as well as increased geographical spread of economic activities (Dicken, 2015: 2). While organizations internationalize, governments, for reasons outlined in more depth below, are increasingly opening their markets to foreign investment in order to speed up economic growth. With few exceptions (examples of some of which will be provided later in the chapter), firms in most countries compete in a global market. Trade barriers to entering foreign markets are being gradually eroded. An exemple of this is the international civil aviation industry (see below). As a result of an increasingly free movement of capital and labour, global competition for goods and services has increased. As a direct result of this, industrialized economies such as the UK and the US have seen jobs in labour-intensive manufacturing sectors such as car production and steel shift to emerging economies, initially to South Korea, but more recently to China and India. This has led to a very different dynamism between 'mature' and emerging markets. Governments in advanced industrial economies (mature markets where labour costs are high) are implementing austerity and labour market reforms to cheapen the cost of labour, and making the terms and conditions on which workers can be hired more employer friendly in attempts to become more competitive with emerging markets. At the same time, emerging economies, notably the 'BRIC' (Brazil, Russia, India and China) have sustained comparably strong GDP growth rates over the past two to three decades, and with rising inflation have seen an increase in labour costs too. India's year-on-year GDP growth rate between 2015 and 2016, for example, was a staggering 7.6 per cent in comparison to only 2.4 per cent in the US and 2.3 per cent in the UK (World Bank, 2017).

As Chapter 3 will highlight in more depth, globalization does not necessarily mean that the above trajectory is inevitable. In fact, the very term 'globalization' needs to be carefully unpicked for clarity regarding the extent to which we view it in *empirical* or *ideological* terms (Dicken, 2015). In empirical terms, we are merely analysing the changes as well as key trends and patterns associated with certain measures of globalization such as the 'transnationality index' provided annually by the United Nations Conference on Trade and Development (UNCTAD). Engaging with globalization in ideological terms is quite different insofar as it involves actively advocating the aforementioned changes (for example through the erosion of trade barriers through deregulation/liberalization of markets). The following case study provides an example of how national governments, in the case of civil aviation, liberalized an industry that was, until recently, heavily regulated in most countries.

CASE STUDY   Deregulation and the global civil aviation industry

The airline industry has traditionally been highly regulated, with a complex series of national and international restrictions on landing right in different countries. Until the 1970s, all countries had restrictions in place that limited the ability of foreign airlines to use their national airports to carry passengers to another country. The main purpose of these restrictions was to protect national airlines (often state-owned carriers) from cheaper foreign competition in order to preserve jobs and employment terms and conditions at these carriers, as governments were well aware of the threat of foreign airlines (particularly from countries with lower labour costs) encroaching into the market share of their national carriers by undercutting their prices. Throughout the 1970s and 1980s, the political climate began to change, with the pro-market Ronald Reagan and Margaret Thatcher administrations introducing neo-liberal reforms (ie reforms which seek to remove government restrictions on the free market forces of supply and demand) to the US and the UK respectively. The United States and some European countries such as the Netherlands and the United Kingdom were among the first nations in the world to loosen the traditionally restrictive bilateral air services agreements and move towards what is known today as 'open skies' (Doganis, 2006: 31). The first agreement between the Netherlands and the United States saw the removal of government ability to intervene in matters of capacity, pricing and frequency of flights. This meant, for example, that Americans on flights to Europe via Amsterdam benefited from stronger competition, as Dutch airlines such as KLM were now able to compete on these routes as well. This agreement put pressure on other European nations to follow suit. After all, countries like Germany and the UK sought to maintain the significance of their international hubs (London Heathrow Airport and Frankfurt Airport respectively) and avoid losing transatlantic travel to Amsterdam. One of the most liberal European bilateral agreements was soon signed between the Netherlands and the UK in 1983. This agreement essentially allowed airlines from both countries full open-route access, removing previous restrictions on points that could be served in each country by the other country's airlines. The result of such liberalization is clearly quantifiable in terms of air fares. Prior to 1983, the cheapest return fare on the London-to-Amsterdam route was an advance fare of £85, with only three discounted alternatives to choose from. Within two years of the new agreement, the cheapest fare was £55, with 22 alternatives to choose from (Doganis, 2006: 35).

The case of the international civil aviation industry illustrates both why governments may seek to protect their markets (preservation of state-owned companies and their jobs) as well as why they liberalize markets (opening to foreign competition and cheapening products and services for the consumer).

The field of IHRM: approaches and level of analysis

The field of international human resource management can be subdivided into three distinct approaches on the basis of their level of analysis, namely the macro (national/regional), meso (enterprise) and micro (individual employee) levels.

Macro level

At the macro level, there is the approach of **comparative HRM**. This is primarily *descriptive* insofar as it describes what is going on in different countries. That is, it examines key similarities and differences between HRM systems in different countries, regions and industrial clusters; it examines HRM at the country and regional level rather than at the individual or enterprise level. It therefore entails an analysis of contextual factors (for example employment systems) as well as relevant institutional factors such as national-level employment legislation and vocational education and training systems and the impact these factors have on HRM within organizations operating in these countries. This approach will be outlined in more depth in Chapter 5.

Meso level

At the meso level (ie company level), the discipline of **international HRM** seeks to understand the impact of a company's international operations on HRM. Contrary to comparative HRM, it seeks to understand what goes on within transnational or multinational enterprises rather than the extent to which external circumstances (such as the institutional factors mentioned above) influence their practices. This approach places more emphasis on functional areas of HRM such as the management of employee voice (eg whether organizations choose to work with or bypass collective bargaining in the form of trade unions and/or works councils) as well as international staffing (ie the factors influencing a firm's decision on who to send for international assignments and the type of pre-assignment training provided). IHRM is underpinned by the assumption that HR practitioners in MNCs have significant capacity to make decisions and act independently of institutional factors, which comparative HRM tends to consider as more binding. Moreover, IHRM tends to be more prescriptive than the comparative approach. In other words, IHRM not only describes key differences in HRM systems in different countries, but tends to offer advice regarding 'best practice' for practitioners. For example, with regards to international staffing, empirical contributions from the IHRM discipline (see for example Scullion and Collings, 2006) not only describe the reasons why international assignments fail, but also offer advice on how to minimize the failure rate of expatriate appointments. Such 'best practice', including pre-screening of candidates for international assignments as well as cross-cultural training, will be discussed in more depth in Chapters 3 and 4 of this book. While the IHRM approach focuses on the firm (meso) level of analysis, it also touches to some extent on the micro (individual) level, for example by dealing with individual (employee-level) psychological factors that may determine effectiveness of expatriates. Nonetheless, there is a significant standalone approach to understanding HRM across cultures, namely that of 'cross-cultural management'.

Micro Level

At the micro level (ie individual employee, group or team level), cross-cultural management has a different approach to IHRM. Rather than describing practices of MNEs, it examines various practices (such as cross-cultural negotiation, communication and teamworking) from the perspective of managers and/or employees. Many scholars in the field of cross-cultural management come from an occupational psychology perspective, which again highlights the role of the individual as a level of analysis. Key contributions to the field of cross-cultural management will be discussed in Chapter 2 of this book.

Reflective questions

1   How would you describe the field of IHRM in your own words?

2   Revisiting the three aforementioned approaches (comparative and international HRM, as well as cross-cultural management), what in your view are some of the key strengths and weaknesses of each approach? Which one do you believe most closely reflects your idea of how IHRM ought to be studied?

Structure of this book

This book is structured in order to provide a logical progression through key contextual factors influencing IHRM activity.

Chapters 2–6 all contribute to your understanding of the context (both culturally and institutionally) within which IHRM activity takes place, and some of the opportunities and constraints IHRM practitioners need to take into consideration when operating across different countries.

Chapter 2 (the cultural context) discusses some of the relevant cultural frameworks that underpin differences in HRM between different countries.

Chapter 3 (leading and managing across cultures) considers some of the critical success factors of sustainable cross-cultural leadership development, highlighted by two case studies from the global fashion industry.

Chapter 4 (cross-cultural communication) assesses the role of cultural differences in communication in multinational companies (MNCs), particularly in the context of expatriate work in international management, as well as some of the methods to mitigate cultural obstacles (such as cross-cultural training). This is demonstrated by a case study using empirical evidence from subsidiaries in Ghana.

Chapter 5 (the institutional context of IHRM) examines some of the key institutional factors that may account for differences in HRM patterns and practices across different national contexts. Factors discussed in Chapter 5 and highlighted by two case studies will include more tangible (also known as 'hard') institutional factors such as legislation on collective bargaining and minimum standards for training and development, as well as 'softer' background institutions such as inter-country differences in customs on rewarding seniority in organizations.

Chapter 6 (global labour governance) seeks to shed some light on the key reasons behind the emergence of a global labour governance regime, and the role played by institutional, structural and political factors in shaping the local impact of global labour norms in various countries, including the Latin American world.

Chapters 7–12 then focus on some of the key functional areas of IHRM activity, ie those practices which IHRM practitioners are likely to deal with on a day-to-day basis.

Chapter 7 (international recruitment, selection and talent management) looks at some of the key processes associated with attracting, recruiting and retaining talent, and the role of employer branding in ensuring that the organization is appealing to potential applicants. Some of the relevant theories and 'best practice' will be applied to various international organizations such as Skullcandy in China.

Chapter 8 (international staffing in multinational companies) then discusses the key decisions multinational companies (MNCs) need to make when staffing their overseas subsidiaries, and some of the best practices to ensure that their international assignees can integrate in their host country. These practices include language and culture training amongst other factors. Case study evidence will be presented from a study with expatriates and managers at MNC subsidiaries in Ghana.

Chapter 9 (international reward) then focuses on one of the major functional areas of HRM, namely the discipline (or perhaps art) of remunerating people fairly within organizations and, in the case of IHRM in multinationals, consistently across countries. This chapter considers reward beyond pay, and discusses the relative value placed on different extrinsic (mainly monetary) but also intrinsic (intangible/unquantifiable rewards more focused on the nature of work and the job itself) such as flexibility and autonomy at work. A case study on a Chinese travel agency's implementation of flexible working will highlight some of the cultural obstacles potentially faced when trying to universally adopt 'western' HRM practices in other countries.

Chapter 10 (international training, development and workforce skills) looks at some of the key inter-country differences in training practices and workforce skills development. We will examine the role of vocational education and training in coordinated market economies such as Germany and compare the outcomes in terms of workforce skills with those countries (such as the US and UK), where a larger proportion of young people opt for general education, and what these differences mean for firms seeking competitive advantage in various sectors, both in manufacturing and services. Chapter 5 (the institutional context of IHRM) provides a useful introduction to the 'varieties of capitalism' debate (Hall and Soskice, 2001), and Chapter 10 will briefly discuss the key features of this framework that can be considered to have an impact on workforce training and development.

Chapter 11 (international employee relations) then looks at the issue of employee voice in organizations and beyond from an international perspective. The chapter will look at different forms of employee voice (union and non-union), different sources of employee bargaining power in the employment relationship, and how globalization has transformed the employment relationship. The latter point is tied together with a case study on civil aviation, which is an industry that is both an antecedent and consequence of globalization.

Chapter 12 (work organization and job design across national contexts) will deal with key global changes to the organization of work in production and services over the past century, and look at some of the recent trends in the organization of work in manufacturing. A case study on the Brazilian automotive industry will examine the extent to which successful models of work organization can be transferred from their country of origin (Japan in the case study) to emerging economies (as in the case of Brazil).

Chapter 13 concludes the book by bringing together some of the key overarching findings of the preceding chapters and by looking at the likely future opportunities and challenges for IHRM practitioners. Globalization is of course one of the key macro-level trends the chapter will deal with, but it will also examine some of the counter trends such as a global political landscape that is becoming increasingly hostile to globalization. We will also look at some of the recent counter-trends to the consequences of globalization, such as the increasing 'reshoring' of services and manufacturing to mature industrial economies such as the UK and US, where wages and labour costs have been stagnant for the last decade or so while those in emerging economies such as China have been rapidly catching up.

References

Bjorkman, I and Lu, Y (2001) Institutionalization and bargaining power explanations of HRM practices in international joint ventures: the case of Chinese–Western joint ventures, *Organization Studies*, **22** (3), pp. 491–512

Dicken, P (2015) *Global Shift: Mapping the contours of the changing world economy*, Sage Publications, London

Doganis, R (2006) *The Airline Business*, Psychology Press

Hall, P A and Soskice, D (2001) *Varieties of Capitalism: The institutional foundations of comparative advantage*, Oxford University Press

Hymer, S (1982) The multinational corporation and the law of uneven development, in *Introduction to the Sociology of 'Developing Societies'*, eds H Alavi and T Shanin, Macmillan Education UK, pp. 128–52

Ngai, P and Chan, J (2012) Global capital, the state, and Chinese workers: the Foxconn experience, *Modern China*, **38** (4), pp. 383–410

Scullion, H and Collings, D G, eds (2006) *Global Staffing*, Routledge

World Bank (2017) Annual GDP growth by country [online] http://data.worldbank.org/indicator/NY.GDP.MKTP.KD.ZG

02
The cultural context of international HRM

DANIEL WINTERSBERGER

Learning outcomes

At the end of this chapter, you should be able to:

- understand the ways in which national culture may influence organizational culture;

- appreciate that culture comprises implicit (underlying beliefs) and explicit (espoused values) dimensions;

- appreciate two different ways (emic and etic) to understand/measure culture and cultural differences between nations and regions;

- understand the role of culture in various business theories and HRM;

- understand and manage cultural differences in applications such as cross-border alliances, international HRM and employment relations;

- understand the way in which national cultural factors underpin and interplay with the institutional factors discussed in Chapter 5.

Introduction

Before jumping to functional areas of international HRM (IHRM), it is important to appreciate the potential role national culture plays for virtually every functional area in the HRM arena. One's cultural orientation may determine one's preference for particular reward, one's propensity to take risk, and one's attitude towards teamwork and towards hierarchy.

But before looking at the link between culture and HRM in more depth, it is important to reflect on what we actually consider culture to be. Some have described culture as behavioural 'patterns', both explicit and implicit (Kroeber and Kluckhohn, 1952), shared by people within a society, organization or nation. Culture can also be viewed as a system of values and norms that guide members of a society, organization or nation on what is acceptable and unacceptable behaviour. Culture can be manifest at multiple levels, and a way of making it perhaps more tangible is to compare it to an iceberg.

The iceberg is a suitable metaphor, for as with culture, only a small proportion of it is above the water level and therefore visible to us. Similar to an iceberg, culture can be envisaged as comprising more and less visible factors. Firstly, at the visible (or 'explicit') level, culture can be observed and sometimes even measured. Examples of such explicit manifestations, often referred to as 'artefacts' (Schein, 1989), include visible aspects of office design and layout. For example, a cubicle system – common up until the 1980s – is often associated with high levels of bureaucracy, whereas the more recent trend towards open-plan offices highlights perhaps an increasing emphasis on post-bureaucratic forms of work organization which are more flexible and foreground informality in interaction between employees.

Figure 2.1   Culture as an iceberg

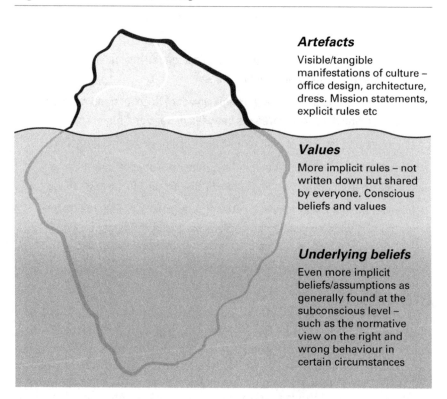

Artefacts

Visible/tangible manifestations of culture – office design, architecture, dress. Mission statements, explicit rules etc

Values

More implicit rules – not written down but shared by everyone. Conscious beliefs and values

Underlying beliefs

Even more implicit beliefs/assumptions as generally found at the subconscious level – such as the normative view on the right and wrong behaviour in certain circumstances

Artefacts might also include visible status differentials such as uniform codes that differ between employees of different ranks, as well as the sizes of offices and other benefits provided (eg better parking) based on employee level in the hierarchy.

It is important to note that such artefacts are only superficial visible manifestations of culture and while they can be easily manipulated (eg changes to company vision statement, office design and dress code), they may not be representative of, or have any meaningful impact on the shared values and beliefs of people within an organization. It is these underlying values and beliefs that are considered relatively impervious to change (Schein, 1989). At organizational level, in fact, managerial attempts to change such values and beliefs in a top-down manner (perhaps in order to make the organization more efficient) sometimes even lead to strong resistance and the perpetuation of the 'old' culture not desired by management (see for example Ogbonna and Harris, 2014). A study of a major culture change initiative at a premier league football club (a new management team seeking to make the club more commercially viable) found that it led to extremely fierce resistance from various stakeholders such as supporters and former players (Ogbonna and Harris, 2014). On the other hand, where management successfully implement a strong culture (for example through the socialization of new employees into what are expected codes of practice and role behaviours) and manage to gain employee 'buy-in' to the new culture at the emotional level (eg through organizing social and teambuilding events such as company barbecues and sporting events), organizational culture can be a powerful source of control insofar as employees control their own behaviours (see for example Kunda, 2009; Wintersberger, Pullen and Williams, 2013).

Similar to culture at the organizational level, culture at national level can be envisaged as comprising explicit and implicit features. Explicit (ie clearly articulated or visible) manifestations may include religious icons, clothing and, very importantly, the food people eat (Choi, 2014). Such explicit manifestations are immediately visible, recognizable and to some extent also measurable. In contrast, implicit manifestations such as deeper underlying (subconscious) beliefs and values are difficult to grasp and measure. As this chapter will outline in more depth, such underlying values may include people's attitudes towards hierarchy and inequality as well as perceptions of gender roles and general lifestyle orientation.

Methodological underpinnings

The way in which we perceive and understand culture is contingent on our approach to studying and measuring it. Firstly, there is the **emic** approach, also known as the inside perspective, which seeks to describe distinctive features of a certain culture (such as level of risk aversion, attitudes toward inequality and hierarchy etc), irrespective of any prior theoretical frameworks or knowledge of any other existing culture. Therefore, the emic approach seeks to describe a culture in its own terms, meaning that a deep understanding of the norms, values and behaviours associated with this culture is essential. The methodological implication of this approach is that often the emic approach requires in-depth case study research featuring unstructured interviews, focus groups or even immersion of oneself within the culture that is being studied, for example in the form ethnographic research. In the context of national culture, the emic perspective would therefore seek to understand culture from the 'native' point of view and is therefore associated with '**interpretivism**'.

Interpretivism: an approach to research underpinned by the assumption that the social world (ie people and their interactions with one another) is not amenable to being studied via the same methods as the natural world. It is the polar opposite of 'positivism', ie the assumption that the social world can be researched and 'measured' in a similar way to the natural world.

In contrast to the emic approach, the **etic** approach (also known as 'outside' perspective) has a more macro-level focus insofar as the culture in question is compared to other cultures based on quantifiable characteristics (such as people's self-reported levels of tolerance of inequality and risk aversion) which can be measured and are directly comparable with other countries and/or regions. In contrast to the emic approach (which aims at eliciting deep, context-specific data on a culture in a particular environment), the etic approach seeks to maximize 'external validity', which means that inferences made from the sample of respondents and participants in the study are in fact applicable to the wider population. For example, findings from an emic ethnographic study on the role and impact of national culture on the way in which relationships are formed between two small firms in an emerging country are unlikely to be generalizable to the country's entire population. Etic approaches, by largely being quantitative in nature and generally entailing large sample sizes, seek to derive findings which are generalizable to the wider population. As a consequence, the etic perspective is about linking cultural practices to external, antecedent factors such as economic conditions. With its emphasis on large sample sizes and high levels of generalizability, the etic perspective is underpinned by the research philosophy of 'positivism'.

Positivism: contrary to interpretivism, positivism is an approach to research that is underpinned by the assumption that only what is objectively measurable (eg counted, observed, rated etc) and quantifiable can be considered valid research. Unlike with interpretivism, research underpinned by positivism is generally quantitative and explanatory in nature (eg determining and confirming the strength and direction of a relationship between two variables such as pay levels and levels of employee self-reported job satisfaction) rather than exploratory.

Reflective exercise

Think about the relative merits and limitations of both aforementioned approaches (emic and etic) to studying and understanding culture. Which one is likely to generate better insights under what circumstances? In summary, what are the key strengths and weaknesses of each?

When considering the strengths and weaknesses of emic and etic approaches, you may have come to the conclusion that each has its own merits and limitations under different circumstances and that the strength of one approach may be the weakness of another. The emic approach might be more effective for exploratory research in a context about which little is known. Moreover, we may mitigate the risk of 'cultural bias' (Thomas and Peterson, 2014). Cultural bias may emerge due to our own (culturally derived) presuppositions about the meaning assigned to certain behaviours, gestures, artefacts and symbols in a new culture about which we know very little. By pursuing the inside (emic) perspective, we seek to understand all observed phenomena from the perspective of those immersed in the culture in question. As a consequence, we might argue that the emic approach is particularly suitable to explore new cultural contexts about which little is known in order to build new theory (rather than simply test existing cultural values). In contrast, the etic approach has its merits when it comes to corroborating findings and testing hypotheses due to its large-scale (quantitative) approach, which enables high levels of generalizability of findings. As a consequence, the etic approach may be better for testing existing theory rather than building new theory. As far as research in IHRM is concerned, a key question we need to ask ourselves in the context of these methodological considerations is whether or not we can meaningfully categorize and measure people's cultural values, and whether or not people can be categorized into meaningful clusters (eg nations, regions, religious groups etc) based on their cultural orientation or whether everyone holds a fairly distinctive set of values, making it impossible to use pre-defined survey questions to simply measure the extent to which they fit into a specific cultural group.

Measuring cultural differences

In this section we discuss some of the most widely known and cited 'etic' contributions in the field of cross-cultural management and IHRM. One such framework emanates from Dutch psychologist Geert Hofstede's indicative work on 'culture's consequences' (Hofstede, 1984). Before looking in more depth at each of Hofstede's cultural dimensions, it is helpful to familiarize ourselves with the origins of this significant contribution to our understanding of national culture. The original survey was first conducted with 116,000 IBM employees (employed in marketing and general services) in 40 countries in the period 1967–69 and repeated between 1971 and 1973. This may seem a long time ago, but the four dimensions of cultural differences emerging from this study (power distance, uncertainty avoidance, masculinity–femininity and individualism–collectivism) are still known and used in more contemporary research (Matusitz and Musambira, 2013). As the survey was repeated (and found largely similar results to the initial one), it lends support to the idea that national culture is relatively impervious to change.

Hofstede's initial (1984) publication generated four dimensions of national culture: power distance, individualism–collectivism, uncertainty avoidance and masculinity–femininity. Subsequent work generated the fifth dimension – Confucian dynamism – also known as long-term versus short-term orientation (Bond, 1987).

Power distance (PD)

This describes the extent to which less powerful members of institutions/ organizations within a country expect and accept that power is distributed unequally (Hofstede, 1991: 262). High levels of PD would be reflected at organizational level in managers pursuing what can best be described as an autocratic leadership style. Decision making would be relatively centralized, running top-down in a relatively steep organizational hierarchy entailing multiple layers. In high-PD societies, one would expect there to be a higher level of power imbalance between an employer and its employees, whereby the employer is viewed as taking some degree of ownership over the welfare of its employees. The resulting management style has often been referred to as 'paternalism' (Purcell, 1987). Under a fairly authoritarian leadership style, paternalism may entail practices which involve substantial managerial concern for employee welfare but also morality (Cheng, Chou and Farh, 2000). Examples of HRM practices of paternalistic employers may include employer-provided housing, but also a company doctor looking after the physiological health of the workforce. Air India, for example, house a significant proportion of their workforce in the Air India colony, located in close proximity to their major hub of Mumbai airport and boasting facilities such an Air India-provided school for the children of staff as well as sports facilities (Wintersberger, Pullen and Williams, 2013). This is quite common practice in India, where employees have been found to trust paternalistic employers to a greater extent, in part at least due to relatively high levels of power distance (see for example Rawat and Lyndon, 2016). Moreover, in high-PD societies, people are likely to be more tolerant towards the privileges that come with high levels of power. At organizational level this implies that we can expect greater status differentials, for example between managerial and non-managerial staff.

In contrast, low levels of power distance at organizational level would imply less autocratic leadership styles and management allowing its workforce more participation in decision making. Organizations in low-PD societies are likely to be less hierarchical and more egalitarian, as individual employees are likely to be more conscious of their rights, and less inclined to tolerate an overly unequal distribution of power and the resources that come with that power. Table 2.1 compares and contrasts the organizational implications of high and low levels of power distance.

Power distance tends to be relatively high in many Southern and Eastern Asian countries such as Malaysia, Indonesia, the Philippines and India, as well as in some Central and South American countries such as Guatemala, Panama and Venezuela. Countries scoring low on power distance tend to cluster in northern and western Europe (eg Denmark, Austria, and Ireland are amongst the countries to consistently score lowest in Hofstede's studies (Hofstede, 2001).

Uncertainty avoidance (UA)

This describes the extent to which members of a culture feel threatened by uncertain/unknown situations (Hofstede, 2001). High levels of (UA) are

Table 2.1 Organizational implications of high and low levels of power distance

High PD	Low PD
• Autocracy in leadership • Authority that is centralized • Paternalistic ways of management • A number of hierarchy levels • The acceptance of the privileges that come with power • A lot of supervisory staff • An expectation of power differences and inequality	• Participative or consultative style of management • Decision-making responsibility and authority decentralized • Flat structure of organizations • Supervisory staff small in proportion • Questioning of authority • An inclination toward egalitarianism • Consciousness of rights

usually linked with high levels of risk aversion, for example in activities such as takeovers, where CEOs from countries with high levels of UA have been found to be significantly more reluctant to engage in the more risky cross-border and cross-industry takeovers (Frijns et al, 2013). Moreover, members of a society characterized by high levels of UA tend to have a preference for very standardized and rigid policies and procedures, and promotion is usually very much based on age and job tenure (Hofstede, 1993), meaning that positions of responsibility tend to be held by older and more experienced people. In contrast, low levels of UA are associated with a higher preparedness to take risk and greater degrees of flexibility in terms of work organization (Hofstede, 1993). There is no clear geographical cluster of countries scoring high or low on UA. Countries scoring highest on UA include Greece, Guatemala, Portugal and Uruguay (Hofstede, 2000: 502). Countries scoring lowest (ie least risk averse) include Singapore, the UK and China (Hofstede, 2000).

Individualism–collectivism

This dimension entails two opposite ends of a continuum, so the opposite of high levels of individualism would be high levels of collectivism. High levels of individualism are usually reflected in relatively loose ties between individuals and low levels of affective commitment towards their organization. People tend to believe that they are better off looking primarily after themselves. In contrast, in societies characterized by high levels of collectivism, individuals are said to have a tendency to see themselves better off in groups rather than simply focusing on their individual fate. Levels of individualism/collectivism may have a strong impact on various HRM areas including teamworking and employee retention. Higher levels of collectivism are linked with a greater preference amongst members of that society to engage in cooperative behaviours with others and to be comfortable with outcomes that emerge from collective (team) rather than individual efforts (Marcus and Le, 2013). Similarly, higher levels of collectivism are positively associated with a firm's ability to retain their workforce due to higher levels of employee loyalty and 'normative commitment' (Allen and Meyer, 1990) to the organization in such societies (Ramamoorthy et al, 2014). There appear to exist clear regional country clusters based on individualism and collectivism. Countries scoring particularly high on individualism include the US, UK and Australia (hence the Anglo-American world). Countries scoring particularly high on collectivism include most Central and South American countries (especially Colombia, Venezuela, Guatemala and Costa Rica), several North African and Gulf countries including Saudi Arabia, as well as many of the Southern and Eastern Asian nations, particularly including South Korea, China and Bangladesh.

Masculinity–femininity

As with individualism and collectivism, this dimension also entails two opposite ends of a continuum where the opposite of high levels of masculinity would be high levels of femininity. This dimension refers to the extent to which a society emphasizes clear distinctions between gender roles, and to what extent men and women are expected to adopt traditional stereotypical roles. For example, to what extent are men expected to be assertive and career oriented or women to be more modest? The dimension of masculinity has clear implications for HRM, for example with regard to management style where, in societies characterized by high levels of masculinity, women are expected to adopt traditional stereotypical behavioural patterns (eg assertive leadership style) when promoted to senior positions involving leading and managing others (Wajcman, 2013). Table 2.2 (below) contrasts high levels of masculinity and femininity.

While Hofstede's study generated influential insights into meaningful dimensions upon which we can categorize national culture, one of the key weaknesses of the initial study was its ethnocentricity. Devised entirely by Geert Hofstede as well as other people from a western context, some have argued that Hofstede's initial study has limited 'content' validity (Bond, 1987). In other words, we cannot be sure that all cultural values held by people from a non-western context have been grasped in this study. Bond (1987), with the help of Chinese scholars, devised a new questionnaire disseminated only in China. Although findings supported three of Hofstede's dimensions (individualism–collectivism, power distance and masculinity–femininity), the dimension of uncertainty avoidance was not corroborated. Instead, Bond's study contributed a fifth dimension to Hofstede's framework:

Table 2.2 Implications of masculinity and femininity

High masculinity	High femininity
• Clearly distinct gender roles	• Overlapping of social gender roles
• Benevolence has little or no significance	• Men, as well as women, are expected to be tender, modest, with focus on the quality of life
• Men are expected to be tough and assertive with a concentration on material achievements	• Emphasis on the non-materialistic angles of success
• Much value is associated with mastery of people, nature, job and the like	• Self-fulfilment/intrinsic satisfaction at work more important than material rewards/status from work
• Strong/autocratic leadership style/assertiveness commonly assumed to be 'good' leadership	• Work–life balance/family more important than career success
	• Leadership style more likely to be more participative/less autocratic

Based on Hofstede (1991: 500) and Sorge et al (2015: 40–41)

Confucian dynamism (also known as long-term versus short-term orientation). Hofstede's later work (see for example Hofstede, 1990) included this dimension in its data collection and analysis, allowing meaningful comparisons to be made between countries based on this dimension.

Members of a society scoring high on long-term orientation would be expected to behave quite similarly to societies characterized by high levels of uncertainty avoidance. As the name suggests, those individuals would be expected to be thrifty with money and resources and to focus on investments with longer-term but potentially also superior returns. The exact opposite would be expected to be the case in societies scoring high on short-term orientation. Beyond looking for quick returns on investment, members of such societies would be expected to value leisure to a greater extent than their counterparts in high long-term-orientation cultures (Hofstede and Minkov, 2010).

Critique of Hofstede's cultural dimensions

Although Hofstede's cultural dimensions make for a clear and appealing framework based upon which meaningful comparisons between countries might be made, there are numerous criticisms. As mentioned earlier, one of the key criticisms is the underlying ethnocentrism associated with relying entirely on a survey devised solely by people from a western context (Kim, 2007). A second issue is that dimensions from the original survey have been devised based on insights from only one company (IBM). Inevitably, the question arises as to whether this really has led to findings that are generalizable to the level of entire nations. It is unlikely, for example, that values and attitudes displayed by certain groups of employees within IBM are representative of those of other members of societies. The nation state as a whole is perhaps an outmoded level of analysis. Nations such as India have long harboured ethnically and religiously very diverse populations. Advanced industrial economies such as the UK and the Netherlands are becoming increasingly ethnically, religiously and certainly also culturally diverse.

Reflective question

Think about the extent to which and way in which Hofstede's cultural dimensions are applicable to your own country of origin, its customs, beliefs and values both in the workplace and beyond. Would you describe your own country of origin as culturally homogenous? If not, why?

Perhaps it is good to be aware of the aforementioned limitations of Hofstede's framework (level of analysis and ethnocentricity) but at the same time not to dismiss it entirely. While potentially ethnocentric and probably oversimplifying culture at the level of the nation state, it provides a useful framework which certainly has informed three decades of international HRM research and practice.

Etic approaches beyond Hofstede: the World Values Survey

One of the criticisms of Hofstede's work introduced earlier was of its largely cross-sectional nature, comparing cultures at a particular point in time. In contrast, the World Values Survey (WVS) allows us to track cultural changes over time in five-year intervals. An additional advantage of the WVS is that it draws on a slightly more representative sample of respondents at national level than did Hofstede's initial study, with a large sample size of over 80,000 respondents from 75 countries (Inglehart, Basanez and Moreno, 1998). The WVS discerns two bipolar dimensions of culture: first, traditional versus rational–secular authority and second, survival versus self-expression values. In traditional societies, religion is said to play an important role, as do traditional values. Work (and success therein) is likely to be an important part of life. Societies scoring high on traditional values also tend to be politically more conservative. The opposite is the case in rational–secular societies. Secondly, in societies valuing survival over self-expression values, financial security is a key priority. Those in societies scoring higher on self-expression values are likely to be prepared to take more risk and are likely to value quality of life over career success (Inglehart, 2007). As a result, where self-expression values predominate, HR practices such as flexible working (including opportunities to work at home) and other family-friendly policies are likely to be valued to a greater extent by employees, as post-materialist values are more important. This needs to be taken into consideration in various IHRM areas such as employee reward (see Chapter 9). Where survival values dominate, base pay and other 'extrinsic' forms of reward (ie rewards such as money, not related to the work itself – more on this in Chapter 9) are likely to be valued to a greater extent than where self-expression values are dominant.

For example, Sweden (a nation scoring particularly high on self-expression values) is a country often used a role model for the rest of Europe when it comes to flexible working practices (Brewster, Mayne and Tregaskis, 1997). Sweden has some of the world's most generous paternity leave policies, and the uptake is very high. In total, Sweden offers 16 months' paid leave which can be split between both parents. In addition, they have recently introduced three months' paid paternal leave for fathers (Agence France-Presse, 2015). Flexible working practices are widely available to employees, allowing people to stay in work alongside family commitments, and as a result, Sweden boasts one of the highest female employment rates in the world (79.6 per cent). In an attempt to further increase worker productivity, the city of Gothenburg has recently announced plans to implement six-hour working days as a trial (Agence France-Presse, 2015). Such a profound societal emphasis on work–life balance seems consistent with a culture scoring high on self-expression values, but does not explain where the emphasis on self-expression values actually comes from in the first place. Recapping on the ideographic perspective of culture, we may look for contextual factors in Sweden that may lead to Swedish society particularly valuing self-expression over survival values. As mentioned earlier, Inglehart et al (2000) argue that self-expression values become dominant in fairly egalitarian, secure and affluent post-industrial societies. Material values become less important than lifestyle factors. Not only is Sweden affluent, but the wealth is also spread fairly evenly throughout society, with high levels of security and healthcare publicly provided. For example, the country has an exceptionally low Gini coefficient (World Bank, 2017) and boasts one of the best social security systems in the world (European Commission, 2013), meaning that the issue of money and housing is largely taken off the table for people and lifestyle factors become more important.

Nature versus nurture?

Those aiming to interpret culture via the etic approach have traditionally assumed that it is something that has emerged in particular ways in societies as a means for survival. In this context, Hofstede (2001: 12) views culture as emerging out of natural (such as climate, natural disasters) and human factors (political environment, armed conflict). Historically, prolonged periods of armed conflict and famine may have led to a society valuing survival values to a greater extent than more secure societies. Culture then continuously adapts to external circumstances. As societies become more affluent, secure and egalitarian, people are likely to increasingly focus on self-expression values. However, in mature industrial economies, in times of austerity, survival values may become more pronounced again.

The adaptive view of culture has its limitations. Changes to our environments occur very quickly and it is questionable whether culture can change at such a rapid rate to adapt to changes in external circumstances. For example, following the cold war period, within only a couple of years, the world transitioned from the brink of a nuclear war to two relatively peaceful decades. Similarly, the onset of the 2008 financial crisis in advanced industrial economies was very rapid, and it is questionable whether cultural changes would have yet occurred as a consequence of the prolonged periods of austerity that followed.

What impact (if any) we would expect such developments to have on culture is largely dependent on the extent to which we believe in either the nomothetic or ideographic view of culture. The **nomothetic** (or 'etic') view believes that our national culture (similar to our personality) is determined by birth and is relatively impervious to change. For example, the nomothetic view would maintain that a Lebanese child born into a family of first-generation Lebanese migrants to the United States would first and foremost be 'Lebanese' in terms of personality traits and subsequently their cultural frames of reference. At the macro level, those buying into the nomothetic perspective would assume that culture is something relatively fixed in a society, so a country scoring high on survival values in the World Values Survey today would be expected to do so in decades to come, regardless of political developments.

In contrast, the ideographic view envisages culture as something more adaptable and therefore continuously changing rapidly in response to external circumstances. This perspective is supported at least in part by some of the profound drifts in cultural orientation some countries have been found to have undergone between the first and second data collection phases for the World Values Survey over a very short period of time. Poland, for example, has moved strongly from traditional towards more rational–secular values in a short period of time. Similarly, Argentina has made a strong leap from survival towards self-expression values (Inglehart et al, 2000).

Reflective exercise

Using examples from your own country of origin, discuss the extent to which local culture may be the consequence of historical survival mechanisms in your natural, social and political environment. To what extent do you see your country's culture as homogeneous and impervious to change?

Conclusions

In this chapter we examined two key contributions (Hofstede's cultural dimensions and the World Values Survey) in the area of IHRM and cross-cultural management. We examined the differences between national and organizational culture, and the way in which national culture impacts on various IHRM applications (eg distribution of pay within organizations, organizational design, hierarchy etc). It is important to note again that with culture, the meaningful is not always measurable insofar as people's values and basic underlying beliefs are implicit in nature and therefore not always quantifiable. Moreover, it is important to keep in mind that, although Hofstede's work and findings from the World Values Survey still receive empirical support today, it is not always possible to neatly categorize people into specific country clusters as nations are becoming increasingly ethnically, religiously and indeed culturally diverse. Having read this chapter, you should have a general understanding of the two cultural frameworks (Hofstede and World Values Survey). Moreover, the chapter should equip you with the foundations for the functional areas of IHRM (such as reward and employee voice) discussed in the latter half of this book. However, culture is not the only variable that impacts IHRM activity, and we need to be aware of the key role institutional factors (such as laws and formalized systems of bargaining) play in shaping IHRM activity within organizations. Some of these factors are discussed in more depth in Chapter 5, which examines the institutional context of IHRM and to some extent how institutional factors may interplay with cultural values.

The next chapter, 'Leadership across cultural contexts', focuses on the critical factors that determine the efficacy of different leaderships styles in different cultural contexts.

Key learning points

- Etic contributions to understanding cultural differences across nations (including Hofstede's cultural dimensions and the World Values Survey) allow us to make systematic comparisons between nations.

- To some extent, these cultural frameworks may explain some variations in HRM patterns in different national contexts. For example, high levels of collectivism in Japan are consistent with the great emphasis placed on loyalty to the company and long-term employment.

- However, the consequences of globalization (multinational companies and migration on a large scale) have made national contexts increasingly ethnically, religiously and therefore culturally diverse, and therefore we need to be careful not to over-rely on the cultural frameworks discussed in this chapter, as cultural values are not impervious to change.

- For practitioners of HRM in an international context, an understanding and appreciation of cultural differences between countries and regions is indispensable, as cultural values have implications for virtually all functional areas of IHRM (including reward, employee voice and work organization).

References

Agence France-Presse, Stockholm (2015) Swedish fathers to get third month of paid paternity leave, *Guardian*, 28 May [online] https://www.theguardian.com/world/2015/may/28/swedish-fathers-paid-paternity-parental-leave

Allen, N J and Meyer, J P (1990) The measurement and antecedents of affective, continuance and normative commitment to the organization, *Journal of Occupational Psychology*, **63** (1), pp. 1–18

Bond, M H (1987) The Chinese cultural connection – returning to the Middle Kingdom: Chinese values and the search for psychological universals, *Cross-Cultural Psychology*, **18** (2), pp. 143–64

Brewster, C, Mayne, L and Tregaskis, O (1997) Flexible working in Europe, *Journal of World Business*, **32** (2), pp. 133–51

Cheng, B S, Chou L. F and Farh, J L (2000) A triad model of paternalistic leadership: the constructs and measurement, *Indigenous Psychological Research in Chinese Societies*, **14**, pp. 3–64

Choi, A (2014) What Americans can learn from other food cultures, *TED* [online] http://ideas.ted.com/what-americans-can-learn-from-other-food-cultures/

European Commission (2013) *Your Social Security Rights in Sweden*, European Commission, Employment, Social Affairs and Inclusion

Frijns, B et al (2013) Uncertainty avoidance, risk tolerance and corporate takeover decisions, *Journal of Banking & Finance*, **37** (7), pp. 2457–71

Hofstede, G (1984) *Culture's Consequences: International differences in work-related values*, Sage Publications

Hofstede, G (1991) *Cultures and Organisations: Software of the mind*, McGraw-Hill, London, New York

Hofstede, G (1993) Cultural constraints in management theories, *The Academy of Management Executive*, **7** (1), pp. 81–94

Hofstede, G (2000) Whatever happened to masculinity and femininity? *Cross-Cultural Psychology Bulletin*, **34** (4), pp. 14–21

Hofstede, G (2001) *Culture's Consequences: Comparing values, behaviours, institutions and organizations across nations*, Sage Publications

Hofstede, G and Minkov, M (2010) Long-versus short-term orientation: new perspectives, *Asia Pacific Business Review*, **16** (4), pp. 493–504

Inglehart, R (2007) Postmaterialist values and the shift from survival to self-expression values, in *The Oxford Handbook of Political Behaviour*, eds R J Dalton and H-D Klingemann, Oxford University Press

Inglehart, R, Basanez, M and Moreno, A (1998) *Human values and beliefs: A cross-cultural sourcebook: political, religious, sexual, and economic norms in 43 societies: findings from the 1990–1993 World Values Survey*, University of Michigan Press, Ann Arbor

Inglehart, R et al (2000) *World values surveys and European values surveys, 1981–1984, 1990–1993, and 1995–1997, ICPSR version*, Institute for Social Research, Ann Arbor, Michigan

Kim, M S (2007) Our culture, their culture and beyond: further thoughts on ethnocentrism in Hofstede's discourse, *Journal of Multicultural Discourses*, **2** (1), pp. 26–31

Kroeber, A L and Kluckhohn, C (1952) *Culture: A critical review of concepts and definitions*, Peabody Museum of Archaeology & Ethnology, Harvard University

Kunda, G (2009) *Engineering culture: Control and commitment in a high-tech corporation*, Temple University Press

Marcus, J and Le, H (2013) Interactive effects of levels of individualism–collectivism on cooperation: a meta-analysis, *Journal of Organizational Behavior*, **34** (6), pp. 813–34

Matusitz, J and Musambira, G (2013) Power distance, uncertainty avoidance, and technology: analysing Hofstede's dimensions and human development indicators, *Journal of Technology in Human Services*, **31** (1), pp. 42–60

Ogbonna, E and Harris, L C (2014) Organizational cultural perpetuation: a case study of an English premier league football club, *British Journal of Management*, **25** (4), pp. 667–86

Purcell, J (1987) Mapping management styles in employee relations, *Journal of Management Studies*, **24** (5), pp. 533–48

Ramamoorthy, N et al (2014) Individualism–collectivism and tenure intent among knowledge workers in India and Bulgaria: moderating effects of equity perceptions and task interdependence, *The Journal of High Technology Management Research*, **25** (2), pp. 201–09

Rawat, P and Lyndon, S (2016) Effect of paternalistic leadership style on subordinate's trust: an Indian study, *Journal of Indian Business Research*, **8** (4)

Schein, E H (1989) The role of the founder in creating organizational culture, *Readings in Managerial Psychology*, **278**

Sorge, A, Noorderhaven, N G and Koen, C I (2015) *Comparative International Management*, Routledge

Thomas, D C and Peterson, M F (2014) *Cross-cultural Management: Essential concepts*, Sage Publications

Wajcman, J (2013) *Managing Like a Man: Women and men in corporate management*, John Wiley & Sons

Wintersberger, D, Pullen, A and Williams, H (2013) HRM at low fares airlines in BRICs: commitment and insecurity, *Nascent Connections 2013*, **72**

World Bank (2017) Gini coefficient by country (World Bank estimate). https://data.worldbank.org/indicator/SI.POV.GINI

03
Leadership across cultural contexts

SHING KWAN TAM

> **Learning outcomes**
>
> At the end of this chapter, you should be able to:
>
> - understand the different theories of leadership and their developments;
> - differentiate between leader and leadership development;
> - gain a better understanding of the critical success factors of sustainable cross-cultural leadership development.

Introduction

Over recent decades, the complexity of organizational leadership has intensified due to rapid changes brought about by globalization and the management difficulties generated by territorial, political and cultural differences (Maria and Arenas, 2009; Sheppard, Sarros and Santora, 2013). Wade (1996) notes that globalization refers to changes in the international economy which are brought by the 'increase in international trade in goods and services, greater flows of foreign direct investment (FDI) and the growth of international financial transactions' (Bamber, Lansbury and Wailes, 2011: 14). As Edwards and Rees (2011: 122) argue, globalization does not necessarily lead to convergence of practices and multinational corporations (MNCs) have been dealing with the standardization tensions by local adaptations in the context of leadership practices. In this vein, with intensifying globalization, development of global leaders becomes increasingly crucial for MNCs. Such need is actually reflected in survey results of Fortune 500 enterprises in which 85 per cent of them have expressed concerns about inadequate supply of global leaders – individuals with organizational and business expertise and the cross-cultural skills enabling them to run organizations under uncertain situations (Evans et al, 2010).

Nevertheless, researchers and practitioners have also long been criticized for adopting an overly 'culture neutral' approach to studying leadership development (Acker, 1990; Broadbridge and Simpson, 2011; Kark, 2004). Whether or not leadership is universal is contended. Some researchers such as Bass (1990) and House et al (2004) argue that certain aspects of leadership, such as supportiveness, excellence orientation (conscientiousness) and honesty may be universally applicable across different cultures (Dickson, Den Hartog and Mitchelson, 2003). These approaches stress a few universal traits to successful leadership and simply deliver the same programmes to all participants regardless of their cultural background. With the ignorance of local context variations and failure to reflect the organizational realities women face, these approaches are 'doomed to failure from the outset' (Steers, Sanchez-Runde and Nardon, 2012: 480). In order to address diversity issues and to provide guidelines for optimizing leadership in contemporary organizations, it is necessary to take an inclusive approach with the inclusion of culture as a factor for the leadership theory development and research (Ayman and Korabik, 2010; Chin, 2010). From a critical perspective, globalization and culture influence institutions, education systems, management and leadership at macro level, and these factors have impact at organizational level in the context of leadership development (Blackmore, 2010). Due to the impact of globalization, 21st-century organizations operate in more complex and diverse forms, and culture can certainly be considered as one of the key factors influencing the expectations people have about what constitutes effective leadership (Ayman and Korabik, 2010; Klenke, 2011).

What is leadership?

Development of leadership theory

Contemporary leadership theory is seen as complex, wide-ranging and contradictory, with no agreement on one definition. Some suggest that leadership is to be understood from the perspectives of person, result, position and process (Jackson and Parry, 2011). It is also suggested that leadership encompasses interacting dimensions of person, process and context (Yukl, 2013). Although many leadership definitions exist, leadership can be summarized as a process that involves influence, occurs within a group with interactions between leaders and followers, and includes aspects related to resulting shared outcomes (Day and Antonakis, 2012; Yukl, 2013). As leadership is a dynamic and democratic process of interaction that creates changes, every organization member performs the leadership function at some point in time (Barker, 1997). These definitions imply that dynamic interplay and mutual goals among leaders and followers and organizational context are crucial.

There has been a wide variety of leadership theories developed in past years. Concepts include a focus on leader traits (ie innate qualities) and behaviours, contingency approaches, leader–member exchange, charismatic and transformational leadership, strategic leadership, and distributed leadership (Northouse, 2016). There is no simple way to study leadership; one of the most useful ways to categorize leadership theory and research is to look into the variables that foster leadership. Generally speaking, there are three key types of variable that are related to leadership study: first, characteristics of leaders, second, characteristics of followers, and third, characteristics of situations (Yukl, 2013).

The trait approach was one of the first ways of studying leadership. This approach focuses on the leaders' characteristics such as personality, motives, values and skills. It was suggested that some individuals are born leaders with effective leadership traits, while others are not (Northouse, 2016). In the early 20th century, the leadership research direction was mainly about differentiation of specific personality traits between leaders and followers (Bass, 1990). This approach has gained much interest in the research area about the influence of traits on leadership (Bryman, 1992). Much research has been conducted on the relationship between traits and perceptions with regard to leadership (see Bass, 1990; Lord, De Vader and Alliger, 1986; Zaccaro, 2007). Nevertheless, there still exists doubt about the impact of traits on outcomes such as team performance and leader progression (Yukl, 2013). Despite these shortcomings, progress has been made regarding the association of traits and leadership behaviours and effectiveness, and as this approach is applicable to all individuals at all levels of organizations, by taking the trait assessments, leaders could use this information as a reference for understanding their strengths and weaknesses in a way that is beneficial to their future leadership development (Northouse, 2016).

The pitfalls of the trait approach stimulated the interest in developing the behavioural approach. Behavioural leadership studies focused on organizational psychology for many years to understand the influence of leader style on group behaviour and resulted in two essential behavioural dimensions – 'task focus' versus 'people orientation' as the key study direction (Storey, 2016). In other words, this approach is concerned with what the leaders do at work regarding goal accomplishment and how they make their followers feel comfortable in the team for the sake of achieving their work objectives. Yet leadership exists in group membership in organizations and is argued as highly situational and contextual, that is, leadership is sensitive to the changes of the broader external environment (Lord et al, 2001).

As Stogdill (1974) asserts, the trait and behavioural leadership research failed to demonstrate solid evidence for a universal theoretical concept of effective leadership. These viewpoints explain precisely the emergence of contingency theory during the 1970s and 1980s. Different theories were developed, such as path–goal theory, situational leadership theory, leader substitutes theory, multiple linkage model, least preferred co-worker (LPC), contingency theory, cognitive resources theory and normative decision models. Although the contributions of contingency theories to the literature are extensively recognized, some researchers are doubtful about the validity of the elusive and lofty leadership construct as the theories are complex and difficult to test (Hernandez et al, 2011).

Dissatisfaction in leadership research that treats leadership as a set of traits and characteristics led to a new research direction that zoomed in on the nature of leadership – the relationship between leaders and followers. That is, the attention was more on what the leaders do (ie their behaviours) in order to drive a better result, instead of who they are (ie in-born traits). In the 1980s, attention shifted to the 'new leadership' theories that promoted the concept of transformational, charismatic, visionary and inspirational leadership (Storey, 2016). The new leadership is redefined with emphasis on the engagement of followers and goal-driven actions that bring about transformation and change (Bryman, 1992; Chin, 2010; Day and Antonakis, 2012). Bass (1985) referred to this type of new universal leadership as **transformational leadership**, which idealized the inspiring leadership behaviour that transforms followers' interests for the greater good.

There are sound reasons to study the 'new' leadership, and specifically transformational leadership (TFL). With the impact of globalization, the increasing convergence of global technologies, institutions and industrial logic contributes to the harmonization of management practices (Zagorsek, Jaklic and Stough, 2004). As employees across the globe are increasingly commonly knowledge workers, Bass (1997) asserts that TFL is effective universally across cultures, as transformational leaders are equipped with these qualities (Ergeneli, Gohar and Temirbekova, 2007). Storey (2011) also argues that TFL's change-focused feature and centric idea of inspirational motivation become critical to organizations in view of deregulation of markets, challenging global competition and increasing use of flexible and looser employment. Eagly, Johannesen-Schmidt and van Engen (2003) further stress that a meta-analysis of 39 studies substantiated TFL's effectiveness by showing the positive correlations between leaders' effectiveness and all components of transformational leadership. In brief, transformational leaders lead as role models through gaining the trust and confidence of followers. In contrast, transactional leaders appeal to the self-interest of subordinates based on the exchange relationship with them. Though these two types are separable empirically, both types of leadership have been found to be effective and generate positive outcomes (Sarros and Santora, 2001).

While all the aforementioned leadership theories are leader-focused, in recent decades, followers have become the focus of research, which has led to the emergence of Implicit Leadership Theory (ILT). Implicit leadership theory is basically a lay theory which focuses on followers' ideas of effective leadership (Shondrick and Lord, 2010). ILTs are defined cognitive structures or prototypes specifying the traits and abilities that characterize leaders

(Lord and Maher, 1991). In other words, perceptions of ideal leadership behaviours are impacted by the expectations of followers; once the followers' schema are established, they are found to be consistent over the time unless there are changes brought by contextual factors (Epitropaki et al, 2013). Formation of leader perception is dependent on the perceived match between leaders' behaviours and the pre-existing leader prototype (ie what features constitute a good leader) implanted in followers' memories. That is, the identity of the leader needs followers' recognition in order to be solidified, and activation of this process is automatic and unconscious in its sensitivity to contextual changes (Fischbein and Lord, 2004). It is noteworthy to assert that national culture as a contextual factor is found to have an impact on the formation of ILTs. Culture is defined as a shared belief that differentiates a group of members from another and is deeply rooted in each country due to past dependency. As leadership perception is formed by ILTs and leader prototypes are affected by the shared beliefs and values that are embedded in national culture, this contextual factor is argued to be an important dimension to be considered when it comes to leadership study (Fischbein and Lord, 2004; Yukl, 2013)

Critically speaking, the assumption of leadership universality provides an insufficient explanation. Leadership does not occur in a vacuum and it is not culture neutral (Ayman and Korabik, 2010; Chin, 2011). Ayman and Korabik (2010: 166) assert that studies on culture matter because they have impact on a 'leader's style, behaviour, emergence and effectiveness'. In view of the importance of culture on the leadership experience, acknowledging an intertwined contextual factor such as culture is critical for enhancing understandings of leadership (Day and Antonakis, 2012; Zagorsek et al, 2004).

Leadership development in organizations

In addition to the understanding of leadership theories, leadership development is crucial for organizations practically, thus it is essential to differentiate the distinction between leader and leadership development for the adoption of an effective approach.

Day (2000) argues that the development of human capital (leader development) as compared with social capital (leadership development) is the core orientation difference of the two approaches. Leader development focuses more on individual capabilities. It aims at developing three main areas of skill – cognitive, social/emotional, and behavioural – which serve as intrapersonal competence foundations.

By contrast, the aim of leadership development is to develop a leadership team with effective work relationships. The focus is on the development of collective leadership capacity and quality with emphasis on contexts such as social processes and structures, and group or team activities, and is related to organizational development concepts. Iszatt-White and Saunders (2014) elaborate further that it is a systemic approach which aims at developing shared understanding or vision regarding the required leadership in an organization and how it is to be enacted. It is also argued that by developing the individual skills and attributes of a leader, leadership quality will eventually be increased. They also suggest organizational factors such as reward and appraisal systems are to be integrated alongside the organizational leadership development. In this sense, rather than leader development, a situation-specific leadership development approach should be adopted in organizations for collective performance improvement and survival.

Traditionally, leadership development is mainly facilitated with training and development interventions in the hope of enhancing collective leadership quality by developing individual leader skills and competence. Most of the time, this approach fails because it is designed according to the unproven assumption that 'leadership is the sum of what leaders do' (Storey, 2011: 189). However, this does not imply that one must choose either leader or leadership development, as development of human and social capitals are intertwined (Day, 2000). In this vein, a situation- and organization-specific education model aligning with an emerging leadership paradigm is crucial. Barker (1997) suggest that skill-based training is still required for those who are in need of subconscious subroutine enhancement. Executive development with a focus on reflection and interpretation will help people to explore and develop personal values, with the aim of facilitating their participation in the leadership development process, and leadership education is for exploring social patterns and moral orders with the integration of experience, insights and values for developing conscious awareness (Barker, 1997). As leadership development is about learning on the job and experiencing within social contexts, in addition to classroom training, interventions such as 360-degree feedback, coaching mentoring, job assignments and trigger events may be adopted in the latter two approaches, and networking and action learning would be particularly useful for social capital development, which is the highlight of leadership education (Day, 2000).

Nonetheless, providing leadership development opportunities to all employees is not sufficient to guarantee and sustain leadership effectiveness. Situational contexts such as strategy, culture, organizational structure and systems play an important role in creating the supportive environment for leadership development (Iszatt-White and Saunders, 2014). Moreover, holistic integration with business strategy and other complementary HR processes and practices such as selection, reward and succession planning are also pivotal to sustain the leadership development impact (Storey, 2011).

Yet difficulties are found in terms of implementation and result measurement. While TFL is recognized as an effective leadership style, large organizations may find it difficult to nurture TFL culture. Decentralized structure and context-focused job design may not be applicable to some organizations due to business needs and difficulties in selecting and developing emotionally stable leaders; internal developers may not be involved in the strategic planning process and further investigation is needed on applicability of the model across different cultures (Jung, Yammarino and Lee, 2009; Menges et al, 2011; Walter and Bruch, 2010; Storey, 2011). Moreover, use of competence-focused evaluation for leadership development effectiveness is also questioned as it fails to capture the benefits of social capital development and ignores the impact of context such as culture (Iszatt-White and Saunders, 2014). Despite the execution difficulties, leadership development chances for all potential leaders are recommended as employees are the sustainable resource of organizations from the resource-based view (RBV) perspective and development of people's collective leadership capacity is deemed crucial for organizations' survival.

Cross-cultural leadership

Cross-cultural leadership research

A majority of leadership research has been conducted in the context of western culture. In recent decades, scholars have started to use a more systematic approach to study cross-cultural leadership across different cultures and organizations (Hernandez et al, 2011). Scholars argue that cultural and institutional factors form the macro environment of organization, and these contextual factors have potential influence on leadership practice (Klenke, 2011). Cross-cultural studies remark clearly that expectations of individuals are influenced by cultural differences; evolution of leadership assumptions and philosophies in organizations are found to be in line with the culture within which they function (Dorfman, 1996; Hofstede, Hofstede and Minkov, 2010; House et al, 2004).

Among contemporary management scholars, Hofstede defines culture as 'the collective programming of the human mind that distinguishes the members of one group or category of people from another' (Hofstede, Hofstede and Minkov, 2010: 6). Broadly speaking, as history is embedded within societies and has a direct impact on people's beliefs and behaviours, it can be concluded that culture is a system of beliefs, values and practices with strong path dependencies, and each culture is enabled to solve universal problems with divergent ways (Greener, 2002). Over the past few decades, many researchers have developed different cultural models to differentiate between national cultures, such as Hall's high/low context system (Shi and Wang, 2011), the Hofstede model (Shi and Wang, 2011), studies by Schwartz and Bilsky (1987), Trompenaars (1993), and the GLOBE Model (House et al, 2004; Shi and Wang, 2011). Of all the different studies, Hofstede's work has had a great impact in leadership and management studies and is still the most widely cited for analysis of phenomena in different cultures (cited 1,800 times through 1999) (Chao and Tian, 2011; Kirkman, Lowe and Gibson, 2006; Shi and Wang, 2011). Hofstede's research covers more than 100,000 employees in more than 40 countries and has provided the first theoretic basis for understanding why and how countries are different from each other, and for helping to understand cross-cultural leadership features (Iszatt-White and Saunders, 2014; Maude, 2011).

Global leadership and organizational behaviour effectiveness (GLOBE)

Building on the work of Hofstede and others, in 1991, Robert House initiated an extensive study, Global Leadership and Organizational Behaviour Effectiveness (GLOBE), in the specific area of culture and leadership (House et al, 2004). It is regarded as one of the most extensive pieces of research of international nature as it is an ongoing programme involving more than 160 investigators covering 61 cultures (Northouse, 2016). The ultimate objective of GLOBE is to build an empirically based theory to 'describe, understand, and predict the impact of specific cultural variables on leadership and organizational processes and the effectiveness of these processes' (House et al, 2002: 4). Specifically, two key matters are addressed in this study: first, the extent of similarities and differences in effective leadership in different countries, and the root causes for these differences; second, the explanation of the cultural influence on leadership beliefs and behaviours. With a large amount of data collected from 17,000 managers in more than 950 organizations as supporting evidence, this multi-phase study has confirmed that effective leadership can be culturally bound and the unique cultural context needs to be paid attention to when it comes to the study of how leadership functions (Hernandez et al, 2011).

The nine value dimensions

GLOBE researchers identified nine value dimensions as follows.

1. Uncertainty avoidance

Uncertainty avoidance measures the degree to which an organization, society or group counts on social norms, rituals, and bureaucratic practices to avoid uncertainty and minimize the unpredictability of future events. In other words, it refers to the extent to which a group looks for order, consistency, formal framework and process, and rules to deal with daily situations. From the view of people from high-UA societies, 'What is different, is dangerous' (Gudykunst, 2004: 61). As a result, they have a strong desire for control of work process through internal regulations, although in this case discretionary power of superiors outweighs internal rules where power distance is large. In countries with high uncertainty avoidance such as Portugal and Greece, people tend to look for consensus and feel more comfortable in structured environments; therefore, deviant behaviour is not acceptable (Hofstede, Hofstede and Minkov, 2010). In addition, their need for clarity is also reflected in communication; they are more expressive and look for a structure in relationships and communication which makes events more predictable and interpretable (Hofstede, Hofstede and Minkov, 2010). In these societies there is a relatively higher degree of formalization and decentralized organizational structure where management by personal control is not preferred (Sully de Luque and Javidan, 2004). In contrast, people in societies with low uncertainty avoidance, such as Egypt, have lower levels of stress, weaker superego, higher willingness to take risks, lower-key communication style, and are more open to different opinions (Northouse, 2016). Rules should only be established in case of necessity and problems can be solved with informal rules (Sully de Luque and Javidan, 2004).

2. Power distance

Power distance refers to the extent to which the group members show expectation and agreement about the unequal sharing of power. Broadly speaking, this dimension describes the degree of a group's acceptance and endorsement of authority, power distance, and status privilege (Carl, Gupta and Javidan, 2004). Organizations with high power distance endorse hierarchies and power; managers tend not to communicate on equal terms and autocratic communication style is adopted. Gudykunst et al (1996) pointed out that high power distance hinders communication in general, and openness, disclosure and informality are not encouraged. Communication styles of subordinates are found to be deferential, while managers' styles are more paternalistic and condescending. The subordinates either prefer such dependence in the form of autocratic or paternalistic bosses or reject it completely, which is also known in psychology as counterdependence (dependence but with negative sign) (Hofstede, Hofstede and Minkov, 2010). Additionally, as power is seen as a basic part of society, coercive or deferent power are stressed. A study by Bazerman et al (2000) found that members of cultures with high power distance tend to avoid conflict with their superiors (cited in Maude, 2011: 9) and the task culture requires discipline (Hofstede, Hofstede and Minkov, 2010). Conversely, in countries with small power distance such as the United States, individuals are viewed as equal, employees expect consultation from their managers, the task culture demands subordinates' initiatives, and communication in the workplace is actually marked by high levels of informality (Hofstede, Hofstede and Minkov, 2010; Maude, 2011).

3. Collectivism

Societal collectivism describes the degree to which an organization or society encourages institutional or societal collective actions and prefers resources to be distributed collectively. In other words, it concerns whether a culture values broader societal interests more than personal goals and achievements. North Korea is regarded as a typical culture with high societal collectivism value, where the Supreme Leader controls and monitors the country's development and how resources are allocated according to societal interests (Northouse, 2016).

In-group collectivism measures the extent to which people demonstrate pride, loyalty and cohesiveness in their organizations or families. That is, it concerns the degree to which individuals are more committed to their organizations or families than to their personal interests. People from cultures with high in-group collectivism see membership of a cohesive in-group as important to their self-identity, and loyalty to a group as a highly valuable attribute. It is remarked that individuals from these cultures (eg China) are less likely to change their jobs, demonstrate a higher willingness to devote extra time to their organizations and display more organizational citizenship behaviours (Jackson et al, 2006).

Those cultures that value collective goals and interests are found to endorse and appreciate collaborative and team-integrating leadership behaviours. People are concerned more about saving face and status but do not view participation as an important factor of effective leadership. More, leaders in collectivist culture are expected to be capable of managing interpersonal dynamics well (Sully de Luque and Javidan, 2004).

4. Gender egalitarianism

This is the degree to which an organization or society strives to minimize gender role differences and gender discrimination in the home, organizations and communities. In other words, it measures the extent of people's beliefs about how the gender of society members should decide the roles they play in their organizations and societies. In cultures with higher gender egalitarianism, there is a smaller gap between gender roles and more available equal opportunities for women to take over important leadership roles, particularly in the public sector. Due to fewer gender-role expectations, there are fewer biases around individuals' behaviours when being evaluated by their followers and superiors. For example, in Sweden, which is such a culture, people have clear expectations that the power and influence should be shared equally between men and women (Northouse, 2016). A well-supported welfare system also helps both sexes to strike the balance between work and family life. In the light of leadership style preferences, people from cultures with higher gender egalitarianism show higher acceptance levels of charismatic leadership behaviours such as enthusiasm and foresight, and participative leader attributes such as delegator and collective orientation. Attributes such as self-protective, self-centred, status conscious and formal are shunned in the organization and societies in such cultures (Emrich, Denmark and Den Hartog, 2004).

5. Assertiveness

Assertiveness is the extent to which people in organizations or societies are dominant, tough, assertive, confrontational and aggressive in their social relationships.

Assertiveness is not viewed as just a behaviour and trait in the GLOBE study but also as a national culture dimension that reflects shared beliefs about whether individuals are assertive and tough or unassertive and tender in social relationships. In countries with a higher assertiveness culture such as Latin America and Southern European countries, open expressions of emotion are seen as a norm, whereas in Scandinavian and Asian countries, for example, people tend to be more conservative about showing emotions in public (Den Hartog, 2004). When assertiveness as a practice is valued by a culture, people from this culture tend to endorse leadership behaviours that are autonomous, individualistic and independent. Humane leader attributes such as modesty and compassion are also preferred because of followers' need for leaders' social support in an assertive and also highly likely threatening environment (Northouse, 2016). On the contrary, a number of leadership behaviours are not desired by followers if the organization values and practises assertiveness. These are behaviours such as being inclusive and participative in terms of decision making, over-emphasis of team collaboration, team orientation, team integration, and too much diplomacy etc (Den Hartog, 2004).

6. Future orientation

Future orientation is the degree to which individuals in organizations or societies endorse and display behaviours with future orientation such as planning, investing in the future, and delaying gratification. That is, people from such culture hold a belief that their current actions will impact their future, and investment in their future is a priority, as the future matters. In other words, the effects of their current actions are assessed by the planning and development of the future. Many Middle Eastern countries, such as Egypt and Turkey, are more highly past oriented and traditional values and ways of handling things are core to them. It is found that they have conservative tendencies in management and can be slow to make changes to things that tie with the past (Northouse, 2016). Contrarily, Americans hold a strong belief that they can control and plan for the future and initiate idealized change for the sake of changing (Northouse, 2016). Organizations that value future-oriented practices are more likely to endorse leadership behaviours such as team integration, collaborative team orientation, modesty, supportive and considerate leadership, and motivational and inspirational attributes. These organizations with stronger future orientation also tend to endorse visionary leadership where leaders are expected to have the foresight to form future plans and make and well-planned preparations for the future. People from societies such as Israel and Ireland are strongly influenced by the vision of promoting the unique identity of their nations, and this may be an explanation for their high endorsement of visionary leadership (Ashkanasy et al, 2004).

7. Performance orientation

Performance orientation describes the degree to which high standards, individual achievement, performance improvement and excellence are encouraged and rewarded by an organization or society. It is concerned with whether the behaviour of setting challenging goals is rewarded. In the United States, the belief that the role of President can be attained by all citizens is a strong indication of performance orientation (Northouse, 2016). This dimension also includes the future-oriented component of the dimension called Confucian Dynamism (Hofstede and Bond, 1988). That is, the Confucian principles which value perseverance, hard work and learning new skills are seen as instrumental in making progress and improvements, particularly in the context of the Southeast Asia region's economic development (Javidan, 2004). At the organizational level, performance orientation is related to the degree to which the organization is concerned about achievement of ambitious and challenging goals through innovative performance improvement. It reflects the requirement for leaders' excellence orientation and continuous pursuit of advancement. As societal culture is also reflected in organizations, leaders from organizations with high performance orientation value are expected to set challenging goals, communicate high expectations for their followers, challenge them intellectually and facilitate their skill development and confidence building. In contrast, cultures with low performance orientation are reported to endorse social and family relations, loyalty and seniority (Javidan, 2004). For example, horizontal coordination (ie collaboration among counterparts) and networks (or guanxi) are essential for success in China (Hofstede, Hofstede and Minkov, 2010).

8. Humane orientation

Humane orientation is the degree to which individuals in organizations or societies encourage and reward individuals for being fair, altruistic, friendly, generous, caring, and kind to others. This dimension is similar to the dimension labelled kind-heartedness by Hofstede and Bond (1988). It is concerned with the extent to which sensitivity to others, social support and community values are emphasized in a society or an organization. In cultures with high humane orientation, members are expected to display supportive behaviours such as providing financial and material help, spending time together, showing empathy and love, solving problems by sharing information etc. Contrarily, low humane orientation involves endorsement of behaviours such as lack of consideration and promotion of self-interest. In paternalistic societies with high human orientation value such as China, participative leadership with emphasis on collaboration and team integration, and consideration of followers' needs and feelings is preferred. Leaders from this culture are expected to provide social support by offering pastoral care for followers' and employees' personal problems, providing mentoring and coaching when needed and behaving in an approachable and accepting manner (Kabasakal and Bodur, 2004; Yukl, 2013).

An understanding of the aforementioned cultural issues has implications for leadership development in organizations. Cultural sensitivity and diversity has been a popular training and development subject in MNCs (Northouse, 2016). This training aims to increase the awareness of leaders about the characteristics of different cultures and how to deal with cultural differences in a sensitive way. Bing (2004) remarks that an understanding of cultural differences is useful for leadership development as it will help leaders to understand the expectations from global teams better, and to adapt their styles and communicate more effectively in the international environment. In this vein, Ng, Van Dyne and Ang (2009) conclude that enhancing leaders' cultural intelligence with extensive cultural understanding and experiences is pivotal for advancement of leadership effectiveness.

CASE STUDY Global leadership development in a global fashion retailer

This case study takes place in a large multinational organization with headquarters in Germany and an Asia Pacific head office in Hong Kong. It is a global casual fashion and lifestyle brand founded in 1960s in the United States. The group has a presence in over 40 countries, with directly managed retail stores and wholesale points of sale which engage in the sale of collections for women, men and kids.

The organization was unified as a single-unit global brand in 2002; before that, the entities in other continents operated with great autonomy. From 2008 to 2012, the CEO was changed twice, and the company went through robust business transformations and cultural changes. Business models and collaborations among the regions changed after the transformation. Productivity and efficiency of channels became the key focus of the business strategy; that is, more synergy between retail, wholesale and franchise units was needed and a global mindset was seen as a key leadership criterion. As a result, the urgent need to develop global leaders emerged and the Global Leadership Development Programme was launched.

The aim of this programme is to prepare the company for future changes with sufficient supply of global leaders who can facilitate the transformation process. As the company has subsidiaries in different markets globally, execution of headquarters' strategy with adaptation to local market practices is crucial; consequently, a 'global mindset' is set as a key competence to be developed through this programme and the content was structured according to this direction. 'High potential' senior leaders from key markets such Australia, China, Germany, Hong Kong, the Netherlands and the UK were selected as the participants. The 18-month programme was designed to reflect a typical MBA programme structure, with inclusion of business modules such as strategy, leadership, supply chain, finance management etc. These modules were all delivered by professors from European business schools or consultants from the United States. In order to help the leaders to have a better self-awareness about their strengths and weaknesses, psychometric assessments, coaching and mentoring were also included. Challenging global projects were another key element of this programme, as on-the-job learning was seen as an effective intervention to stretch the leaders and enhance their global management experience.

While a global mindset was seen as a key leadership competence for the potential future leaders, the programme was lacking elements about cross-cultural leadership. It was basically a western-centric programme with a focus on the MBA knowledge. During the transformation process, execution of initiatives at subsidiary level was crucial but most of the time that was also where implementation problems happened. This important leadership issue about cross-cultural management and local adaptation was not included or discussed in any part of the programme. The impact of this daily operation leadership problem was reflected in the global project collaboration during the programme. Similar problems were found in this context. For example, there was lack of consideration about subsidiaries' situations and local adaptation from the project leaders who were from the company headquarters. Project members who were from subsidiaries in Asia Pacific (particular in China) complained about their local business needs being neglected and were reluctant to execute the initiatives put forward by headquarters, yet they were not very vocal about the problems they faced as the headquarters-based project leaders were seen as people who were more senior in the organization hierarchy.

The programme has its strength regarding the enhancement of the participants' business knowledge and provided them with career exposure opportunities as a preparation for their planned future promotions. Some of these high-flying leaders who showed excellent performance were promoted to more senior positions. Nevertheless, the overall quality of these leaders as global leaders was doubted by their counterparts at subsidiary level because the leadership problems mentioned were not tackled; similar issues were still found and caused failures regarding global initiative implementation, which harmed the pace of business transformation and effectiveness.

Reflective questions

1 Does the one-size-fits-all leadership development approach work in this organization? What is missing?

2 What were the key gaps reflected in this case about the cross-cultural collaboration between the headquarters and subsidiaries? How could leadership as a possible solution improve the situation?

3 What role did cultural values play in this context?

4 What would be a culturally intelligent way for the Group CHRO to manage the leadership development strategy globally?

CASE STUDY   Global leadership in the 'fast-fashion' industry:
the case of Gap

Gap was founded in California in 1969 by wealthy real estate developer Don Fisher and his wife (Joslin et al, 2010). The brand proved to be an immediate success and became a publicly listed company two years later; by 1975, Gap was already a brand with 186 stores and sales worth US $100 million. As of the end of 2016, the global apparel retailer has a presence in 90 countries with 3,300 company-owned and 400 franchised stores operating under the brands Gap, Old Navy, Banana Republic, PiperLime, Athelta, and Intermix (Gap, 2016).

Nevertheless, the apparel giant has been struggling in the past two decades in the face of challenges brought by fast-fashion rivals such as Zara, H&M and Forever 21 (Brandchannel, 2016). The landscape of fast-fashion retailing is ever changing and highly competitive due to increased globalization and unique market characteristics (Caridi, Perego and Tumino, 2013). Fast-fashion retailers typically adopt the 'speed to market' approach with fast responsiveness and greater flexibility to maintain the relationship between customers and suppliers (Bhardwaj and Fairhurst, 2010). Zara has been seen as the most successful fast-fashion retailer, with continuous international expansion supported by its well-known vertical integration business model (Carugati et al, 2008). This nimble model has the features of a short production cycle and high responsiveness to the ever-changing customer and market needs due to the fact that Zara owns its factories; this allows them to maintain low supply chain costs and to control productivity.

Zara's model became an inspiration for market players and Gap is one of those wanting to take advantage of globalization to stay ahead of the competition (Mayrhofer, 2010; Tokatli, 2008). Gap does not own its own factories, so product manufacturing is subcontracted to over 700 suppliers in the United States and Asia (Mayrhofer, 2010). Since the 1980s, the company has been expanding its business in countries with certain cultural affinities with the United States such as Britain, Canada, France and Germany. In 2012, Gap executed their key expansion plans with more than 30 new Gap stores in China and Japan (Gap, 2012). In 2015 there were already 100 stores in China, and Japan has also become one of Gap's largest foreign subsidies (Gap, 2015).

However, due to the intensification of competition in the past decade, Gap has had difficulties, leading to the reduction of stores in the aforementioned countries (Mayrhofer, 2010). When Art Peck was appointed as the new CEO of

Gap in 2014, 'product to market' business transformation initiatives were put in place to support the long-term growth strategy with a focus on global growth, product, experience, and talent (Gap, 2014). Yet the impact of these initiatives was not reflected in business results for quick turnaround, and the closure of 175 stores in 2015 did not help the bottom line a lot; the profits for that year were US $920 million – a 27 per cent decline from 2014 (Gap, 2014; 2015; Li, 2016). Cost impact is now an important consideration with regard to stabilizing the shaking business that has seen the targeting of cash balance, the closure of an entire fleet of 53 Old Navy stores in Japan. Further development of a responsive supply chain with a supplier network heavily built in China and Vietnam, and continuous growth in Asia became the key business directions in 2015 and 2016 (Gap, 2015; 2016).

The change of CEO and frequent shifts of business direction, particularly in the Asia market in the past few years, have reflected the uncertainties issues faced by the Gap leadership team. These changes create big losses for the company and leadership effectiveness appears to be crucial for the future.

Reflective questions

1 What are the implications of Gap's transformation on cross-cultural leadership?

2 What are the possible leadership risks in this situation when Gap has been going through constant and drastic changes?

3 Whilst Asian countries (particularly China and Vietnam) are seen as key in support of the future business development, what strategies could the American leaders from headquarters employ to better integrate different groups outside the United States?

4 What kind of leadership styles/attributes would you suggest to the Gap leaders to better manage global integration and team dynamics?

Conclusions

Culture is a set of common beliefs and values shared amongst individuals with the same cultural background, and has an impact on the sense-making mechanism of people's values and preferences (Yukl, 2013). As the influence of culture is reflected and translated in the context of leadership and organizational processes, its impact is significant when it comes to leadership effectiveness (House et al, 2002). In the light of increasingly dynamic and international business contexts, leaders who are able to understand, operate and manage in the global environment are seen as a valuable and inimitable competitive advantage for organizations (Ng, Van Dyne and Ang, 2009). As it is acknowledged that there is an insufficient supply of global leaders, in view of the importance of these leaders in the complicated international business environment, the task of global leadership development should without doubt be a priority for multinational organizations (Evans et al, 2011).

Key learning points

- Have an awareness of the cultural differences and possible challenges faced by global leaders.

- Pay more attention to the followers' perspectives and expectations in the context of global leadership.

- Cross-cultural understanding and experience is crucial in the light of leadership development and this element should be incorporated in the organization's culture and training and development programmes

References

Acker, J (1990) Hierarchies, jobs, bodies: a theory of gendered organizations, *Gender and Society*, **4** (2), pp. 139–58

Ashkanasy, N M et al (2004) Future orientation, in *Culture, Leadership, and Organizations: The GLOBE study of 62 societies*, eds R House et al, Sage Publications, pp. 282–31

Ayman, R and Korabik, K (2010) Leadership: why gender and culture matter, *American Psychologist*, **65** (3) pp. 157–70

Bamber, G J, Lansbury, R D and Wailes, N (2011) *International & Comparative Employment Relations Globalisation and Change*, 5th edn, Sage Publications

Barker, R A (1997) How can we train leaders if we do not know what leadership is? *Human relations*, **50** (4), pp. 343–62

Bass, B M (1985) *Leadership and Performance Beyond Expectations*, Free Press, New York, Collier Macmillan, London

Bass, B M (1990) *Bass and Stogdill's Handbook of Leadership: Theory, research, and management applications*, 3rd edn, Free Press, New York

Bass, B M (1997). Does the transactional–transformational leadership paradigm transcend organizational and national boundaries? American Psychologist 52 (2), 130–139

Bazerman, M H et al (2000) Negotiation, *Annual Review of Psychology*, **51** (1), pp. 279–314

Bhardwaj, V and Fairhurst, A (2010) Fast fashion: response to changes in the fashion industry, *The International Review of Retail, Distribution and Consumer Research*, **20** (1), pp. 165–73

Bing, J W (2004) Hofstede's consequences: the impact of his work on consulting and business practices, *The Academy of Management Executive (1993–2005)*, pp. 80–87

Blackmore, J (2010) Leadership and gender, in *International Encyclopedia of Education*, eds P Peterson, E Baker and B McGaw, Elsevier, pp. 797–802

Brandchannel (2016) Gap Inc trims Old Navy and Banana Republic in brand overhaul [online] http://brandchannel.com/2016/05/19/gap-inc-051916/ [accessed 5 June 2017]

Broadbridge, A and Simpson, R (2011) 25 Years on: reflecting on the past and looking to the future in gender and management research, *British Journal of Management*, **22** (3), pp. 470–83

Bryman, A (1992) *Charisma and Leadership in Organizations*, Sage Publications

Caridi, M, Perego, A and Tumino, A (2013) Measuring supply chain visibility in the apparel industry, *Benchmarking: An International Journal*, **20** (1), pp. 25–44

Carugati, A, Liao, R and Smith, P (2008), Speed-to-fashion: managing global supply chain in Zara, in *Management of Innovation and Technology*, ICMIT 2008, 4th IEEE International Conference, pp. 1494–99

Carl, D, Gupta, V and Javidan, M (2004) Power distance, in *Culture, Leadership, and Organizations: The GLOBE study of 62 societies*, eds R House et al, Sage Publications, pp. 513–63

Chao, C C and Tian, D (2011) Culturally universal or culturally specific: a comparative study of anticipated female leadership styles in Taiwan and the United States, *Journal of Leadership & Organizational Studies*, **18** (1) pp. 64–79

Chin, J L (2010) Introduction to the special issue on diversity and leadership, *American Psychologist*, **65** (3) pp. 150–56

Chin, J L (2011) Women and leadership: transforming visions and current contexts, *Forum on Public Policy* [online] http://forumonpublicpolicy.com/vol2011.no2/archivevol2011.no2/chin.rev.pdf [accessed 5 June 2017]

Day, D V (2000) Leadership development: a review in context, *The Leadership Quarterly*, **11** (4), pp. 581–613

Day, D V and Antonakis, J (2012) *The Nature of Leadership*, 2nd edn, Sage, London

Den Hartog, D N (2004) Assertiveness, in *Culture, Leadership, and Organizations: The GLOBE study of 62 societies*, eds R House et al, Sage Publications, pp. 395–436

Dickson, M, Den Hartog, D and Mitchelson, J (2003) Research on leadership in a cross-cultural context: making progress, and raising new questions, *The Leadership Quarterly*, **14**, pp. 729–68

Dorfman, P W (1996) International and cross-cultural leadership research, in *Handbook for International Management Research*, eds B J Punnett and O Shenkar, University of Michigan Press

Eagly, A H, Johannesen-Schmidt, M C and van Engen, M I (2003) Transformational, transactional, and laissez-faire leadership styles: a meta-analysis comparing women and men, *Psychological Bulletin*, **129** (4) pp. 569–91

Edwards, T and Rees, C (2011) *International Human Resource Management: Globalization, national systems and multinational companies*, 2nd edn, Pearson

Emrich, C G, Denmark, F L and Den Hartog, D N (2004) Cross-cultural differences in gender egalitarianism: implications for societies, organizations, and leaders, in *Culture, Leadership, and Organizations: The GLOBE study of 62 societies*, eds R House et al, Sage Publications, pp. 343–94

Epitropaki, O et al (2013) Implicit leadership and followership theories 'in the wild': taking stock of information-processing approaches to leadership and followership in organizational settings, *The Leadership Quarterly*, **24** (6), pp. 858–81

Ergeneli, A, Gohar, R and Temirbekova, Z (2007) Transformational leadership: its relationship to culture value dimensions, *International Journal of Intercultural Relations*, **31** (6), pp. 703–24

Evans, P et al (2010) Leadership development in multinational firms, *Leadership in Organizations: Current issues and key trends*, ed J Storey, Routledge, p. 207

Fischbein, R and Lord, R G (2004) Implicit leadership theories, in *Encyclopedia of Leadership*, eds G Goethals, G Sorenson and J M Burns, Sage Publications, pp. 700–06

Gap (2012) Annual Report [online] http://phx.corporate-ir.net/External. File?item=UGFyZW50SUQ9MTc3ODA0fENoaWxkSUQ9LTF8VHlw ZT0z&t=1 [accessed 05 June 2017]

Gap (2014) Annual Report [online] http://www.gapinc.com/content/ attachments/gapinc/GPS%202014%20Annual%20Report.pdf [accessed 05 June 2017]

Gap (2015) Annual Report [online] http://phx.corporate-ir.net/External. File?item=UGFyZW50SUQ9MzMxMzk4fENoaWxkSUQ9LTF8VHlwZ T0z&t=1&cb=635954753332651759 [accessed 05 June 2017]

Gap (2016) Annual Report [online] http://www.gapinc.com/content/ dam/gapincsite/documents/GPS%202015%20Annual%20Report.pdf [accessed 05 June 2017]

Greener, I (2002) Theorising path-dependency: how does history come to matter in organizations? *Management Decision*, **40** (6) pp. 614–19, available from Emerald eJournals

Gudykunst, W B (2004) *Bridging Differences: Effective Intergroup Communication*, 4th edn, Sage Publications, London

Gudykunst, W B et al (1996) The influence of cultural individualism-collectivism, self construals, and individual values on communication styles across cultures, *Human Communication Research*, **22** (4), pp. 510–43

Hernandez, M et al (2011) The loci and mechanisms of leadership: exploring a more comprehensive view of leadership theory, *The Leadership Quarterly*, **22** (6), pp.1165–85

Hofstede, G and Bond, M H (1988) The Confucius connection: from cultural roots to economic growth, *Organizational Dynamics*, **16** (4), pp. 5–21

Hofstede, G, Hofstede, G J and Minkov, M (2010) *Cultures and Organizations: Software of the mind*, revised and expanded, McGraw-Hill, New York

House, R et al (2002) Understanding cultures and implicit leadership theories across the globe: an introduction to project GLOBE, *Journal of World Business*, **37** (1), pp. 3–10

House, R J et al, eds (2004) *Culture, Leadership, and Organizations: The GLOBE study of 62 societies*, Sage Publications

Iszatt-White, M and Saunders, C (2014) *Leadership*, Oxford University Press

Jackson, B and Parry, K (2011) *A Very Short, Fairly Interesting and Reasonably Cheap Book About Studying Leadership*, 2nd edn, Sage Publications

Jackson, C L et al (2006) Psychological collectivism: a measurement validation and linkage to group member performance, *Journal of Applied Psychology*, **91** (4), p. 884

Javidan, M (2004) Performance orientation, in *Culture, Leadership, and Organizations: The GLOBE study of 62 societies*, eds R House et al, Sage Publications, pp.239–81

Joslin, R et al (2010) Gap, Inc: has the retailer lost its style? *Understanding Business Strategy: Concepts and Cases*, pp.1–18

Jung, D, Yammarino, F J and Lee, J K (2009) Moderating role of subordinates' attitudes on transformational leadership and effectiveness: a multi-cultural and multi-level perspective, *The Leadership Quarterly*, **20** (4), pp. 586–603

Kabasakal, H and Bodur, M (2004) Humane orientation in societies, organizations, and leader attributes, in *Culture, Leadership, and Organizations: The GLOBE study of 62 societies*, eds R House et al, Sage Publications, pp. 564–601

Kark, R (2004) The transformational leader: who is (s)he? A feminist perspective, *Journal of Organizational Change Management*, **17** (2) pp. 160–76

Kirkman, B L, Lowe, K B and Gibson, C B (2006) A quarter century of culture's consequences: a review of empirical research incorporating Hofstede's Cultural Values Framework, *Journal of International Business Studies*, **37** (3) pp. 285–320

Klenke, K (2011) *Women in Leadership: Contextual dynamics and boundaries*, Emerald Group Publishing, Bradford

Li, S (2016) Does Gap have an identity problem? Why the retailer's sales keep dropping, *LA Times* [online] http://www.latimes.com/business/la-fi-gap-struggles-20160517-snap-story.html [accessed 5 June 2017]

Lord, R G, De Vader, C L and Alliger, G M (1986) A meta-analysis of the relation between personality traits and leadership perceptions: An application of validity generalization procedures, *Journal of Applied Psychology*, **71**, pp. 402–10

Lord, R and Maher, K (1991) *Leadership and Information Processing: Linking perceptions and processes*, Unwin Hyman, Boston

Lord, R G et al (2001) Contextual constraints on prototype generation and their multilevel consequences for leadership perceptions, *The Leadership Quarterly*, **12** (3), pp. 311–38

Maria, J F and Arenas, D (2009) Societal ethos and economic development organizations in Nicaragua, *Journal of Business Ethics*, **88** (2), pp. 231–44

Maude, B (2011) *Managing Cross-Cultural Communication: Principles and practice*, Palgrave Macmillan

Mayrhofer, U (2010) International distribution: the paradoxical logics developed by retail groups, in *The Paradoxes of Globalisation*, eds E Milliot and N Tournois, Palgrave Macmillan UK, pp. 132–44

Menges, J I et al (2011) Transformational leadership climate: performance linkages, mechanisms, and boundary conditions at the organizational level, *The Leadership Quarterly*, **22** (5), pp. 893–909

Ng, K Y, Van Dyne, L and Ang, S (2009) From experience to experiential learning: cultural intelligence as a learning capability for global leader development, *Academy of Management Learning & Education*, **8** (4), pp. 511–26

Northouse, P G (2016) *Leadership: Theory and practice*, Sage Publications

Sarros, J C and Santora, J C (2001) The transformational-transactional leadership model in practice, *Leadership & Organization Development Journal*, **22** (8) pp. 383–94

Schwartz, S H and Bilsky, W (1987) Toward a universal psychological structure of human values, *Journal of Personality and Social Psychology*, **53**, pp. 550–62

Sheppard, J A, Sarros, J C and Santora, J C (2013) Twenty-first century leadership: international imperatives, *Management Decision*, **51** (2) pp. 267–80

Shi, X and Wang, J (2011) Interpreting Hofstede model and GLOBE model: which way to go for cross-cultural research? *International Journal of Business and Management*, **6** (5), pp. 93–99

Shondrick, S J and Lord, R G (2010) Implicit leadership and follower-ship theories: dynamic structures for leadership perceptions, memory, and leader-follower processes, *International Review of Industrial and Organizational Psychology*, **25** (1), pp. 1–33

Steers, R M, Sanchez-Runde, C and Nardon, L (2012) Leadership in a global context: new directions in research and theory development, *Journal of World Business*, **47** (4), pp. 479–82

Stogdill, R M (1974) *Handbook of Leadership: A survey of theory and research*, Free Press

Storey, J (2011) *Leadership and Organizations Current Issues and Key Trends*, 2nd edn, Routledge

Storey, J (2016) Changing theories of leadership and leadership development, *Leadership in Organizations: Current issues and key trends*, p. 17

Sully de Luque, M and Javidan, M (2004) Uncertainty avoidance, in *Culture, Leadership, and Organizations: The GLOBE study of 62 societies*, eds R House et al, Sage Publications, pp.602–53

Tokatli, N (2008) Global sourcing: insights from the global clothing industry—the case of Zara, a fast fashion retailer, *Journal of Economic Geography*, 8 (1), pp. 21–38

Trompenaars K (1993) *Riding the Waves of Culture: Understanding cultural diversity in business*, Nicholas Brealey, London

Wade, R (1996) Globalization and its limits: reports of the death of the national economy are greatly exaggerated, *National diversity and global capitalism*, 8, pp. 60–88

Walter, F and Bruch, H (2010) Structural impacts on the occurrence and effectiveness of transformational leadership: an empirical study at the organizational level of analysis, *The Leadership Quarterly*, 21 (5), pp. 765–82

Yukl, G (2013) *Leadership in Organizations*, 8th edn, Prentice Hall, London

Zaccaro, S J (2007) Trait-based perspectives of leadership, *American Psychologist*, 62 (1), p. 6

Zagorsek, H, Jaklic, M and Stough, S J (2004) Comparing leadership practices between the United States, Nigeria, and Slovenia: does culture matter?' *Cross Cultural Management: An International Journal*, 11 (2), pp. 16–34

04
Cross-cultural communication

JAMES BABA ABUGRE

Learning outcomes

At the end of this chapter, you should be able to:

- understand the complexities associated with communication across different cultural contexts;
- recognize the significance of cross-cultural communication to expatriates in international management;
- understand the key challenges associated with expatriate communication in different contexts of MNC subsidiaries;
- recognize the need for cross-cultural training when communicating across cultures;
- understand that competence in cross-cultural communication is the key tool for expatriates' efficiency in and adjustment to local subsidiaries;
- acquire practical learning examples from the empirical case study.

Introduction

The goal of this chapter is to explain the role of cultural differences in communication and their importance to multinational companies (MNCs) in international business. In the face of globalization, MNCs send out global managers – expatriates – to work in their foreign subsidiaries in distant locations around the world. An expatriate, by this definition, is a person who has been sent by his or her company to another country to work in a subsidiary. You are likely to find the term expatriate also used sweepingly for people from Europe, North America or Australia, working in emerging economies such as China, despite being locally recruited there. A British national taking up employment with a language school in China, for example, is not an expatriate according to this definition.

Therefore, in international human resource management (IHRM), expatriates are staff or employees who are transferred to a country other than their own to work in the subsidiary MNC. Their role in international assignments is usually to establish a relationship between the MNC headquarters (HQ) and the MNC subsidiary in a distant location or country. This presupposes that expatriates must be able to understand and communicate effectively in the subsidiary locations in order to competently transfer knowledge and skills from the MNC HQ to the MNC subsidiary location. This is possible if expatriates are skilful in cross-cultural communication, which involves the communication between people from different cultures, who share different value attributes and social relations.

Globalization has succeeded in bringing the world and its different cultures under one umbrella. Phatak, Bhagat and Kashlak (2005: 60) describe globalization as the growing economic interdependence of countries worldwide and the increasing integration of economic life across national boundaries, through the increasing size and variety of cross-border transactions in goods, services, capital flows, and rapid and widespread diffusion of technology. This increase in global business has led to more employees being sent on foreign assignments than ever before, and therefore an enormous pressure has been exerted on the IHRM activity of MNCs. Consequently, administrators of MNCs, including international corporations, are confronted daily with the task of how to manage people from diverse nationalities and cultures working together to achieve organizational goals (Stahl et al, 2017). Managing people from diverse cultures in an organization can be described as cross-cultural management, and a critical element of cross-cultural management is cross-cultural communication. Cross-cultural communication is a process that involves the interaction between people who are culturally different from each other in such important areas as their value orientations, preferred communication codes, role expectations, and perceived rules of social relations (Moran, Harris and Moran, 2011). The approach and style of communication adopted in cross-national businesses can make the business either successful or unsuccessful (Okoro, 2012; Padhi, 2016). Communicating across cultures requires a well-planned effort that will embrace the cultural differences and similarities among the people working together in the company under consideration (Padhi, 2016). Hence, cross-cultural communication can be described as the recognition of diverse communicative behaviours of expatriates and local employees of MNCs across diverse cultures. It enables expatriate managers and local employees from different cultures to co-exist and to coordinate their work activities in a concerted effort towards the achievement of corporate goals (Nakayama and Halualani, 2010; Abugre, 2016).

Cross-cultural communication is indispensable to expatriates' work in the subsidiary MNC (Abugre, 2016). According to Stahl et al (2017), expatriates who are able to effectively manage cross-cultural communication are able to appreciate the way cultural differences and distance can improve business effectiveness and performance of the MNC.

In the coming paragraphs, this chapter will describe in detail what cross-cultural communication is and its significance to IHRM; we will discuss the context and cultural dilemmas of cross-cultural communication, cross-cultural training and cross-cultural communication. A case study will underpin this discussion by drawing on the views of expatriates on the essence of cross-cultural communication.

Cross-cultural communication in international business

It is an undeniable fact that communication is one of the most important human processes, and that people cannot live without communicating with each other. Different human behaviours arise from variations in responses to and interpretations of messages of communication (Samovar and Porter, 1997). This is because there is a wide multicultural make-up of people working together and yet they may not understand each other due to variations in communicative behaviours. Thus, understanding the interactions between people is crucially related to an understanding of the ways in which messages are relayed through spoken and written languages.

In international management, the ability to effectively communicate with people from other cultures has become an increasingly important skill in the corporate life of multinational companies. The increasingly competitive nature of global business presupposes that MNCs must rely more and more on their employees having the skills and competencies to appreciate issues across cultures. Hence the significance of cross-cultural communication competence in international business.

As corporations move toward employing global teams across all levels, expatriate managers who come from different parts of the world have to increase their knowledge of the complex nature of team interaction so as to develop the skills required not only to be team members but also to plan, organize, lead and sustain these teams. This advocates the importance of understanding team interaction through cross-cultural communication competence. Accordingly, there is a need for expatriates to develop competence in cross-cultural communication in order to manage cultural diversity, cultural differences, and cross-cultural conflicts which may have become common sources of tension and conflict among multicultural team members in the subsidiary. People can easily misinterpret and misunderstand each other due to the differences in their cultural upbringings. Therefore, understanding the differences in the individual team members' preferences in interpersonal and impersonal communication behaviours at the initiating stages of their work can help prevent potential intercultural barriers among these multicultural team members as they work together within the MNC (Zhu, Nel and Bhat, 2006).

The next section will discuss the significance of cross-cultural communication in international management using expatriates as the conduit and link between multinational businesses.

The significance of cross-cultural communication to expatriate work in international management

Though communication comes in many different forms, global managers are still getting themselves into problems by assuming that communication is the same everywhere (McFarlin and Sweeney, 2006). This results from the fact that there are fundamental differences in the ways various cultures view the essential facts of the lives of a group of people, and it is important to gain an understanding of the values and deep structures of the cultures with which one is communicating or negotiating (Samovar and Porter, 1997). Consequently, understanding the value system of another culture can help an expatriate worker appreciate the behaviours of its people and know how to communicate with them appropriately. For example, knowing that the Sub-Saharan African business terrain is complex and multi-faceted because of the multiplicity of linguistics and language usage arising from multiple cultural values would help a Western expatriate working in that region to appreciate the difficulties the indigenous employees go through in order to process an official work communication, since they have to shift between the indigenous language and the official languages like English, French and Portuguese adopted from their former colonial masters (Abugre, 2016). Hence, cross-cultural communication competence demonstrates the importance of learning to understand the cultural differences in the manner in which diverse people undertake their business actions. While there is evidence for the universal experience of communication behaviours, culture influences the expression of emotion through cultural display rules or norms which prescribe the kinds of feelings that should be displayed or expressed in a particular context (Lutz and White, 1986). This is why there are no universally acceptable display rules on non-verbal expressions of communication (eg the terminologies and jargons used) as non-verbal expressions vary from culture to culture without fixed symbolic meanings. But, to effectively understand these non-verbal expressions, one has to learn them in the context in which they are used. Thus, for expatriates to be successful in international management, they must communicate with the local or indigenous employees who share different cultures, and they (expatriates) must be able to identify the communicative behaviours such as norms or rules of interaction in the local subsidiary. For example, when expatriates sojourn to subsidiary locations they definitely come into contact with local employees who are host-country nationals from where the MNC subsidiary is located.

These host-country nationals have their own cultural values and linguistic orientations, and the expatriates working with them will only succeed if they learn to adapt to the indigenous behaviours and attitudes of the local people, for example, the way they think and do things differently from the expatriates.

Cross-cultural communication competence deepens expatriates' understanding of and proficiency in the delicate behaviours and attitudes embedded in the host cultural language.

Having competence in cross-cultural communication means having the ability to communicate effectively with co-workers or team members who are culturally different from you in the host subsidiary community. Therefore, cross-cultural communication competence is the overall internal capacity to decode and encode information in accordance with the communication practices of the host culture (Kim, 1988; 1995). When expatriates acquire sufficient levels of cross-cultural communication competence, they become more mature members of the host society and less reliant on local workers for protection in managing their daily activities. The host communication competence indicates the ability of expatriates to properly identify and realize messages from the host environment in different situations of interaction. Consequently, cross-cultural communication is very significant to expatriates' ability to work and manage the multinational subsidiary in a distant environment.

Having explained the significance of cross-cultural communication in international management, the next section deals with the difficulties and dilemmas of cross-cultural communication faced by MNCs due to different business contexts and locations in their international operations.

Context and cultural dilemma of cross-cultural communication

The multinational corporation (MNC) is an organization composed of several business units and diverse work groups spread across the globe. As a result, MNCs send expatriate executives from subsidiary to subsidiary and from one country to another in order to build their global relationships and also to develop a common corporate culture within their human resource management practices. This also guarantees that the MNCs have the necessary talent in the right location at the right time. Consequently, MNCs use multiple types of employees who hail from different countries and cultures to operate their various transnational businesses, which presupposes the usefulness and application of multiple language usages or multilingualism in international business. This linguistic divergence of the staff which results from the different speech communities they come from can pose a contextual dilemma of cross-cultural communication to international business. This is even more problematic when the language of the HQ does not share any common knowledge or similarities with that of the local subsidiary. As a diverse group of people within the MNC in the various local subsidiaries, the expatriates or assignees to these foreign subsidiaries must learn the communicative behaviours of the local employees in order to be able to understand and appreciate their behaviours. 'Communicative behaviours' refers to the various linguistic forms and non-verbal arrangements pertaining to a specific culture, which foreigners and people who do not hail from that culture can find difficult to understand (Abugre, 2016).

Therefore, the context of subsidiary operations brings about the dilemma of cross-cultural management and communication due to the social and cultural differences and the wide geographical distance between the expatriate's home country and the subsidiary location. The geographical origins of people working together in a subsidiary have a strong impact on their cultural value orientations, which can impede the level of cultural aggregation of expatriates in the subsidiary if a common basis of language or communication is lacking. Wide differences in cultural upbringing and contextual languages generate communication gaps and differences amongst people. The differences are created and sustained by a complex set of values and behaviours that are deeply embedded within the members of a culture (Lustig and Koester, 2006). Since the value systems are firmly linked to the individual employee or staff identity, it is critical that both expatriates and local staff understand the others' cultural values and their importance, as disrespect for people's values can lead to conflict and a turbulent multinational subsidiary. Thus, cultural patterns and orientations in the form of contextual communicative behaviours are significant determinants of different organizational behaviours which MNCs cannot afford to overlook in the operations of their subsidiaries in distant cultures. This is why cross-cultural communication competence is of great significance for expatriate management and operations in complex subsidiary cultures. Complex subsidiary cultures mean that MNCs are branded as multilingual communities, as they consist of groups of subunits dispersed across a variety of cultures, each workforce having its own native language, form of discourse and cultural environment (Babcock and DuBabcock, 2001; Phillips, Lawrence and Hardy, 2004). In transnational business, communication boundaries are not clear cut; however, multiple languages are often and concurrently used within a subunit, between subunits, and between subunits and headquarters (Luo and Shenkar, 2006). Therefore, effective application of communication strategies and proper language design for foreign assignees or expatriates can improve intra-network communication, inter-unit learning, parent–subsidiary coordination and integration, and intra-unit value creation within the geographically dispersed network of the MNC (Luo and Shenkar, 2006).

It is therefore important that, to communicate more effectively in global business environments, foreign assignees or expatriates understand basic features about cultures and subcultures. Foreign assignees or expatriates also have to recognize cultural diversity and differences and acquire intercultural sensitivity towards such differences across the globe. Specifically, they should understand acceptable and unacceptable communicative styles that are associated with the various national and cultural values and beliefs. In addition, extensive practical knowledge of how to cope with problems has been directed toward international business communicators, revolving around such issues as verbal (oral and written) and nonverbal communication patterns, business etiquette, business and social customs, and intercultural negotiation processes in different countries (Harris and Moran, 1996). Thus, communication in international business has become an important issue, not only to MNCs transacting business abroad, but to most educational institutions where people are required to gain knowledge of business communication.

Effective communication necessitates an understanding between expatriates and local employees so that the needs of both expatriates and local employees are met in the relationship of work in the subsidiary. Confusions and breakdowns in communication can come about through inability to speak the local language, poor translation, ignorance of idioms, and lack of perception of the meaning of non-verbal language and symbols (Christopher, 2012). Hence, awareness of communicative behaviours, and being careful and ready to learn from people are widely understood to be necessary for interacting successfully with different others (Guirdham, 1999). Being aware of the communicative behaviours of other people is possible through training. Thus, when expatriates are trained in the languages and behaviours of the local people, including the local cultural values, they (expatriates) can become competent in the understanding of issues in the subsidiary. This competence will enable them to work better and also to adjust socially within the local communities. The next section will discuss the perspective of cross-cultural training in cross-cultural communication.

Cross-cultural training and cross-cultural communication

It has become an acceptable norm that people do well in new environments when they understand the norms and protocols governing these new environments. They can start to do this by simply learning to adapt to these foreign norms and protocols; hence, the significance of training in cross-cultural communication of expatriates in foreign multinational subsidiaries.

Expatriate staff in multinational subsidiaries face many inherent problems associated with their assignments, both in the overseas workplace and in the foreign society in which they reside. These problems may involve culture shock (ie the painful effects of being exposed to unfamiliar behaviours in another culture), differences in work-related norms, differences in social relations, and language. Moreover, they may experience personal and family problems that can trigger or increase their level of stress in their professional lives and work. Given this stream of obstacles encountered by expatriates in their line of their work, many are likely to fail in their overseas assignment or may not even be able complete it. As a result, preparing expatriate managers for foreign assignments should be the focus of managers of MNCs. Thus, it is very important for MNCs to train and develop employees in all subsidiary locations so that they can perform their task and accomplish the objectives for which they were sent to the subsidiary locations.

Generally, training is a term often used casually to describe almost any effort initiated by an organization to foster learning among its members. On the other hand, cross-cultural training can be described as the processes and tools used to enhance learning across cultures. It is the knowledge acquired from learning the behaviours and value systems of different cultures.

Cross-cultural training is considered extremely important by international HR practitioners as it helps in developing essentials skills needed for global managers who are expected to work with culturally diverse teams, manage overseas clients, travel to different countries for business purposes, and perform effectively in the field of their assigned job (Pandey, 2012). Thus, cross-cultural training in cross-cultural communication can help expatriates to become competent in cross-cultural issues; it can also help facilitate rapid adjustment to the foreign subsidiary, helping expatriates promptly develop their capabilities in foreign value systems, thereby enhancing their performance and adaptability to the local or subsidiary community (Abugre, 2016).

Language training

As language is regarded as a very important instrument in the operations of international business (Babcock and Du-Babcock, 2001), so is the significance of cross-cultural communication and understanding of a diverse multinational staff working together. Accordingly, Ashamalla (1998) proposes that foreign language training should be an obligation in cross-cultural training of personnel because knowledge of the language of the host country is critical to successfully living and working in that country. This is because linguistic skills and competency of the expatriate can be a significant antecedent to expatriate adjustment and can also enhance expatriates' effective negotiation skills in the foreign culture. Thus, for expatriates assigned to an English-speaking country, pre-departure English language training would facilitate their cross-cultural adjustment and the development of their cross-cultural communication skills (Ko and Yang, 2011). The fact is that there are marked divergences of work behaviours between local or indigenous employees and expatriates, and differences in points of reference, expectations and approaches to work; it is only by training expatriates in this area of cultural specifics that they will better understand the typical indigenous cultural behaviours of the multinational subsidiary. More importantly, cross-cultural training can help to minimize any negative work behaviour of expatriates in the subsidiaries by increasing their cultural awareness.

Thus, through cross-cultural training in cross-cultural communication, MNC executives may be able to disseminate their strategies and policies and implement them effectively with little or no ambiguity in the operations of their foreign businesses.

CASE STUDY Insights from subsidiary locations in Ghana

This case study draws on the views of expatriates (at middle or senior management level) within MNC subsidiaries operating in Ghana. This comprises MNCs from all sectors, including mining, banking and finance, communication, food and beverage, automobile and electronics, and others.

The subsequent section presents empirical information of the views expressed by expatriate executives on specific thematic areas of cross-cultural communication, the significance of cross-cultural communication to expatriates, the importance of cross-cultural training in cross-cultural communication, and strategies to deal with problems of cross-cultural communication in multinational subsidiaries. These themes are grounded in the objectives of the study as indicated below.

Objective 1: To determine the factors that precipitate training in cross-cultural communication for expatriates within MNCs in local subsidiaries.

To address this objective, an open-ended question to the expatriates was asked: *Could you please suggest ways in which expatriates can benefit from training in cross-cultural communication?* Consequently, Table 4.1 below shows the results of respondents' direct answers to the question.

Table 4.1 Benefits of training in cross-cultural communication

Levels of expatriates' opinions on cross-cultural training	Number	Percentage
1 Helps expatriates and their dependent family members integrate into the local subsidiary society	4	2.0%
2 Helps expatriates to understand the two cultures, which will influence decision-making processes at work in the subsidiary	10	4.9%
3 Enables mutual respect of cultural differences, especially from the side of expatriates	9	4.4%
4 Effective communication makes an expatriate's life outside work easier and effective since he/she has learnt the values	6	2.9%

(continued)

Table 4.1 *(Continued)*

Levels of expatriates' opinions on cross-cultural training	Number	Percentage
5 Expatriates become more tolerant and accepting of others when they participate in cross-cultural training	9	4.4%
6 Expatriates learn to understand the way people think, deal with issues and what drives them to behave the way they do	21	10.3%
7 No response	145	71.1%
Total	**204**	**100%**

The table above presents the empirical accounts of expatriates on the importance of cross-cultural communication. The various accounts presented illustrate the fundamental role of cross-cultural communication competence of expatriates in a foreign subsidiary. For instance, training in cross-cultural communication can facilitate and support expatriates, including their dependent family members, to be able to integrate well in the local subsidiary community where the expatriate works. By learning and knowing how to communicate and understand people in different environments, the expatriate and the members of his/her family who have sojourned to this new environment are able to appreciate the 'dos' and 'don'ts' of their new community and thereby can easily integrate with the local people. This can further facilitate the expatriate's adjustment and comfort in the foreign land and consequently enable the expatriate to enhance his/her productive work life for the MNC.

Additionally, training in cross-cultural communication means the expatriate is able to learn and understand the new culture in addition to his/her own culture. This helps the expatriate executive understand why people from different cultures behave differently and thereby inform them on how to formulate and implement decisions about work in the subsidiary's local community.

Similarly, by understanding the 'dos' and 'don'ts' of the local subsidiary culture through training in cross-cultural communication, expatriates are able to appreciate better the communicative behaviours of the local staff, thereby enhancing mutual respect for both cultures. This will improve teamwork between local staff and expatriates of the MNC, resulting in a healthier relationship between the two groups.

Expatriates on foreign assignment interact not only with MNC subsidiary workers, but the entire community where the MNC is located. This means that foreign assignees attend the social gatherings, religious services, markets and festivals of the indigenous people. This presupposes an interaction between the expatriate or assignee and the outside world of the MNC. By training in cross-cultural communication, the expatriate enhances their effective communication skills required to meet the value systems of the local community.

Furthermore, the expatriate or assignee is able to become more tolerant and accepting of others, including co-workers' views and behaviours. This is because, by participating in cross-cultural communication training, expatriates learn to understand the way people think, deal with issues and what drives them to behave differently from the way others do.

Reflective question from Objective 1

What are the main benefits of training in cross-cultural communication?

Objective 2: To examine the sources of misunderstanding arising from lack of cross-cultural communication between expatriates and local employees in the subsidiary location.

To address this objective, an open-ended question was asked: *Could you please mention some of the factors that are common sources of tension/disagreements between expatriates and the local staff in this company?* Table 4.2 below shows the results of respondents' direct answers to the question.

Table 4.2   Sources of disagreement due to lack of cross-cultural communication skills

Levels of common sources of conflict arising from misinterpretations	Number	Percentage
1 The use of indigenous languages in the presences of expatriates	15	7.4%
2 Lack of knowledge of expectations of local staff, hence they sometimes ignore instructions by giving excuses like 'I did not understand'	5	2.5%
3 Timescale differences due to cultural orientation of time, which affects production schedules at work	24	11.8%
4 Inappropriate use of mobile phones by local staff during work	10	4.9%

(continued)

Table 4.2 *(Continued)*

Levels of common sources of conflict arising from misinterpretations	Number	Percentage
5 Feeling of superiority by expatriates to the local staff and therefore the local staff are not comfortable in the presence of expatriates	7	3.5%
6 No response	143	70.1%
Total	**204**	**100**

Our empirical narratives on the factors that are common sources of tension/ disagreements between expatriates and the local staff in subsidiary MNCs showed that most local staff would normally communicate in their indigenous languages in the presence of expatriates, even though the official language of the company may be English. This sometimes creates anxiety among the expatriates since they do not understand what the local staff are saying. For example, it is common for an expatriate executive to issue an instruction at work, especially to those in the field (for example in the mining and extractive industries) and the local staff may be speaking their indigenous language and even laughing, which may not necessarily have anything to do with the expatriates' instruction. Yet this can make the expatriate suspicious of what might have been communicated between them.

Similarly, there are times when it is just difficult to understand exactly what the local staff's expectations are. For example, in this case study, some expatriates have complained that the local staff can be erratic and moody at work, and this can lead to slow work; when they question why work or an instruction has not been followed well, the usual answer is 'I don't know' or 'I don't understand'. All these behaviours stem from the fact that the expatriates do not fully understand the way of life of the indigenous people and how they work. Another source problem of misunderstanding regarding the actions and comportment of local staff that affects work in local subsidiary is the differences in the perception of time management. Expatriates and local staff sometimes apply different timescales and time management to the work in the subsidiary.

This divergence or differences in the management and use of time between expatriates and local employees should do with points of reference and expectations resulting from the different cultural orientations which can create a major rift between the two groups of employees. Additionally, cross-cultural misunderstandings do arise between expatriates and local staff because the latter feel that the former display arrogance due to a feeling of superiority over the indigenous people. Ethnocentrism is a major impediment to cross-cultural communication and cross-cultural relationships between diverse people working together. Thus, when local staff perceive expatriates' behaviours as superior to them or as ethnocentric, then the possibility of a conflict can occur between the two groups of employees.

Reflective question from Objective 2

What are the main sources of disagreement arising from lack of cross-cultural communication skills to be drawn from this case?

Objective 3: To determine the strategies that expatriate managers can employ to deal with cross-cultural communication problems in MNCs in local subsidiaries.

One major objective of this project was to find out management strategies to deal with problems of communication in the subsidiary, particularly conflict arising from miscommunication between expatriates and local staff. To address this objective, an open-ended question was asked: *What are some of the tactics/strategies that you use to facilitate effective communication between you and the local staff at work?* Table 4.3 below shows the results of respondents' direct answers to the question.

Table 4.3 Management strategies to facilitate effective cross-cultural communication

Management strategies to facilitate effective cross-cultural communication	Number	Percentage
1 Assign younger expatriate staff who are eager to associate with local people in subsidiary locations	2	1.0%
2 Expatriates should explain further what has been communicated to the local people	22	10.8%
3 Expatriates should be friendly and show greater respect to the local staff in order to earn their respect too	21	10.3%
4 Expatriates should have regular meetings and training sessions with local staff in order to build a greater bond between them	20	9.8%
5 Expatriates should repeat their instructions and also ask follow-up questions to see if the local people understand whatever the expatriates have said	24	11.8%

(continue)

Table 4.3 *(Continued)*

Management strategies to facilitate effective cross-cultural communication	Number	Percentage
6 Expatriates should learn to communicate well in the local language to facilitate better understanding of contextual issues	16	7.8%
7 Expatriates should involve local staff in the decision making of the MNC	4	2.0%
8 Expatriates should share their work experiences together with the local staff so that the latter can build on the former's skills	27	13.2%
9 No response	68	33.3%
Total	**204**	**100%**

In order to facilitate effective cross-cultural communication, the empirical findings from the survey suggest that during communication between expatriates and local employees, the former (expatriates) should endeavour to explain further what has been sent as communication to the local staff. Expatriates should repeat their instructions and also ask follow-up questions to see if the local people understand what has been said, because of the differences in intonations and modulations of voices between them. By clarifying and emphasizing what has been said or the instructions given, the local staff are able to better understand what the message is all about, and as a result they can effectively work on or respond to it.

Additionally, expatriates need to be friendly by demonstrating respect to the local people during communication and interactions. This then can be reciprocated by the local staff if they find the expatriates approachable, thus reducing anxieties which can cause miscommunication and misunderstanding between the two groups. Equally, the study findings recommend regular meetings and team training sessions between expatriates and local staff in order to build a greater bond between them; this increases interactions and social relationships, thereby enhancing effective cross-cultural communication in the subsidiary. Similarly, by building bridges between them, it will be easier for expatriates to share their work experiences with the local staff so that the latter can build on the former's skills and improve their work in the subsidiary.

Another management strategy that was proposed by a few participants in the study is that the MNC HQ should try to assign much younger staff who are more ready and eager to associate with the local people. The suggestion is that older expatriates do not feel the need to associate themselves as freely with the local people, either at work or socially, although this certainly will not always be the case.

Importantly, by being encouraged to participate in the management and decision-making processes of the subsidiary, local staff will be enthusiastic to give their all, since they may wish to prove themselves as capable of managing the affairs of the local subsidiary instead of always depending on every instruction from HQ and the expatriates. Through this, the expatriates will learn to understand effective contextual issues of successful management. This will further improve their knowledge of the local language to facilitate better understanding of complex multinational subsidiary operations.

Reflective question from Objective 3

What management strategies can you draw from this case to solve cross-cultural communication problems in your organization?

Conclusions

Internal conflicts in the international business operations of MNCs are complicated and usually occur between expatriates and local indigenous employees due to differences in their value systems. Differences in value systems can cause a rift between workers in the same company if they are not managed through effective understanding of each other. This is possible through effective cross-cultural communication. Therefore, cross-cultural communication is undoubtedly the solution for effective expatriate teamwork, since it can facilitate expatriates' skills in understanding themselves and others from different cultures.

Consequently, cross-cultural communication is critical in the operations of MNCs, because expatriates and local staff in the subsidiaries must communicate to understand the objectives of the organization they work for. Work schedules and tasks are efficiently achieved through a better understanding of the individual employee's job function, so competence in cross-cultural communication is extremely important if expatriates really wish to effectively work with and understand the local staff in the various MNCs. The chapter suggests that as part of MNCs' staffing strategies, PCNs (parent-country nationals) and TCNs (third-country nationals) must develop their knowledge of the language of communication and behaviours of local employees, particularly by adapting to the jargon, slang, values, symbolic meanings and interpretations, including the code systems of the local communities. This will certainly give expatriates the desired skills to transmit the required knowledge, skills and abilities to the local staff in the various subsidiaries.

Reflective questions

1 What is the significance of studying cross-cultural communication?

2 Should cross-cultural communication competence be a requirement for international assignment of expatriates?

3 What is the essence of learning the communicative behaviours of people?

4 Does context matter in communicating effectively? Explain your reasons.

5 Is it necessary to acquire cross-cultural training before embarking on a long-term voyage to a different culture to study or work?

Key learning points

• People communicate differently across cultural contexts, and IHRM practitioners need to be aware of this.

• In order to increase the likelihood of expatriate appointments being effective, firms need to ensure that they provide their international assignees with extensive cultural awareness and language training prior to their international assignment.

References

Abugre, J B (2016) The role of cross-cultural communication in management practices of multinational companies in Sub-Saharan Africa, in *Sustainable Management Development in Africa: Building capabilities to serve African organisations*, eds H H Kazeroony, Y Du Plessis and B B Puplampu, Routledge, New York, pp. 123–40

Ashamalla, M H (1998) International human resource management practices: the challenge of expatriation, *Competitiveness Review: An International Business Journal*, **8** (2), pp. 54–65

Babcock, R D and Du-Babcock, B (2001) Language-based communication zones in international business communication, *Journal of Business Communication*, **38**, pp. 372–412

Christopher, E (2012) *Communicating Across Cultures*, Palgrave Macmillan, London

Guirdham, M (1999) *Communicating Across Cultures*, Macmillan Press, London

Harris, P R and Moran, R T (1996) European leadership in globalization, *European Business Review*, **96** (2), pp. 32–41

Kim, Y Y (1988) *Communication and Cross-Cultural Adaptation: An integrative theory*, Multilingual Matters, Clevedon, England

Kim, Y Y (1995) Cross-cultural adaptation, in *Intercultural Communication Theory*, ed R Wiseman, Sage, Thousand Oaks, CA

Ko, H C and Yang, M L (2011) The effects of cross-cultural training on expatriate assignments, *Intercultural Communication Studies*, **XX** (1), pp. 158–74

Luo, Y and Shenkar, O (2006) The multinational corporation as a multilingual community: language and organization in a global context, *Journal of International Business Studies*, **37**, pp. 321–39

Lustig, M W and Koester, J (2006) *Intercultural Competence: Interpersonal communication across cultures*, 5th edn, Pearson Education Inc, Boston

Lutz, C and White, G M (1986) The anthropology of emotions, *Annual Review of Anthropology*, **15** (1), pp. 405–36

McFarlin, D B and Sweeney, P D (2006) *International Management: Strategic opportunities and cultural challenges*, Houghton Mifflin Company, Boston

Moran, T R, Harris, P R and Moran, S V (2011) *Managing Cultural Differences: Leadership skills and strategies for working in a global world*, Butterworth-Heinemann, Oxford

Nakayama, T K and Halualani, R T (2010) *The Handbook of Critical Intercultural Communication*, Wiley-Blackwell, Chichester

Okoro, E (2012) Cross-cultural etiquette and communication in global business: toward a strategic framework for managing corporate expansion, *International Journal of Business and Management*, **7** (16), pp. 130–38

Padhi, P K (2016) The rising importance of cross-cultural communication in global business scenarios, *Journal of Research in Humanities and Social Science*, **4** (1), pp. 20–26

Pandey, S (2012) Using popular movies in teaching cross-cultural management, *European Journal of Training and Development*, **36** (2), pp. 329–50

Phatak, A V, Bhagat, R S and Kashlak, R J (2005) *International Management: Managing in a diverse and dynamic global environment*, McGraw-Hill Irwin, Boston

Phillips, N, Lawrence, T B and Hardy, C (2004) Discourse and institutions, *Academy of Management Review*, **29** (4), pp. 635–52

Samovar, L A and Porter, R E (1997) *Intercultural Communication: A reader*, 8th edn, Wadsworth Publishing Company

Stahl, G K et al (2017) The upside of cultural differences: Towards a more balanced treatment of culture in cross-cultural management research, *Cross Cultural & Strategic Management*, **24** (1), pp. 2–12

Zhu, Y, Nel, P and Bhat, R (2006) A cross-cultural study of communication strategies for building business relationships, *International Journal of Cross Cultural Management*, **6** (3), pp. 319–41

05
The institutional context of international HRM

DANIEL WINTERSBERGER

Learning outcomes

At the end of this chapter, you should be able to:

- understand the extent to which institutional factors may account for differences in HRM patterns and practices across different national contexts;
- make informed decisions regarding the implementation of HRM practices across different institutional contexts;
- differentiate between tangible (hard) and intangible (soft) institutions and understand their role in shaping HR systems in different countries directly and indirectly;
- gain a deeper understanding of some of the differences between liberal and coordinated market economies.

Introduction

The preceding chapter introduced you to national culture as a key factor influencing HRM and employee relations outcomes at national level. IHRM practitioners need to be aware of these cultural factors in order to manage effectively (and sensitively) across different countries. Building on these cultural factors, this chapter will introduce you to *institutional* factors which may lead to distinctive contexts for HRM across countries. After a brief introduction into what actually constitutes an 'institution' in the context of international HRM (IHRM), the chapter will outline and highlight the ways in which different 'varieties of capitalism' (Hall and Soskice, 2001) and their institutional contexts lead to different HRM and employment relations outcomes in different countries. We will examine in more depth some of the key institutional factors at national level that lead to distinctive pressures on HRM practitioners. There will be some recap of the material from Chapter 2 on culture, so you would benefit from reading that chapter. After all, as you will probably agree upon having read both chapters, culture and institutions do not exist in isolation; they complement each other.

As highlighted in the introductory chapter of this textbook, traditional, mainstream HRM is often ethnocentric insofar as it proposes a (seemingly) universally applicable array of 'best practices' (Pfeffer, 1998) that lead to success regardless of the context within which the firm is operating. When perpetuating this approach, we run the risk of cultural myopia and an inability to learn from insights from those contexts (such as the Asian Tiger economies) where firms are using increasingly successfully and productively despite (or perhaps precisely as a result of) not emulating the HRM strategy and practices of Anglo-American companies. Much of the existing IHRM literature is prescriptive. This means that rather than looking at differences and comparing international cases, it seeks to establish what firms 'ought to do', not what they actually do and why they do it. This prescriptive literature predominantly emanates from a 'western' perspective, and very rarely are practices from other contexts (such as emerging economies) diffused 'westwards'. A notable exception is Japanese management principles, some of which underpin various HRM 'best practice' frameworks. For example, high levels of job security and autonomous work groups, as featured in Pfeffer's seven best practices (Pfeffer, 1998) are arguably the direct result of American practitioners and academics trying to emulate the manufacturing principles which made Japanese products so competitive in the 1980s and 1990s. However, as will be demonstrated by the case study at the end of this chapter, the extent to which management practices can be transplanted from one institutional context to another might be limited.

The background to institutional analysis

In order to understand the way in which institutional factors may lead to different HRM practices and systems in different countries, it is essential to understand what actually constitutes an institution in the context of IHRM. An important starting point is clarity about the level of analysis at which we might look at institutions. As highlighted in Chapter 1, there are three levels of analysis in IHRM: the macro (national) level, the meso (organizational) level, and the micro (individual) level. When looking at IHRM from an institutional perspective, we are largely dealing with the interaction between macro and meso levels. Therefore, the institutional perspective might be informed by the work of political economists (macro level) as well as the contributions of work sociologists at the organizational level.

In accordance with these perspectives, institutions can be viewed as 'constraints that structure political, economic and social interaction' (North, 1991: 97). It is explicit in this definition that institutions are often restrictive (hence the use of the term 'constraints'), limiting the extent to which organizations exercise discretion on how to operate or interact with other firms. In the context of IHRM, this perspective would imply that practitioners of HRM across different countries have to align their HRM strategy with national institutional factors. As a result, even the largest multinationals would find it difficult to implement a globally homogenous HRM strategy as a result of institutional constraints in different countries. However, multinationals often do attempt to implement a globally homogenous HRM strategy, regardless of relevant institutional factors, demonstrating the ability of firms to exercise 'strategic choice' (Kochan, McKersie and Cappelli, 1984), rather than simply having to adapt to the context within which they operate. Take for example the case of American multinational fast-food MNCs such as McDonald's, Yum brands and Burger King. Royle (2010) found that such giants exhibit substantial degrees of independence from various institutional factors at country level around the globe. McDonald's has developed a reputation as an employer with strong anti-union sentiment, engaging in quite fierce union suppression tactics such as bullying and the use of anti-union consultants even within continental European countries such as Germany, where legislation generally provides a more employee- and union-friendly context than for example in the United States (Royle, 2002).

Hard versus soft institutions

We can meaningfully categorize institutions into soft (intangible and implicit) as well as hard (tangible and explicit) institutions. Soft institutions might entail customs and traditions at national level. They may also include rituals and codes of conduct (North, 1991: 97), and as such exist in implicit form. In other words, customs, values, rituals and beliefs are not formally written down as laws, but still exist in people's minds. In contrast, hard (or 'tangible') institutions entail formal rules and policies such as employment law. Such rules by implication are not pliable. For example, companies operating in countries which have minimum wages (such as the UK) cannot pay their workforce less than the minimum wage. In contrast, an example of a soft institution with regard to pay determination would be a country's customs and practices regarding pay increases based on seniority as opposed to merit. In this chapter, we will discuss the traditional Japanese 'Nenko' (seniority-based pay) system as a soft institution that still to some extent exerts some influence in Japanese firms. Table 5.1 below provides some examples of hard institutions and their corresponding soft institutional factors.

Table 5.1 Hard versus soft institutions

Hard institutions	Soft institutions
Employment law	'Good practice'
Minimum wage	Typical industry rates
Legal context	Political context

As you may notice, informal, or 'soft' institutions, by referring to customs, values, rituals and beliefs are actually quite closely aligned with national culture, making it difficult to differentiate meaningfully between the two. This chapter will focus mainly on the more tangible institutions while providing examples of how these might be complementary to some of the more well-known intangible institutions or cultural values in the respective country. It is therefore the institutionalized rules (for example regarding company corporate governance, employment law, legislation on training etc) which we shall focus on in this chapter.

The institutional perspective maintains that all transactions within a country are rooted in social settings and explicit rules. This also applies to organizations. In order to function effectively, an organization has to align its modes of operation or 'ways of doing things' with various institutional factors that prevail within the host country. Such institutional factors may include employment law, patterns of collective bargaining, the political environment (for example the extent to which it is more employer or employee friendly), as well as established norms on work and employment. For example, how much training is to be provided, as well as the question of whether or not to engage in individualized or collective bargaining at enterprise or sectoral level are all rooted in institutional factors. Consistent with the 'institutional complementarity' (Hall and Soskice, 2003), organizations are said to derive benefits from congruency with their institutional context and in contrast are often at a distinctive disadvantage when operating inconsistently with their environment. For example, many commentators have linked Walmart's failure to successfully expand in Germany with cultural resentment on the side of the population. In a country where employment legislation tends to be more employee friendly than in the United States, and where unions are more influential, it may simply have been the case that Walmart's 'low road' approach to human resource management and employee relations (especially the use of video surveillance to spy on their staff) was not acceptable either for workers or for customers. Although there are many other potential explanations for Walmart's failure in Germany, one of the key reasons may well have been that Walmart simply 'couldn't hack the pro-labour union culture of Germany' (Macaray, 2011).

Institutional factors vary across different countries, and therefore it is difficult to create meaningful clusters of countries based on their institutional factors. However, it is more feasible to categorize countries on the basis of the type (or variety) of capitalism which they have embraced, as this allows us to make some inferences about the nature of institutional constraints present in that country.

The varieties of capitalism approach

As the name suggests, the varieties of capitalism (VoC) approach seeks to compare different types of capitalism, ultimately categorizing them and developing 'ideal types'. According to the seminal publication by Hall and Soskice (2001), there are two ideal types of capitalism: liberal market economies and coordinated market economies. In order to understand these better, it is worthwhile examining their historical development. In liberal market economies, economic policy is informed by neo-liberalism.

> **Neo-liberalism**: a governmental approach that aims to provide as few constraints as possible on the free market and its 'natural' economic forces such as supply and demand.

Although neo-liberalism dates back earlier, to the works of economists such as Friedrich Hayek and later Milton Friedman, neo-liberalism permeated government policy strongly for the first time in the 1970s. A traditional argument by neo-liberals such as Margaret Thatcher in the UK and Ronald Reagan in the United States throughout the 1970s and 1980s was that too much intervention in the free market is not good. Such exponents of neo-liberalism (ie the logic that the state should not intervene in the free market) at the time pointed to the failure of soviet communism as an exemplar of the consequences of too much state intervention in the 'free' market. Instead of intervening on the side of governments, the 'invisible hand' of the market is said to ensure the most effective use of resources and fairest distribution of gains from productivity increases, ultimately making such economies driven by a free market logic more efficient and successful. However, throughout the 1980s, 1990s and beyond, we have observed how countries such as Germany and Japan, as well as some of the 'Tiger' economies mentioned earlier, have been highly productive and successful 'despite' strong government intervention in their markets. This has led many to conclude that there are different patterns in the social organization of capitalism, rather than a single best way. Accordingly, each variety of capitalism has its own distinctive advantages and disadvantages.

Although slightly more nuanced approaches exist (see for example Nölke and Claar, 2013), for the sake of simplicity, we will stick to the aforementioned two most widely known ideal 'types' (varieties) of capitalism: liberal market economies and coordinated market economies (Hall and Soskice,

Table 5.2   Market versus non-market mechanisms

Market mechanisms	Non-market mechanisms
Government economic policy: laissez-faire – don't intervene in the free market.	Government economic policy: correct deficiencies of the market – eg by ensuring minimum quality standards for products and levelling the bargaining position of labour through minimum wages.
Inter-firm relations: arm's length. Formal contracting (eg for supplying components at a set price). No obligations beyond what is in the contract.	Inter-firm relations: collaborative – beyond contractual obligations. Extensive knowledge-sharing and partnership, eg. firms collaborating on vocational training schemes for workers (Hall and Soskice, 2001: 10).

2001). Each of these forms of capitalism includes a set of complementary institutions that form the basis of a country's competitiveness and lead to good economic outcomes. In order to develop, produce and distribute goods and services profitably, a firm must effectively coordinate with a wide range of **actors**. Such actors might include **investors, employees, unions,** as well as **the state.**

As mentioned earlier, institutions can be viewed as tangible (proximate) as well as more intangible (implicit) factors that shape how firms behave. In liberal market economies (LMEs), firms resolve coordination problems mainly through free **market mechanisms**. This means that they make limited commitments towards other firms and do not behave very collaboratively. Table 5.2 below compares and contrasts market and non-market mechanisms.

Inter-firm relations in liberal market economies can therefore best be described as 'arm's length', characterized by high degrees of competition. In contrast, firms operating in coordinated market economies (CMEs) often resolve coordination problems through non-market institutions. Such implicit institutions might include strategic interaction with other firms as each specializes in a different market niche, hence reducing the need to compete with one another and increasing the benefits derived from collaboration.

Both the aforementioned approaches to firm interaction (collaboration and competition) create distinctive advantages and disadvantages. In LMEs, firms are comparably more likely to derive a competitive advantage from the flexibility associated with relatively arm's-length relationships with other companies. In contrast, firms in CMEs derive benefits from highly cooperative behaviours, including the exchange of information between firms as well as stronger 'punishment' of those who don't play by the rules such as minimum standards for training provision. The comparably greater ability to sanction those who deviate from commonly agreed good practice stems from the relative strength of trade unions and employers' associations in coordinated market economies, resulting in these organizations exerting a stronger influence on their members (Masczyk and Rapacki, 2012). For example, as a consequence of more legislative intervention, universal minimum standards for training provision in coordinated market economies ensure a level playing field for employers, avoiding the risk that companies have a free ride on the skills provided by the education system and competitors (more on this later).

Company funding and corporate governance are further criteria on the basis of which we can distinguish between LMEs and CMEs. LMEs are characterized by well-developed capital markets and 'outsider' forms of corporate governance (Wailes, Bamber and Lansbury, 2011:14). Under those circumstances a large proportion of company shares are owned by people or institutions with no affiliation to the company, and potentially no particular vested interest in its long-term survival or job creation, with shareholders often looking for short- to mid-term return on investment. In contrast, a large CME firm is likely to have a substantial proportion of its shares owned by 'insiders' such as employees, management or indeed local government, as in the case of Volkswagen (more on this later), where at least a quarter of shares are owned by the government of Lower Saxony, the province in Germany where the VW headquarters are located (Milne, 2015).

'Ideal types' of varieties of capitalism

With the exception of North Korea and (increasingly less so) Cuba, most countries in the world have embraced some form of capitalism to run their economies. The extent to which neo-liberalism has been pursued determines whether economies can be categorized as liberal or coordinated market economies. It is important to note that countries are likely to fit each typology only to a certain extent, and there may be features of liberal market economies within what we might categorize as a coordinated market economy and vice versa. With such blurred boundaries between the two types of capitalism, it is useful to look at 'ideal types'. The United States is most frequently viewed as the epitome of a liberal market economy as it meets several of the relevant criteria. For example, with regard to corporate governance, US firms are dominated by outsider shareholders, with organizational performance being viewed in the short term (current earnings and share prices). Senior management in US firms are likely to act primarily in the best interests of shareholders and the aforementioned dimensions of short-term performance, as shareholders exert a lot of influence on them.

In the same way as there are arm's-length relationships between businesses in liberal market economies, there are also arm's-length relationships between employers and their employees. 'Hire and fire' is a term often used to connote the American employment system. Employment relations in the United States are indeed generally more short-term than in coordinated market economies. Management tend to exert unilateral control over employees due to unions being largely absent from the workplace. In 2015, only 10 per cent of the overall workforce were union members, compared to nearly 20 per cent in Germany and nearly 70 per cent in Sweden (OECD Stat, 2017). An obvious consequence of weak trade unions in the United States is that wage setting tends to be a rather unilateral managerial activity. Where wage bargaining does occur in LMEs, it generally does so at the individual (employee) rather than collective level. This is facilitated by the 'laissez faire' approach of successive governments in the United States over the last 40 years. As mentioned earlier, neo-liberals view too much state intervention in firm governance and relations between different stakeholders (including employers and employees) as bad, potentially making markets inefficient. Therefore, much of the bargaining process is left to individual employees and their direct line managers. It is important to note again that liberal and coordinated market economies are only ideal types, and that features might overlap in different countries. In the context of wage setting, for example, several US states have set their own federal minimum wages. These range from as little at $5 per hour in states such as Georgia to up to $15 per hour in cities such as Seattle (NCSL, 2017). Some states (such as Alabama) have no minimum wage at all. Instead of 'sectoral agreements' (more on these later), employees in the United States are not represented by unions at occupational level, meaning that there are likely to be significantly larger salary differentials between individual workers than in coordinated market economies.

Within LMEs such as the United States, the laissez-faire approach taken by the state extends well beyond collective bargaining. In contrast to CMEs, LMEs pose few constraints (ie minimum standards) for training provision at enterprise level. In contrast to CMEs, where the state often coordinates the planning of training provision with employer representative bodies as well as trade unions, such state intervention is generally absent in LMEs such as the US and the UK, though increasingly less so in the UK, where the government is in the process of introducing an 'apprenticeship levy'. Employers in LMEs can be said to operate in a rather more 'voluntarist' setting than employers in CMEs. Vocational education and training (VET) is therefore less likely to be offered by employers, or is often of inferior quality in LMEs. Consistent with the free market ideology prevalent in LMEs, young people are expected to be responsible for obtaining the necessary skills before entering the labour market. As a result, organizations operating in LMEs will find a more ready supply of skilled graduates, but a lower supply of those with 'middle-range skills' such as electricians and mechanics, as the labour force, largely having undergone tertiary education, will have more general skills. It is probably not a coincidence that LMEs tend to have a comparative advantage in the service sectors (demanding general and 'soft' skills) as opposed to CMEs, where manufacturing is comparatively more prevalent and stronger. As a consequence of the rather voluntarist training system in LMEs, firms are often found to be reluctant training providers. Voluntarism creates a culture of free riding (Streeck, 1997) whereby firms, well aware of there being few or no government sanctions for low levels/quality of training, adopt a minimalist stance towards training, also due to fear of competitors 'poaching' their most skilled employees after they have been trained (often at high cost) by the organization. With substantial proportions of young people undergoing tertiary education, another key feature of LMEs is a ready supply of skilled graduates, hence creating a further disincentive for firms to train. In the next section, we examine some of the key features of coordinated market economies in more depth, using the case of Germany as an example.

Germany: the epitome of a coordinated market economy

The extant literature on varieties of capitalism often treats Germany as the epitome of a coordinated market economy (see Hall and Soskice, 2001). Indeed, there are many features in the German employment system and German HRM that make it very distinctive from LMEs such as the United States and the UK. Before looking at the outcomes in terms of work, HRM and employment, we need to consider some of the distinctive institutional factors which, in the German case, lead to these outcomes.

One such distinctive feature is certainly the more long-term nature of company funding, often referred to as 'patient capital' (see for example Hall and Soskice, 2001: 22). As the name suggests, this term refers to company funding that is more patient insofar as there are longer planning horizons. The most notable difference lies in the relative importance of equity-based and public bond market finance, which plays a greater role in LMEs than in CMEs, where firms are more dependent on bank loans rather than shareholders. The consequence of this is of course that the planning horizon in LMEs becomes shorter for firms, eager and pressurized to ensure short-term return on (shareholder) investment. In contrast, bank loans, which are more common in CMEs, are more long term, enabling firms in CMEs to engage in more long-term planning. As you would imagine, the planning horizon (long versus short term) can have a profound impact on an organization's HR practices.

Institutional complementarity (Hall and Soskice, 2003) refers to the notion that institutional factors (such as training and development infrastructure as well as the source of capital) often work together to create a distinctive institutional context. There is certainly institutional complementarity between sources of capital and the training and development context. On the one hand, we have already discussed how the rather 'voluntarist' system in LMEs creates a strong disincentive for employers to train their workforce. The rather low minimum standards of company-provided training, coupled with lax enforcement of training standards leads to a greater reluctance amongst LME firms, well aware of the risks associated with competitors 'poaching' their well-trained workforce, to invest in workforce training and development. On the other hand, the lack of 'patient' capital creates a further disincentive. One of the key issues with training is that it is often costly (consider the cost of training provision itself as well as the productive time lost by employees and perhaps also managers involved in the training process) and its benefits are difficult to quantify, often only visible in the long term. The two disincentives to train in liberal market economies (fear of poaching and lack of patient capital) are complementary with another key institutional feature in LMEs, namely the ready supply of highly skilled graduates in the labour market (Bosch and Charest, 2008) as the lower company-level investments into training (including vocational education and training) encourage more young people to attend university as a means to develop their skills and improve their position in the labour market. In a sense, therefore, firms in LMEs are more likely to attempt to 'free ride' both on the high-quality talent (graduates) in the labour market and potentially on skilled workers poached from competitors. In coordinated market economies such as Germany, the Netherlands and Sweden, the 'free rider' phenomenon can be seen to exist less than in LMEs, firstly because of stronger legislation and minimum standards for training provision and secondly because of the more patient forms of capital that exist. A bank issuing a long-term loan, for example, is likely to care less about the short-term profitability of the firm it lends to than would, for example, shareholders who bought shares in the hope of short-term increase in value.

In CME contexts such as Germany, it is common for a significant proportion of shares in large companies to be owned by so-called 'insiders' (Höpner, 2001). Such insiders might be current employees as well as members of the management team but also other people or bodies (such as local government) who share in common a vested interest in the long-term sustainability of the organization and subsequently the creation and maintenance of secure employment (see the second case study in this chapter). It has been well established that employee share ownership, coupled with extensive employee involvement and participation and decision making, as traditionally associated with European CMEs (Thelen, 2001) is likely to lead to greater degrees of organizational resilience (Lampel, Bhalla and Jha, 2014), and hence longer-term job security for workers. This is turn is complementary with another key institutional factor in CMEs, namely the generally lower rates of employee turnover and voluntary resignation (Bosch and Charest, 2008). So, in other words, while business, due to higher degrees of 'insider' forms of corporate governance (employee share ownership programmes and participation in decision making) takes a more long-term approach to workforce planning, the higher degrees of job security that ensue are reciprocated by greater employee loyalty, as we would expect where there is a stronger, less arm's-length and more long-term psychological bond or 'contract' between employer and employees (Rousseau, 1990).

Another key feature on which to compare and contrast LMEs with CMEs is that of collective bargaining. As mentioned previously, the United States, being the epitome of an LME, is characterized by decentralized bargaining and trade unions that are weaker in influence, on the one hand due to weaker legislative support by government and on the other hand by the closely related consequence of lower membership levels as discussed earlier. Quite the opposite is the case in Germany (and CMEs in general). First and foremost, the wage bargaining process in Germany is decentralized insofar as it takes place at sectoral (industry) level. The same also applies to some other CMEs such as Austria and to some extent France, but not to Japan (more on this later). Sectoral-level pay bargaining in Germany allows employers' associations at industry level to negotiate with unions at industry level. For example, the metalworkers' union (IG Metall) negotiates minimum sectoral wages for all groups of workers in metal refining and the wider manufacturing industry. Such sectoral agreements are legally binding, and employers who are represented by an employers' association may not undercut these sectoral-level agreements. Germany has only very recently (2015) introduced a minimum wage in order to protect the most vulnerable workers such as those employed in service SMEs, many of which are not members of an employers' association, and don't have to adhere to sectoral agreements.

While the bargaining process in Germany is centralized, operating at industry level, there is also employee representation at workplace level in the form of company or 'works' councils. Works councils are elected by employees and while they do not negotiate pay (which is done by unions at sectoral level – see Exhibit 1 below for an example), they do often have a lot of say in company decision making. A works council may participate in management decision making on issues such as organizational restructuring, offshoring, downsizing as well as production processes and the quality of the working environment. The role of the works council is reinforced by a particular institution associated closely with some CMEs (including Germany and Austria) but not all (for example Japan), namely that of 'co-determination'. In the German case, co-determination is embedded in the law, which stipulates firstly a 'two-tier' board structure for all large companies and secondly a fixed representation of employee representatives within this structure. The two-tier board structure means that German firms have both a supervisory and a management board, unlike in the LME case, where firms are governed unilaterally and solely by a management board. The management board in Germany is appointed by the supervisory board. The supervisory board, consistent with the law of 'parity', must comprise shareholder and employee representatives in equal proportion. The German law of co-determination cedes substantial power to the supervisory board including full veto rights on management board decisions. It is therefore common for the management board to consult the supervisory board prior to making decisions and announcing changes.

Exhibit 1: IG Metall: Germany's largest union

The industrial union of metal workers (IG Metall), while originally founded to represent the interests of metal workers in Germany's formerly large steel industry, now represents workers across many manufacturing sectors including automotive, electronics and printing. With a membership of well over 2.7 million workers, it is also Germany's largest union and its sectoral-level pay negotiations with employers' associations in manufacturing receive substantial media attention as pay settlements in these industries tend to set the tone for deals in other sectors (IG Metall, 2008).

Figure 5.1 Levels of bargaining in Germany

National level:	Bund Deutscher Arbeitgeber (Association of German Employers)	Deutscher Gewerkschaftsbund (German Trade Union Federation)
Sectoral/industry level	Industry-level employers' association – eg Association of Employers in Manufacturing	Industry-level trade union – eg IG Metall (Union of Metal and Manufacturing Workers)
Enterprise level	Company-level works council consulting with management on issues such as quality of working, job creation, downsizing etc. Company council representatives represented in supervisory boards in large companies.	
Workplace Level	Works councils in individual workplaces and subsidiaries of the company in different locations. Liaise with company council (above).	

Japan: A different type of coordinated market economy

Japan is always listed alongside other continental European countries (such as Germany, Austria and Sweden) as a CME (Soskice, 1999; Streeck and Yamamura, 2001). This is problematic because the institutional context affecting HRM, work and employment in Japan, while sharing some similarities with the German 'ideal type' of a CME also bears distinctive differences. One key institutional factor in Japan has traditionally been 'lifetime employment' (Ono, 2010). Under this system of lifetime (or at least long term) employment, large Japanese firms traditionally followed a policy of hiring young school or university graduates and guaranteeing them a steady career progression. This approach was reinforced by relatively low starting salaries but a policy of steady seniority-based pay progression.

There has been a lot of debate on the extent to which 'lifetime' employment is still a key institution in Japan. There are no reliable figures on today's state of lifetime employment in Japan, though it can be assumed with some certainty that the influence of this key institution is waning (Kawaguchi and Ueno, 2013). The traditionally secure employment system in Japan has arguably come under attack from similar crises (such as the 2008 global financial crisis) as other advanced economies. It is quite telling that 'regular' (ie permanent) employment has fallen from 80 per cent of all jobs in Japan in 1990, to 65 per cent more recently (Bamber, Lansbury and Wailes, 2016). This may be associated with the fact that smaller firms (less than 500 employees) in the private sector, usually associated with lower levels of employment security, have accounted for much of the job creation in recent years. Although it might be argued that 'lifetime' employment may no longer play the same role as it did prior to the 1990s, long-term employment is certainly still a key feature of Japanese HRM (Kambayashi and Kato, 2016).

As mentioned previously, institutions can be hard and soft. It might be argued that the relative role of employment security in Japan has shifted from being a hard institution, enshrined firmly in company policy and employment law, to being a softer 'background' institution. As mentioned in Chapter 2, Japan scores high on Hofstede's cultural dimension of 'collectivism', so it may well be that loyalty to the company complements company commitment to job security, even in challenging times.

Beyond long-term employment, Japan bears a further distinctive institutional factor, namely 'enterprise unionism'. As you may recall, the preceding section discussed 'decentralized' collective bargaining (at industry/sectoral level) as a key distinctive feature of CMEs such as Germany. The situation in Japan is different insofar as collective bargaining takes place at enterprise level and there are therefore no collective agreements at sectoral level. It is noteworthy that in the Japanese context, relationships between enterprises and their unions are generally cooperative, involving activities such as information sharing and consultation on managerial decisions. At the same time, wage restraint is exercised by the enterprise union in return for job security. We will revisit these enterprise unions in more depth in Chapter 12 where we will examine international employment relations.

Critique of the VoC approach

As the VoC approach works on the basis of two 'ideal types' of capitalism, inevitably one of the key criticisms is lack of diversity due to having only these two ideal types. There are countries (such as France and Italy) which simply do not fit any of the ideal types particularly well. Then there is the problem that many of the emerging economies have developed very distinctive types of capitalism from mature markets and therefore new categories or ideal types may have to be created. As the preceding subsection on Japan has demonstrated, there is substantial diversity within these ideal types. Japan may well be a coordinated market economy (by virtue of relatively strong state involvement in the market), but it does not include one of the key characteristics of a CME, namely centralized bargaining. At the same time, some LMEs are adopting features of CMEs (notably more state intervention in training and development) and vice versa (for example the extensive neo-liberal reforms under Chancellor Gerhard Schroeder in Germany), meaning that the boundaries between the two ideal types may be increasingly eroded. In fact, the UK and the US, by introducing minimum wage(s) (notably before Germany did), display some features of state intervention in the bargaining process. In 2016, British Prime Minister Theresa May (Conservative Party) raised some eyebrows and fierce responses from the Confederation of British Industry (CBI) by proclaiming that she wants employee representative seats at board level in the UK. Although she has since weakened her case (following pressure from the CBI), this shows that countries are not immune to 'importing' successful practices from other varieties of capitalism. Similarly, in the UK context, politicians have recently called for tighter legislation on training and the Conservative Party has even committed to encouraging the generation of 3 million new apprenticeships by 2020.

While some LMEs such as the UK may be attempting to adopt some of the best practices of CMEs (namely fostering of apprenticeships and employee representation at senior management level), CMEs seem to increasingly closely resemble LMEs. It is argued that globalization and multinationals are leading to global convergence (Quintanilla and Ferner, 2003) in employment patterns towards the LME model (Edwards, 2004). Multinational corporations (more on these later) may be acting as the key vehicle of the transfer of LME HRM practices towards economies traditionally categorized as CMEs (see for example Royle, 2004 and Gamble, 2006).

While we need to be acutely aware of the potential limitations of the VoC approach, we should not dismiss it completely. Actually, it will be very relevant for subsequent chapters in this book and we should not view IHRM as an activity influenced by culture alone. In fact, culture and institutional factors may complement each other. For example, high levels of 'collectivism' (see Chapter 2) as prevalent in Japan, according to Hofstede's work, may act as an antecedent of enterprise unionism and long-term employment – two key distinctive institutions in the Japanese context.

Reflective activity

As mentioned previously, Jeffrey Pfeffer's (1998) seven HR practices for 'successful organizations' are perhaps the most prominent contribution to the HRM 'best practice' literature. Pfeffer argues that, regardless of context within which the firm might be operating, employers derive advantages from implementing the following practices:

1 employment security;

2 selective hiring;

3 self-managed teams and decentralization of decision making;

4 comparatively high pay contingent on performance;

5 extensive training;

6 reduction of status differentials;

7 extensive information sharing across the entire organization.

(Based on Pfeffer, 1998.)

To what extent are these seven best practices consistent with the institutional context in your country of origin and/or the country you currently live in?

Consider institutional factors such as the political (current government) and legal context (key employment legislation – is it more employer or employee friendly), systems of collective bargaining (industry/sectoral or company level) as well as the prevalent system of corporate governance. To what extent would you be able to implement each of these practices in your chosen context? Would their implementation be beneficial or detrimental to organizational performance?

CASE STUDY Transplanting Japanese models of HRM to the UK

In this case study we examine the consequences of managerial attempts to introduce the Japanese model of production and work organization to the UK. The case highlights the challenges associated with the transfer of specific models of work organization and employment from one institutional context (coordinated market economy) to another (liberal market economy). In order to understand the issue of institutional complementarity (Hall and Soskice, 2003) in this context, we need to understand two traditional models of work organization as means to achieve comparative advantage in manufacturing. The first one is 'scientific management' or 'Taylorism' (Taylor, 1911), which arguably has long dominated work organization in the US and UK manufacturing industries. We will compare this with the Japanese form of work organization widely known as 'just in time', 'total quality management' and 'lean manufacturing' (Womack, Jones and Roos, 1990). This approach to manufacturing is epitomized well in the 'Toyota Production System' (TPS). In order to understand the implications of transferring Japanese management practices to the UK, we need to first compare and contrast the Japanese model of production with the traditional Anglo-American model of scientific management.

The Anglo-American model: 'scientific management'

Frederick Taylor's Principles of Scientific Management (Taylor, 1911) have long been the dominant mode of work organization in US and UK manufacturing. Taylor, an industrialist (iron industry in the US) himself at the time of writing his book, viewed workers as inherently work-shy, needing to be monitored, controlled and told what to do by management. Taylor used the term 'soldiering' to describe a tendency amongst workers to perform only the minimum necessary level and standard of work (in terms of quantity as well as quality). Under circumstances where everyone is paid the same, regardless of output, Taylor argued that those more able to perform at a higher level are likely to withhold discretionary effort due to a sense of injustice towards them if they were to perform at a superior level to their co-workers despite earning the same salary. For this reason, Taylor introduced the 'piece-rate' system of pay whereby workers received a bonus for reaching particular performance targets. Under scientific management, these targets are unilaterally set by management. Taylor envisaged that workers are paid to work and managers are paid to think and that there ought to be no overlap between mundane operational tasks and more complex conceptual tasks. As a result, workers had very low levels of autonomy at work, being prescribed the scientifically devised 'one best way' to carry out operations.

As a consequence of such forms of work organization, which also permeated service sectors throughout the 1970s and 1980s (Levitt, 1972), critics have pointed towards their dehumanizing nature and the resulting 'deskilling' and worker 'alienation' (Braverman, 1972) from the labour process. Alienation is the consequence of workers not understanding the full scope and value of their input into the production process. Alienated workers are likely engaged in various forms of 'misbehaviour' (Ackroyd and Thompson, 1999) such as sabotage of production processes for example by deliberately damaging machinery (Taylor and Walton, 1994). In service contexts, alienated workers often resist by venting their frustration towards the customer (Van Maanen, 1999; Leidner, 1993). Worker alienation and resulting lack of commitment to the work and the company may have been one of the key reasons why, throughout the 1980s and 1990s, numerous US scholars, managers and consultants looked to the Japanese model for inspiration (Drucker, 1971) for how to become more productive via a highly committed and polyvalent workforce.

The Japanese model: Total Quality Management

The Toyota Production System (TPS) is often seen as exemplary of what made Japanese products superior in quality throughout much of the 1990s. It is also viewed as the earliest form of what would later be known as 'lean manufacturing' or 'just in time' (JIT) production. The TPS aims to eliminate overburden (muri), inconsistency (mura) and waste (muda). There are several types of waste categories, but the most significant ones are overproduction and production errors. The effective utilization of human resources is absolutely crucial within this system and integral components of the TPS are high levels of employee involvement in management decision making as well as high levels of employee autonomy, especially relative to the standardization approaches outlined previously.

Although the development of the system goes back into the 1950s, it was not until the late 1980s that European and North American managers, consultants and academics developed a keen interest in it and managers began adopting it in western contexts. Critics have argued that such modes of work organization intensify work and subject workers to additional managerial control (Delbridge and Turnbull, 2002). Proponents of such systems claim that workers are required to work 'smarter rather than harder' and that their implementation in western contexts presents opportunities for workers to become more highly skilled and to have greater autonomy and control over the work that they do than under traditionally standardized work organization (Womack, Jones and Roos, 1990).

In this case study, we examine the challenges associated with the implementation of TQM production principles in a UK context. It is based on an example study of a Japanese car manufacturing company that has committed to a five-year contract for producing its small and mid-size range in the north of the UK. Under the new production arrangements, the company, which has its head office in Tokyo, has decided to strengthen its emphasis on tried-and-tested Japanese modes of work organization and production. Previously, the UK plant operated a conventional assembly line system. Individual employees working 'on the line' had a very narrow range of job tasks, sometimes as narrow as attaching a single component to cars as they moved along the line during an entire shift. Hourly wages for those working on the production line were only slightly above the national minimum wage, and a large proportion of the workforce opted to top this up by working night and weekend shifts. As a result of low wages and relatively monotonous work, employee turnover was high. However, due to the simplicity of the tasks, employee turnover was never seen as an issue by management. In fact, if anything, it was viewed as a potentially beneficial strategy to keep the workplace union free. Indeed, many of the (predominantly young) workers, when dissatisfied with pay and working conditions, simply chose to resign rather than attempting to organize collectively.

For the new production deal, a radically new model of work organization was implemented. Applying technologies and practices directly from their Japanese plants, the aim was to implement a production process that foregrounds quality over quantity and customization over standardization. Doing so, however, required drastic changes to work organization and employment relations, and for their implementation, the organization sent members of management from Japan to the UK plant. Substantial changes were made to work organization on the production line. Where previously individual employees carried out repetitive, narrowly defined tasks, the new production system involved workers working in self-managed teams or 'autonomous work groups'. Under the new production system, each work group (comprised of between 12 and 20 assembly line workers) became accountable for specific outcomes which could be quantitative (eg production targets) or qualitative (errors made in the process). Under the new system of work organization, management sought to reward good performance (and penalize underperformance) at the collective (team) rather than individual level. Each work group was assigned a 'team leader' who was generally a longer-serving member of staff. Team leaders were not only accountable for production issues, but also for employee relations and welfare-related issues (such as attendance, punctuality and general worker wellbeing).

The new production system around autonomous work groups required an increased emphasis on what is known in Japanese as *hourensou*. This entails a more collaborative working environment centred around an increased number of meetings and information sharing within and between different teams. Moreover, the new production system emphasized a practice referred to by Japanese management as *genchi genbutsu*, which is the expectation that workers and line managers will go to the source of problems and solve them proactively.

In the previous production process, plenty of parts were always readily available, allowing workers to pre-produce buffer inventory in order to take lengthy breaks once production targets had been achieved. Consistent with the 'just-in-time' imperative that is crucial for customization, a key feature of the new production system was that buffer inventory was made deliberately thin. Parts were delivered from other plants only upon request, and were usually only delivered the day before a new assembly activity commenced. This heavily restricted the extent to which individual workers or teams were able to manage their pace of work.

Consistent with the new emphasis on quality, each individual's accuracy (number of defects) was logged on a daily basis and displayed above their workstation. No more than 20 defects were permitted per month, and if this target was exceeded, workers received a written warning. Persistent failure to meet these targets could result in dismissal. At the same time, poor-quality records at individual level would affect collective (team) performance. Within the new production system, more senior, long-serving members of staff were expected to supervise newer team members to ensure that their performance met the company requirements.

After a year of operating the new production system, the company experienced unprecedentedly high levels of labour turnover and a higher number of defects than under the old production system. Moreover, in consultative meetings, workers reported high levels of stress and fatigue as a result of always having to pace themselves in the just-in-time method of production. A common complaint raised by senior members of staff was the additional burden of having to coach and supervise newer members of staff and those who did not display the commitment and attitude necessary to meet the quantitative and qualitative performance targets. Younger workers in turn complained about 'micro-management' and pressure from more senior team members. Overall plant productivity was around 25 per cent lower than that of a comparable plant in Japan. Management were puzzled about why the Japanese production system was not yielding the desired productivity gains in the UK.

Reflective questions

1 Compare and contrast the UK and Japanese institutional contexts. What are the key differences? Are there any similarities?

2 Discuss to what extent the apparent failure of the Japanese mode of production in the UK plant can be accounted for by institutional factors and explain the nature of these factors. What could the management have done differently for their UK subsidiary?

CASE STUDY The Volkswagen system of corporate governance

The Volkswagen Group (VW AG), founded in 1937 with headquarters in Wolfsburg, Lower Saxony in Germany, manufactured nearly 10 million motor vehicles in 2015, making it the second-largest vehicle manufacturer in the world after Toyota. You may associate VW only with the VW badge, but actually the company owns the car brands Skoda, Seat, Audi, Bugatti, Lamborghini and Bentley, as well as selling commercial vehicles, buses and trucks under the MAN and Scania brands. Launched in the 1970s, the VW Passat Polo and Golf models have been linked with the group's reputation for high-quality, reliable cars. While the main markets for the group have long been Europe and the Americas, China has recently become its largest market.

The corporate governance model of VW entails substantial degrees of 'insider governance' as essential for coordinated market economy models of employment relations and which has long been viewed as exemplary of the 'deep connections between management, workers and local politicians' (Milne, 2015) that have arguably contributed to the German post-war economic miracle and strong manufacturing sector. Consistent with the CME model of employment relations, VW is subject to the German law of co-determination (Mitbestimmungsgesetz) which preserves the rights of workers to participate in management decision making. The law permits employees in companies with 2,000 or more employees to elect representatives (usually from the works council) to make up half the supervisory board of directors. Consistent with the German system of co-determination, VW are governed by a two-tier board structure with a supervisory board and a management board. The supervisory board not only appoints the management board, but also has full veto power on any decisions made by the management board.

In theory, the system of co-determination ought to give employees and shareholders an equal say in management decision making. The presence of works council representatives at supervisory board level has been linked (amongst other institutional factors discussed in the preceding chapter) with the relatively low levels of earnings inequality and limited excesses of executive compensation in Germany compared to similarly advanced industrial economies (Streeck, 1997; Coffee, 2005). However, in the case of VW, the system of co-determination and insider corporate governance has recently come under critique due to a series of scandals (including corruption and bribery) dating back to the early 1990s and culminating in the 2015 emissions scandal. However, the VW system of co-determination deviates a little bit from what we understand

Figure 5.2   Co-determination and the two-tier board structure in Germany

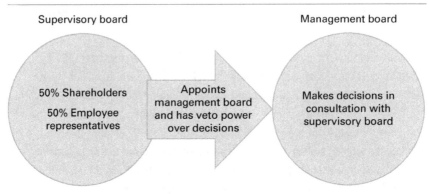

Supervisory board   Management board

50% Shareholders

50% Employee
representatives

Appoints
management board
and has veto power
over decisions

Makes decisions in
consultation with
supervisory board

about co-determination based on what this chapter has covered. At VW, half
the supervisory board seats are reserved for employee representatives. One of
the board seats has long been held by the head of the IG Metall union and the
remainder by works council representatives. In theory, the remaining half of the
board seats are to be held by outsider shareholders, but at VW, four of the 10
seats reserved for shareholders are members of the Porsche and Piëch families
(the Porsche brand being one of VW's brands) who own 31.5 per cent of VW's
equity; two seats are filled by the government of Lower Saxony, which holds 12.4
per cent of shares and Qatar Holding, which owns 15.4 per cent as an outside
investor (Milne, 2015). The only other 'outsider' is Annika Falkengren, CEO of the
Swedish SEB bank, which in turn is an advisor to Scania trucks – a subsidiary of
VW (ibid.).

These peculiarities (over-representation of insiders including local
government) has led a quite a distinctive system of corporate governance at
VW. While in principle, the chairperson would discuss sensitive issues with
shareholders in the first instance before bringing it before the full board at
German companies, sensitive issues would first be taken to the works council
by the chairperson, and a common position agreed before it is taken up with
shareholders (Milne 2015). Some have linked this system to a series of bribery
and corruption scandals affecting VW since the 1990s (see Odell, 2015). The
most notable one was the recent 'emissions scandal' where it has been revealed
that VW has long been involved in a large-scale emissions regulation evasion
scheme (Hotten, 2015). Specifically, the company cheated on federal emissions
tests through the installation of a so-called 'defeat device' on at least 11 million
of its diesel vehicles. The software would detect when the car was being tested

and suppress emissions at the time of test in order to meet stringent emissions requirements in various countries.

How was such endemic, large-scale cheating possible with such elaborate control mechanisms (supervisory board and outsider forms of governance)? Some have blamed the VW system of co-determination, which has become something more 'akin to co-management' (Milne, 2015). The strong representation of the works council and local government on the supervisory board meant that difficult decisions such as job losses were almost impossible to unilaterally implement by management and worker resistance to the prospect of such difficult decisions was strong, owing to the high union density at VW, with some 95 per cent of employees said to be members of IG Metall (Tatje, 2016) As a result, it might be expected that any change initiative aimed at increasing overall productivity (inherently likely to entail downsizing and/or work intensification) is likely to be fiercely resisted. Indeed, some have linked the current shortfall in productivity – VW made around the same number of cars as Toyota in 2014 with almost double the number of employees (Milne, 2015) – with the strong influence of employee representatives at board level.

Reflective questions

1 What are the key features of the corporate governance model at Volkswagen in Germany?

2 In what ways and to what extent is there institutional complementarity between the system of co-determination at VW and the ideal type of a coordinated market economy?

3 What do you see as the system's main advantages?

4 What do you see as the system's main disadvantages?

5 To what extent and in what ways should VW continue to consult their workforce/representatives in decision making?

Conclusions

In this chapter we examined the role of institutional factors in shaping distinctive national level patterns of HRM and employment relations. We considered the role of hard institutions (eg employment law) and soft institutions (such as the 'Nenko' system of promotion in Japanese companies). We have also considered institutions as embedded in particular cultural values, looking at practical IHRM applications such as pay bargaining and systems of employee voice across different countries such as the United States, Germany and Japan). By looking at the case of Volkswagen cars, we highlighted the extent to which co-determination, a distinctive model of collective bargaining in some of the continental European countries, can lead to superior firm performance, but also has its challenges.

Key learning points

- Cross-national differences in cultural values (as discussed in Chapter 2) often lead to distinctive institutional contexts in different countries:

  - these institutional contexts can be crudely subdivided into liberal market economies (LMEs) and coordinated market economies (CMEs).

- The institutional contexts in each type of market economy pose distinctive constraints and opportunities for firms operating in these countries:

  - For example, tighter restriction on staff dismissal and higher standards for minimum training provision in CMEs, legally enforced through penalties and incentives, may be viewed by firms as a key constraint. However, they may also be viewed as an opportunity insofar as they ensure a context within which firms can train their workforce to a higher standard.

  - Similarly, compulsory employee representation on supervisory boards may be viewed by organizations as restrictive, but this form of co-determination may also build trust and more constructive management–worker relations.

References and further reading

Ackroyd, S and Thompson, P (1999) *Organizational Misbehaviour*, Sage Publications

Bamber, G J, Lansbury, R D and Wailes, N, eds (2016) *International and Comparative Employment Relations*, Sage Publications

Bosch, G and Charest, J (2008) Vocational training and the labour market in liberal and coordinated economies, *Industrial Relations Journal*, **39** (5), pp. 428–47

Braverman, H (1972) *Labor and Monopoly Capital*, Monthly Review Press, New York

Coffee, J C (2005) A theory of corporate scandals: why the USA and Europe differ. *Oxford Review of Economic Policy*, **21** (2), pp. 198–211

Delbridge, R and Turnbull, P (2002) Human resource maximization, *Industrial Relations: Labour Markets, Labour Process and Trade Unionism*, **2**, p. 104

Drucker, P F (1971) What we can learn from Japanese management, *Harvard Business Review*, **49** (2), p. 110

Edwards, T (2004) Corporate governance, industrial relations and trends in company – level restructuring in Europe: convergence towards the Anglo – American model? *Industrial Relations Journal*, 35 (6), pp. 518–35

Gamble, J (2006) Introducing Western-style HRM practices to China: shopfloor perceptions in a British multinational, *Journal of World Business*, **41** (4), pp. 328–43

Hall, P A and Soskice, D, eds (2001) *Varieties of Capitalism: The institutional foundations of comparative advantage*, Oxford University Press

Hall, P A and Soskice, D (2003) Varieties of capitalism and institutional complementarities, in *Institutional Conflicts and Complementarities*, eds R J Franzee Jr, P Mooslechner and M Schürz, Springer US, pp. 43–76

Hotten, R (2015) Volkswagen: The scandal explained, *BBC Business News* [online] http://www.bbc.co.uk/news/business-34324772 [accessed 19 July 2017]

Höpner, M (2001) Corporate governance in transition: ten empirical findings on shareholder value and industrial relations in Germany, *Max-Planck-Institute for the Study of Societies Working Paper* (05)

IG Metall (2008) Services of IG Metall [online] https://www.igmetall. de/0161455_Leistungen_Aug2008_gesamt_Englisch_28c4f7286cd82fa0 3678012a851a6f0c8131a413.pdf [accessed 30 June 2017]

Kawaguchi, D and Ueno, Y (2013) Declining long-term employment in Japan, *Journal of the Japanese and International Economies*, **28**, pp. 19–36

Kambayashi, R and Kato, T (2016) Good jobs and bad jobs in Japan: 1982–2007, Working Paper 348, Columbia Business School, Centre on Japanese Economy and Business

Kochan, T A, McKersie, R B and Cappelli, P (1984) Strategic choice and industrial relations theory, *Industrial Relations: A Journal of Economy and Society*, **23** (1), pp. 16–39

Lampel, J, Bhalla, A and Jha, P P (2014) Does governance confer organizational resilience? Evidence from UK employee-owned businesses, *European Management Journal*, **32** (1), pp. 66–72

Leidner, R (1993) *Fast Food, Fast Talk: Service work and the routinization of everyday life*, University of California Press

Levitt, T (1972) Production-line approach to service, *Harvard business review*, **50** (5), pp. 41–52

Macaray D (2011) Why did Walmart leave Germany? *Huffington Post* [online] http://www.huffingtonpost.com/david-macaray/why-did-walmart-leave-ger_b_940542.html

Masczyk, P and Rapacki, R (2012) *Varieties of Capitalism in Transition Countries*, Warsaw School of Economics

Milne, R (2015) Volkswagen: Systems Failure, *Financial Times*, 4 November [online] https://www.ft.com/content/47f233f0-816b-11e5-a01c-8650859a4767 [accessed 19 July 2017]

NCSL (2017) Minimum wages by state in 2017 [online] http://www.ncsl.org/research/labor-and-employment/state-minimum-wage-chart.aspx [accessed 19 July 2017]

North, D (1991) Institutions, *Journal of Economic Perspectives*, **5** (1), pp. 640–55

Nölke, A and Claar, S (2013) Varieties of capitalism in emerging economies, *Transformation: Critical Perspectives on Southern Africa*, **81** (1), pp. 33–54

Odell, M (2015) Volkswagen: A history of scandals, *Financial Times* [online] https://www.ft.com/content/22ca0e9a-6159-11e5-9846-de406c-cb37f2 [accessed 191 July 2017]

OECD Stat (2017) Trade union density by country [online] https://stats.oecd.org/Index.aspx?DataSetCode=UN_DEN [accessed 19 July 2017]

Ono, H (2010) Lifetime employment in Japan: concepts and measurements, *Journal of the Japanese and International Economies*, **24** (1), pp. 1–27

Pfeffer, J (1998) *The Human Equation: Building profits by putting people first*, Harvard Business Press

Quintanilla, J and Ferner, A (2003) Multinationals and human resource management: between global convergence and national identity, *International Journal of Human Resource Management*, **14** (3), pp. 363–68

Rousseau, D M (1990) New hire perceptions of their own and their employer's obligations: a study of psychological contracts, *Journal of Organizational Behaviour*, **11** (5), pp. 389–400

Royle, T (2002) Just vote no! Union busting in the European fast-food industry: the case of McDonald's, *Industrial Relations Journal*, **33** (3), pp. 262–78

Royle, T (2004) Employment practices of multinationals in the Spanish and German quick-food sectors: low-road convergence? *European Journal of Industrial Relations*, **10** (1), pp. 51–71

Royle, T (2010) 'Low-road Americanization' and the global 'McJob': a longitudinal analysis of work, pay and unionization in the international fast-food industry, *Labor History*, **51** (2), pp. 249–70

Sorge, A, Noorderhaven, N G and Koen, C I (2015) *Comparative International Management*, Routledge

Soskice, D (1999) *Divergent Production Regimes: Coordinated and uncoordinated market economies in the 1980s and 1990s*, Cambridge University Press, pp. 101–34

Streeck, W (1997) German capitalism: does it exist? Can it survive? *New Political Economy*, **2** (2), pp. 237–56

Streeck, W and Yamamura, K, eds (2001) *The Origins of Nonliberal Capitalism: Germany and Japan in comparison*, Cornell University Press

Tatje, C (2016) Volkswagen: unheimlich maechtig' *Die Zeit* [online] http://www.zeit.de/2016/16/volkswagen-ig-metall-betriebsrat-unternehmenskultur [accessed19 July 2017]

Taylor, F (1911) *The Principles of Scientific Management*, Harper & Brothers, USA

Taylor, L and Walton, P (1994) Industrial sabotage, in *Organizations and Identities: Text and readings in organizational behaviour*, eds H Clark, J Chandler and J Barry, Cengage Learning, pp. 321–25

Thelen, K (2001) Varieties of labor politics in the developed democracies, *Varieties of Capitalism: The institutional foundations of comparative advantage*, eds P A Hall and D Soskice, Oxford University Press, pp. 71–103

Van Maanen, J (1999) The smile factory: work at Disneyland, in, *Sociology: Exploring the architecture of everyday life – readings*, eds D Newman and J O'Brien, Sage Publications, pp. 210–26

Wailes, N, Bamber, G and Lansbury, R D (2011) International and comparative employment relations: an introduction, in *International and Comparative Employment Relations: Globalisation and change*, eds Bamber et al, Sage, London, pp. 1–35

Womack, J P, Jones, D T and Roos, D (1990) *The Machine That Changed the World: The story of lean production: how Japan's secret weapon in the global auto wars will revolutionize western industry*, Rawson Associates, New York

06
Global labour governance and core labour standards

CHRISTINA NIFOROU

Learning outcomes

At the end of the chapter, you should be able to:

- understand the reasons behind the emergence of a global labour governance regime;

- analyse the advantages and challenges of the different public and private forms of global labour governance;

- understand the role of institutional, structural and political factors in shaping the local impact of global labour norms;

- apply theory to practice with regards to compliance with global labour standards in MNC subsidiaries and suppliers.

Introduction

An emergent global labour governance regime

The establishment of the International Labour Organization (ILO) in Geneva in 1919 was the first significant effort to provide protections for employees and trade unions at the global level. Until the mid-1990s, attempts to regulate labour rights at the global level and impose minimum standards worldwide were perceived to interfere with economic development, particularly in less-developed and emerging economies. Since the mid-1990s, the efforts to institutionalize global labour regulations have multiplied and, as we will see below, they have resulted in the proliferation of different types of instruments. These global instruments have been the source of heated debate among academics and practitioners in the fields of human resource management, employment relations, business ethics and labour geography. Experts argue that there is a global labour governance regime (Hassel, Hensen and Sander, 2010; Egels-Zandén, 2009) in the making that serves to fill gaps in global governance.

There are three types of market institutions that explain the gaps in global governance (Gereffi and Mayer, 2004). There are those that facilitate the operation and expansion of markets (eg financial institutions), those that regulate the markets (eg employment legislation) and those that compensate for market failures (eg welfare provisions). At the global level, there are strong facilitative institutions and weak (if not non-existent) regulatory and compensatory institutions. In other words, the globalization of economic activity has resulted in the emergence of supporting global financial and other mechanisms, whereas market regulation and compensation for the unintended consequences of market operations remain a national matter. Gaps in global market governance have in turn resulted in the emergence of public and private forms of labour governance.

The chapter begins by presenting key debates on core labour standards and attempts to link them to trade agreements, and proceeds to outline the different public and private regulatory mechanisms at the global level that have emerged as a response to governance deficits. It discusses their strengths and limitations and concludes with an analysis of their impact at the local level. A critical review of key up-to-date studies reveals that there are institutional, legal, structural and political obstacles to local compliance with global norms. The chapter will substantiate these arguments by discussing the impact of the Telefonica International Framework Agreement (IFA) in Ireland, Peru and Argentina. The case study will help you link theory to practice with regards to the contribution and challenges of a somewhat recent (since early 2000) global labour instrument (ie IFAs).

Public forms of labour governance

Table 6.1 Examples of key global labour governance actors and instruments

Actors	Instruments
International organizations: ILO, United Nations, OECD	Conventions Declarations and compacts Guidelines
NGOs	GRI, SA8000
Global trade union federations	International framework agreements

Core labour standards

An important public response to the governance deficit is ILO activity. The establishment of international labour standards has been the core activity of the ILO, which has elaborated two forms of standard setting: Conventions that need to be ratified by member states, and Recommendations. Despite the binding status of Conventions (at least in principle) and the existence of reporting systems and quasi-judicial arbitration mechanisms, labour rights have been repeatedly violated (Gibb, 2005). For Leary (1996), although violations do not negate the legality of the norm, they nonetheless challenge the organizational ability of the ILO to impose conformity with its fundamental principles. The enforcement capacity of the ILO has been largely questioned by the ascending number and heterogeneity of members. Since the early 1950s, the accession of a significant number of developing and less developed countries that rely on informal economy, cheap labour and flexible working conditions in order to attract foreign direct investment (FDI) not only increased the economic asymmetry and disparity among ILO members, but also undermined ILO claims for universal validity and application of labour standards (Senghaas-Knobloch, 2004). Moreover, the legal status of the Conventions generated further debates on whether they fall under international law agreements or treaty contracts or whether they are binding by virtue of membership regardless of whether they have been ratified (Leary, 1996; Senghaas-Knobloch, 2004). The ILO has been self-critical on the relevance of 'hard' mechanisms (ie binding regulation that can be invoked to court) in the face of its increased membership and has therefore shifted towards 'softer' approaches based on awareness raising, persuasion and capacity building of local (social and administrative) actors (Senghaas-Knobloch, 2004).

It is within this context of softer techniques that the ILO Declaration of Fundamental Principles and Rights at Work was adopted in 1998. The Declaration reiterated the binding status of Conventions by virtue of membership and prioritized the promotion of eight Conventions on human rights that have become known as Core Labour Standards (CLS). These include the freedom of association and the right to organize, the right to collective bargaining, abolition of forced labour, abolition of child labour, equal remuneration and non-discrimination. The Declaration builds on 'the obligation to policy targets rather than precise rules' (Senghaas-Knobloch, 2004) regarding CLS and has therefore attracted considerable criticism by both academics and practitioners. Alston (2004) makes a distinction between CLS and the remaining conventions on labour standards, arguing that the former have a lower status, based on the notion of 'principles' rather than 'rights'. Gibb (2005) questions the effectiveness of moral suasion or else, the 'mobilization of shame' and technical assistance as ILO mechanisms aimed at generating compliance. In that respect, the absence of trade sanctions is considered an institutional weakness (Van Roozendaal, 2005).

The Core Labour Standards as stipulated in the 1998 ILO Declaration on Fundamental Principles and Rights at Work

1 Freedom of association and the right to collective bargaining.

2 Elimination of all forms of forced labour.

3 Effective abolition of child labour.

4 Elimination of discrimination in respect of employment and occupation.

Linking trade to labour standards

The ILO's policy turn to soft law needs to be situated within wider debates of linking trade to labour standards. Provisions on labour standards have been included in unilateral or bilateral trade agreements where the country that gives preferential treatment to the product of a developing country expects 'some good will' (Gereffi and Mayer, 2004) regarding labour practices. Examples include the North Atlantic Free Trade Agreement (NAFTA) 'side agreements', and the US–Jordan and US–Cambodian Free Trade Agreements where labour and environmental provisions were incorporated in the main text of the accords. However, linking trade with labour standards has been a contentious issue for global regional economic organizations and trade zones. The effectiveness of the labour clauses in trade agreements has been largely questioned. Usually such clauses stipulate the application of local labour laws (ie the NAFTA side agreements), whereas references to labour regulation are absent from other important regional arrangements, as for instance in the ASEAN Free Trade Agreement. Another example is MERCOSUR, where there is a Social and Labour Commission charged with the task of monitoring labour standards, but it is rather weak and lacks formal authority (Gereffi and Mayer, 2004). Indeed, the text of the MERCOSUR Declaration states that the Commission 'shall play a promotional role rather than involving sanctions'.

Moreover, attempts to integrate core labour rights in the World Trade Organization (WTO) agreement (the so-called social clause debate) were unsuccessful (Van Roozendaal, 2002). The failure to link trade with labour standards reflects the negative stance of developing countries that consider the improvement of labour conditions as the result of economic growth rather than the cause, and hence resist any regulation linked to trade as protectionism (Gadbaw and Medwig, 1996). Finally, apart from concerns about protectionism, a social clause in the WTO regime would raise further questions on the capacity of developing countries to control and regulate the behaviour of private market actors and especially the MNCs (Gereffi and Mayer, 2004).

MNCs and public labour governance

Labour governance at the MNC level has been at the core of developments of the European Social Dialogue that culminated in the enactment of the 1994 Directive on the establishment of European Works Councils (EWCs). The latter are 'transnational, pan-European forums of employee representatives within multinational corporate groups for the purposes of information disclosure and consultation with group-level management' (Gold and Hall, 1994: 177–78). EWCs are the first 'genuinely European' institutions of employee interest representation at MNC level, reflecting the need to respond to the Europeanization of business which has been largely a result of the single European market (Patriarka and Welz, 2008). Although they have often been characterized as 'passive' bodies that receive information without actually being consulted (Telljohann, 2005), there have been instances where EWCs have gone beyond the rights stipulated by the Directive, developing a growing negotiating role in corporate practice. Similarly, recent scholarly research advocates that EWC representatives are developing a European identity that goes beyond national interests and the content of EWC agreements is progressively shaped to meet representatives' objectives while a number of EWCs engage in activities that extend beyond the boundaries of the states that have implemented the Directive (Waddington, 2011).

Given their key role in directing capital mobility and their increasingly strong position to control, coordinate and even set their own standards of production, MNCs have also become the focus of regulatory efforts by international institutions. The idea behind these efforts is to compel leading corporations to set higher labour and environmental standards, which would be subsequently imposed to suppliers in the face of company vulnerability to charges of violations that could damage their public image (Gereffi and Mayer, 2004). International efforts to 'mainstream' and 'standardize' CLS (Hassel, 2008) resulted in instances where responsibilities are shared between the public and private realms. The OECD Guidelines for Multinational Enterprises, adopted in 1976 (and significantly revised in 2000), and the UN Global Compact, adopted in 1999, provide a general framework for the employment of codes of conduct by MNCs. Both instruments are 'soft' and encourage companies to abide by certain principles and to extend them to their supply network (Hassel, 2008).

Both the Global Compact and the OECD Guidelines have inspired immense debates. International monitoring mechanisms are deliberately excluded from the UN Global Compact (Hassel, 2008) and MNCs are expected to provide information on implementation in their business reports. The OECD Guidelines, on the other hand, foresee the establishment of national contact points with governments and the preparation of an annual report. On the one hand, the absence of sanctions for non-compliance makes both initiatives attractive to companies (Hassel, Hensen and Sander, 2010) and this could eventually lead to benchmarking processes and spill-over effects (Ruggie, 2008). However, opponents emphasize the contested transparency in monitoring procedures and argue that, in essence, the initiatives are used as a way to prevent harder measures (Clapp, 2005).

Private forms of labour governance

MNC codes of conduct

Private initiatives include the proliferation of corporate codes of conduct adopted by MNCs initially as a response to consumer campaigns and gradually as a response to demands for socially responsible corporate behaviour (Hassel, 2008). Corporate Social Responsibility (CSR) emerged as a fashionable discourse during the 1990s and has even developed into an industry in its own right. CSR can be broadly defined as the way in which companies take responsibility for their activities and societal impact. They can do so by 'integrating social and environmental concerns in their business operations and in their interaction with their stakeholders on a voluntary basis' (European Commission, 2011, p. 366). Proponents of the concept argue that CSR is integral to the sustainability, competitiveness, as well as innovation of businesses. However, critics advocate that the proliferation of CSR codes of conduct seems to be far from a viable solution to address the governance deficit since their objective in most cases is to bypass regulation and collective representation of worker interests, therefore avoiding provisions that would establish dialogue with trade unions (Pearson and Seyfang, 2001). Since private codes of conduct are unilateral initiatives serving managerial prerogatives to avert bad publicity, MNCs follow a 'choose and pick' approach to the recognition of labour standards while there is an absence of pragmatic commitments for compliance and monitoring (Tørres and Gunnes, 2003). Furthermore, they stipulate only minimal (if any) responsibilities for suppliers and subcontractors (Tørres and Gunnes, 2003; Gibb, 2005).

Private multi-stakeholder initiatives

Apart from MNC codes of conduct, private responses embrace a wide range of multi-stakeholder initiatives which are largely triggered and driven by non-governmental organizations (NGOs). The Global Reporting Initiative (GRI) and Social Accountability 8000 (SA8000) are the most prominent among these developments. The GRI is an alliance of NGOs, consultants, academics and companies whose purpose is to outline principles and indicators that companies can use to benchmark their social and environmental performance. GRI indicators cover different areas of the economy (eg economic performance, market presence, anti-corruption) and society (eg employment, occupational health and safety, labour/management relations, non-discrimination, human rights assessment etc). SA8000 is also a prominent social certification standard that was established by Social

Accountability International (a non-governmental organization). SA8000 builds on ILO CLS, the UN Convention on the Rights of the Child, and the Universal Declaration of Human Rights. Key elements of the SA8000 include abolition of child and forced labour, health and safety, freedom of association and right to collective bargaining, discrimination, working hours and remuneration. Both initiatives are voluntary, while the main criticism has to do with the contested legitimacy and accountability of NGOs (Trubec, Mosher and Rothstein, 2000) as their founders and leaders.

Questions on the legitimacy of NGO-driven developments are situated within wider discourses on the underdeveloped and even antagonistic relationship between NGOs and Global Union Federations (GUFs) (Senghaas-Knobloch, 2004). NGOs have been mostly engaged in lobbying initiatives regarding human and labour rights and, over the last few decades, their focus has shifted from governmental institutions towards corporations (Egels-Zandén and Hyllman, 2006; Sullivan, 2003). GUFs are distinguished by industrial sector and have a network of national affiliate organizations from over 120 countries (Croucher and Cotton, 2009). In contrast to NGOs, GUFs aim more at creating and defending space for local unions while their methods include solidarity work, education and, since 1988, the negotiation of international framework agreements (IFAs) (Croucher and Cotton, 2009).

International framework agreements

IFAs constitute an alternative attempt by GUFs to address the inefficacy of existing national and international mechanisms for labour governance and also to enhance their own independency and capacity as global social actors (Gibb, 2005). The first agreement was concluded in 1988 between Danone and IUF and since then IFAs have increased in number to about 100, the majority of them having been negotiated after 2002. In the absence of a formal, universal definition, IFA definitions can be encountered in various global union position papers, statements and guides to affiliates. The definitions are very similar and essentially involve the signature by the MNC and the GUF, the reference to international labour standards and the application to the global MNC operations.

The IMF has been particularly proactive in that area and we find the IMF definition the most comprehensive. According to an IMF model agreement (IMF, 2006: 1):

All IFAs must:

- contain the Core Labour Standards of the International Labour Organization (ILO), clearly referenced by number;
- cover all company operations throughout the world;
- include a strong and unequivocal commitment by the TNC that suppliers and sub-contractors adopt similar standards for their workers.

The definition provided by the International Organization of Employers in their IFA guide to employers reveals much softer language, especially with regard to suppliers (IOE, 2007):

> Ostensibly [IFAs] usually are an agreement signed between a multinational enterprise (MNE) and a Global Union Federation (GUF), which principally concerns international core labour standards. They generally apply throughout the relevant company, but in some instances also have implications for suppliers.

Now that we have presented the key actors and instruments of global labour governance, the remainder of the chapter will discuss issues of compliance at the local level.

Local impact of global labour governance

Institutional barriers to compliance

Whether unilateral, bilateral or multilateral, MNC management adopts a rather 'soft' and voluntary approach to global labour governance, avoiding the establishment of local enforcement and monitoring mechanisms. Research reveals that bilateral instruments are more likely to be implemented in multinationals with a strong tradition of corporate social responsibility (CSR) and trade union presence (Niforou, 2012). It is therefore common practice to integrate global labour governance instruments into existing company CSR policies, while managements often complain that there is a strong overlap among the different instruments that subsequently makes compliance a complicated task. Moreover, global instruments are not legally binding and therefore, when it comes to enforcing compliance, subsidiaries resort to local labour laws, thereby defeating the purpose of having global labour regulation in the first place. This becomes more important when considering that in many less-developed countries, local institutions are weak. For example, the exercise of collective rights in the Latin American region is not automatic and compliance is usually enforced via judicial means, as for instance in Puerto Rico and Argentina.

Legal barriers to compliance

Sometimes, the references to ILO conventions within the texts of global instruments contradict local legislation. For instance, the ratification by Argentina of ILO Convention 87 on freedom of association has generated debates on whether it enhances trade union democracy or whether in practice it leads to further fragmentation of the union movement. In 2008, a landmark ruling of the Argentinean Supreme Court challenged the right to the freedom of association as this is established by the National Constitution. The Court recognized the right of two trade unions to enjoy collective bargaining rights within the same branch, therefore signalling an important departure from the nation's system of statutory trade union monopoly. The Court decided that ILO Convention 87 takes precedence over national laws, while the ruling has been interpreted by legal experts as essentially giving Convention 87 a constitutional status.

Structural barriers to compliance

Research shows that differences in business activity and ownership structure are very important in informing local practice (Donaghey and Reinecke, 2017; Yu, 2015; Niforou, 2014; Xu and Li, 2013; Niforou, 2012). MNC management advocates that they are unable to enforce compliance with core labour standards in minority-owned subsidiaries and suppliers. Minority participation essentially means little (if any) control over day-to-day operations and labour practices, while the relationship between MNCs and suppliers is an arm's-length contractual one. Moreover, practices of restructuring (ie subcontracting and offshoring) further impede local compliance as they result in new companies which are distinct legal entities and therefore do not fall under MNC governance. In order to avoid disputes and scandals, a number of MNCs opt for rather prescriptive language regarding scope and application when adopting global labour governance instruments. An example of such language is when the text dictates the reach of an instrument to companies where headquarters 'exercise control' (Niforou, 2014). However, there have been instances in the apparel and electronics industries where MNC headquarters of lead firms have taken actions to enforce labour standards to suppliers (see Yu, 2015; Xu and Li, 2013). Those actions, though, are usually taken in response to big scandals that jeopardize firm image and reputation, and usually in collaboration with global and local labour activists whose campaigns serve to publicize the scandals.

Political barriers to compliance

Finally, we find that power relationships, political prerogatives and economic interests further determine the local impact of global labour standards (Niforou, 2012; 2014; Yu, 2008; 2015). Global headquarters are interested in maintaining and safeguarding local business, institutional and cultural independency. They also tend to adopt a very flexible stance towards core labour standards during the early stages of internationalization in order to safeguard the future of their investments and expansion. Global unions are largely reactive and mostly intervene to resolve local disputes rather than prevent them. Local unions experience GUFs as 'distant' and bureaucratic in that they put too much emphasis on 'formality' rather than action. In contrast, NGOs and global activist groups tend to be more proactive but are impeded by the barriers discussed earlier. At the subsidiary level, the exercise of power by local actors differs according to expectations. The (threat of) disputes and exposure of violations by local unions, when combined with the mediation of global actors and the reference to global instruments may suffice to enforce compliance. Senior local management has the power to choose between compliance with global norms and compliance with local institutional and industry standards. However, they tend to opt for the latter as they seem to enjoy a high degree of autonomy which global headquarters are cautious not to circumscribe (Niforou, 2012). With regard to suppliers, compliance with the lead firms' standards seems to be impeded by the tensions between firms' imperative for profit maximization and their commitment to workers' rights, and also hard market competition between suppliers (Yu, 2008).

Summary of key barriers to local compliance with global rules

Legal: The legal character of global instruments is ambiguous and the language they use can be subject to multiple interpretations.

Institutional: The content of global norms often conflicts with the content of local laws, particularly in the Global South.

Structural: MNC HQs often find it difficult to enforce standards in minority-owned subsidiaries and suppliers.

Political: In many instances, non-compliance is an issue of strategic choice.

Reflective questions

1 How did the gaps in global governance result in the proliferation of public and private labour instruments?

2 What are the key strengths and shortcomings of the different types of global labour governance?

3 What are the key barriers to compliance with global labour instruments in local MNC subsidiaries and suppliers?

CASE STUDY Compliance with the Telefonica international framework agreement

Source: Author, adapted from Niforou (2012); (2014).

Background

The presentation of this case study builds on primary and secondary data collected in 2008 and 2009. Primary data sources include face-to-face interviews, a small-scale survey, organizational documents, case law as well as the texts of the Telefonica IFA and Business Principles. Interviews were conducted with HR managers and trade union officials at the global headquarters and subsidiaries in Peru, Argentina and the UK. The survey was distributed to management and union officials in 21 subsidiaries. Secondary data included company annual reports and UNI publications.

Introducing the company and the GUF

At the time of the research (2008–2009), **Telefonica** operations were spread across 25 countries (since then, the company has restructured its operations and is now present in 21 countries). Main activities comprised fixed and mobile telephony, broadband services and call centres, while peripheral businesses included media and management consultancy. The company had 257,000 direct and 333,000 indirect employees. Fifty-one per cent of direct employees worked in call centres while 61 per cent of call centre employees were women. Latin America was (and still is) the biggest market of Telefonica products and services, and employees in the region accounted for 67 per cent of the total workforce. In Spain, Telefonica employees are represented by the telecom branches of the two major trade union confederations CCOO and UGT. Seventy per cent of the Spanish workforce are covered by collective agreements. CCOO enjoys the majority of the representation.

In terms of social responsibility, the company had incorporated the Global Compact in 2002 and had also elaborated an internal code of ethics, named 'Business Principles' (Telefonica, 2017). The Business Principles entail rather generic provisions on trust and integrity, respect for the laws and human rights, but also more specific provisions addressing clients, employees, shareholders, the community as a whole and finally suppliers. Telefonica produces annual social responsibility reports in 17 countries, all of which are externally verified using the GRI and AA1000AS indicators.

Summary of Telefonica Business Principles

General principles: honesty and trust, respect for the law, avoidance of bribery and anti-corruption, respect for human rights.

Employee-related principles: commitment to professional development, fair compensation, health and safety, respect for human rights (the latter principle involves brief references to child labour, harassment and respect for employees' right to join a trade union).

Customer-related principles: commitment to high-quality products and services, communications and advertising.

Shareholder-related principles: commitment to highest standards of corporate governance, shareholder value, transparency, provision of appropriate internal controls and efficient use of company assets.

Community-related principles: commitment to the social, technological and economic development of the countries where Telefonica operates; environmental protection.

Supplier-related principles: management of conflicts of interest, commitment to fairness and transparency, responsibility (the latter refers to requirements to meet similar ethical standards and to comply with existing legislation and regulations in the countries where they operate).

The global union federation UNI has more than 3 million members in the information and communication technology services (ICTS) industry in more than 130 countries (UNI Global Union, nd). In terms of governance, it is organized into four divisions: 'UNI-Europa', 'UNI-Americas', 'UNI-Africa' and 'UNI-Asia Pacific'. IFAs, or 'global agreements', as GUFs prefer to call them, are at the core of UNI campaigns targeting MNCs. UNI perceives IFAs as global strategies that foster cross-border cooperation between local and national trade unions and ensure that 'multinationals come to the bargaining table in good faith in every country in which [they] operate' (personal interview with UNI-Americas official, 2008). However, in the case of Telefonica, the negotiation of an IFA was not triggered by UNI. The signing of the agreement was the culmination of union efforts from Latin America to bring their local issues to the attention of global corporate management. The text was signed in 2001 by the CEO, UNI and the telecom representatives of CCOO and UGT.

The IFA

Content

The public origins of Telefonica, management objectives to enhance company image and reputation that were damaged by labour violations in Latin America, and the company's established CSR tradition facilitated the adoption of the agreement and essentially mean that negotiations of substantive and procedural clauses were rather smooth. The text makes references to 12 areas: free selection of employment, child labour, discrimination, freedom of association and collective bargaining, employee representatives' rights, health and safety, working environment, minimum salaries, working time, training and development, employment stability, and respect for the environment. It also goes beyond basic labour rights and covers minimum wages, working day, training and employment stability. However, the language used to stipulate compliance with those rights is generic and foresees the application of local legislation. As explained by the global headquarters, they were keen to respect local traditions.

Issues covered by the UNI-Telefonica IFA and references to ILO

Free selection of employment: references to ILO Conventions 29 and 105.

Employment discrimination: references to ILO Conventions 100 and 111.

Child labour: references to ILO Conventions 138 and 182.

Freedom of association and the right to collective bargaining: references to ILO Conventions 86 and 98.

Worker representatives' rights: references to ILO Convention 135.

Minimum wages: references to national legislation and collective agreements (as set out in ILO Conventions 94, 95 and 131).

Working day: references to national legislation, collective agreements and industry standards (as set out in ILO Conventions 1, 47 and Recommendation 116).

Health and safety: references to ILO Convention 155.

Working environment: commitment to harmonious relations and respect at the workplace.

Development and training: commitment to training, especially with regard to the use of new technology.

Employment stability: references to national legislation and agreements.

Respect for the environment: commitment to ensure that all environmental concerns are met.

Dissemination to local levels

The 2001 IFA text dictated that both parties – management and unions – would be responsible for the administration and implementation of the agreement and to that end they would engage in an ongoing dialogue supported by regular meetings. Management used company intranet to disseminate the IFA to company subsidiaries in Spain and abroad. The text clearly stipulates that the company will disseminate information on the agreement to all companies of the group. However, headquarters prioritized dissemination of the IFA to the unionized subsidiaries of the group. Their explanation was that local managers in operations with no union tradition would find it hard to understand the spirit and letter of the agreement. In other words, their view is that the IFA covers only majority-owned unionized operations where trade unions are affiliated to UNI. They also argued that the IFA is not applicable to Telefonica suppliers. This interpretation of the IFA is shared by unions in Spain and also UNI. Both Spanish unions and UNI believe that the IFA is an agreement between two signatories who represent two groups (unions and managers) and, therefore, when one of the groups is absent, any compliance claims are difficult to meet. However, the objective of UNI was to use the IFA as a vehicle for increasing its membership through trade union recognition and organization.

Enforcement of compliance: the cases of Peru, Argentina and Ireland

Peru: 'Telefonica del Peru' was established after a series of acquisitions of previously public companies with rather strong trade union presence. The restructuring led to extensive redundancies while the employees who were re-employed to different parts of the company were obliged to sign new contracts with inferior terms and conditions of employment. In 2001, trade unions reached an agreement with management. The text provided guarantees that the employees would maintain their trade union rights. Besides local laws and policies, the text made references to the IFA. However, those references were very brief and symbolic while serving political purposes: the local agreement was signed just a few months after the adoption of the IFA and it was the only instance of the IFA being explicitly cited in a local document.

Argentina: In 2004, there was a serious and long dispute over pay in Telefonica Argentina, where employees were on strike for 34 working days. Global headquarters intervened by getting information on the dispute and attempting to mediate its impact. The IFA text was not invoked during the negotiations because, in the words of the Argentinean Group HRD, 'pay is a local issue'. The dispute was therefore resolved locally. There is nonetheless one case where the Telefonica IFA contributed to resolving a local dispute on trade union recognition. The company refused to recognize Cepetel (a small Argentinean union of engineers and technicians) as a legal collective bargaining actor. Cepetel resorted to local labour tribunals and used the IFA through UNI as a vehicle to make the dispute public beyond the borders of Argentina. There were two trade unions representing different segments of the Telefonica Argentina workforce at the time. Both unions perceived Cepetel as a threat to their majority of representation. They therefore joined forces with the company and engaged in a legal battle against Cepetel. Additional motives behind their hostility had to do with political and ideological differences. Cepetel eventually won the case and, in 2008, it was recognized by the company for collective bargaining purposes.

O2 **Ireland** became part of Telefonica following the acquisition of the O2 assets in the UK, Germany and Ireland in 2006 (although it was sold in 2014 and is no longer part of the Telefonica group). O2 Ireland did not recognize trade unions for collective bargaining purposes. The Communications Workers Union (CWU) represented around 3 per cent of the staff in grievance and disciplinary proceedings. In 2007, the company decided to outsource its network technology division to external IT providers – a move that would result in redundancies. Given that a number of the affected employees were union members, the CWU was formally involved in the process. However, the CWU's requests for formal recognition after the outsourcing was over were denied. O2 management invoked the low membership rates and argued that the rest of the employees had not expressed any interest in joining a union. The CWU sent a letter to the HRD of O2 Ireland arguing that O2 Ireland, as a subsidiary of Telefonica, should respect the spirit and letter of the IFA clause on trade union recognition and the right to collective bargaining as specified in ILO conventions 87 and 98. During a global Telefonica–UNI meeting in 2009, the CWU asked for the support and intervention of the CEO and the global HR director. However, the CWU's request was rejected again. The European and Global HR directors explained in a letter to UNI that their interpretation of the IFA is that it foresees neutrality and, as such, it stipulates 'rights for employees, not for trade unions'.

Assessment

The Telefonica IFA was reviewed and renewed in 2007. The outcome of the review was a re-writing of the clause on 'neutrality' triggered by excessive local disputes on trade union recognition. The new wording on neutrality now reads as 'aimed at not preventing or hindering the trade union from setting up in workplaces'. Overall, local trade unions viewed the IFA as a positive development but would prefer a legally binding agreement. However, for local management, the 'soft' and generic language of the IFA text is a one-way road, given the vast institutional and cultural differences in MNC operations worldwide – a view also shared by corporate management and surprisingly, by home-country unions. According to the global HR team, a major success of the IFA is that it 'makes both parties enter into dialogue or at least consider the possibility of dialogue', something which in countries like Colombia or Ecuador is still unthinkable. The IFA was further renewed in 2015 and the new text includes explicit references to the company supply chain. The new agreement between UNI and Telefonica was celebrated as being 'on the cutting edge of labour relations between multinational corporations and global unions' (UNI Global Union, 2015).

Reflective questions

1 What are the barriers to local compliance with the Telefonica IFA? Use the summary of key barriers to local compliance with global rules to help you organize your responses.

2 What are the differences in compliance in Peru, Argentina and Ireland, and why?

3 Discuss the extent to which you agree or disagree with the statement made by O2 Ireland that *the IFA stipulates rights for employees, not for trade unions.*

Conclusions

The chapter has outlined the strengths and limitations of the different public and private forms of global labour governance that reflect efforts to fill regulation gaps at the global level. Key global labour instruments include the ILO conventions, international framework agreements, MNC codes of conduct and multi-stakeholder initiatives such as the GRI and SA8000. These instruments offer companies the opportunity to integrate social standards with business imperatives. However, the nature of these initiatives is voluntary and, ultimately, local compliance often depends on the discretion of management combined with the proactive involvement of trade unions and other lobbying groups.

Key learning points

- The globalization of economic activity has resulted in the creation of gaps in global governance: markets are now global but regulation and compensation remains a national matter.

- There are different types of global labour governance – both public and private – that emerged as a response to the above deficit. These include ILO Conventions, the OECD guidelines for MNCs, unilateral codes of conduct and IFAs among others.

- The local impact of the above global instruments depends on a number of factors: institutional and legal, structural and political.

- Overall, there is evidence to suggest that both management and labour actors adopt a reactive and rather flexible stance towards global labour instruments. The latter seem to be more successful in companies with a long tradition of CSR and strong union presence which in turns defeats the purpose of having global norms in the first place. However, there have been positive cases of compliance in non-unionised subsidiaries and suppliers albeit following the exposure of local disputes and violations.

References

Alston, P (2004) 'Core labour standards' and the transformation of the international labour rights regime, *European Journal of International Law*, **15** (3), pp. 457–21

Clapp, J (2005) Global environmental governance for corporate responsibility and accountability, *Global Environmental Politics*, **5** (3), pp. 23–34

Croucher, R and Cotton, E (2009) *Global Unions, Global Business*, Middlesex University Press

Donaghey, J and Reinecke, J (2017) When industrial democracy meets corporate social responsibility – a comparison of the Bangladesh Accord and Alliance as responses to the Rana Plaza disaster, *British Journal of Industrial Relations*, in press

Egels-Zandén, N (2009) Transnational governance of workers' rights: outlining a research agenda, *Journal of Business Ethics*, 89, pp. 169–88

Egels-Zandén, N and Hyllman, P (2006) Evaluating strategies for negotiating workers' rights in transnational corporations: the effects of codes of conduct and global agreements on workplace democracy, *Journal of Business Ethics*, 76, pp. 207–23

European Commission (2011) Communication from the Commission to the European Parliament, the Council, the European Economic and Social Committee and the Committee of the Regions: a renewed EU strategy 2011–14 for Corporate Social Responsibility /* COM/2011/0681 final */

Gadbaw, M R and Medwig, M T (1996) Multinational enterprises and international labor standards, in *Human Rights, Labor Rights, and International Trade*, eds L A Compa and S F Diamond, University of Pennsylvania Press, Philadelphia, pp. 141–62

Gereffi, G and Mayer, F W (2004) The demand for global governance, Working Paper Series SAN04-02, Terry Sanford Institute for Public Policy, DUKE.

Gibb, E (2005) International framework agreements: increasing the effectiveness of Core Labour Standards, *Global Labour Institute* [online] http://www.globallabour.info/en/2006/12/international_ framework_agreem.html

Gold, M and Hall, M (1994) Statutory European Works Councils: the final countdown? *Industrial Relations Journal*, 25 (3), pp. 177–86

Hassel, A (2008) The evolution of a global labor governance regime, *Governance: An International Journal of Policy, Administration, and Institutions*, 21, pp. 231–51

Hassel, A, Hensen, H and Sander, A (2010) Global Labor, in *The International Studies Compendium Project*, ed R A Denemark, Blackwell, Oxford

IMF (2006) Recommendations of the International Framework Agreement (IFA) Conference, *International Metalworkers Federation* [online] http://library.fes.de/pdf-files/gurn/00251.pdf

IOE (2007) International industrial relations, *International Organization of Employers* [online] www.ioe-emp.org.preview11.net4all.ch/en/policy-areas/international-industrial-relations/index.html

Leary, V A (1996) The paradox of workers' rights as human rights, in *Human Rights, Labor Rights, and International Trade*, eds L A Compa and S F Diamond, University of Pennsylvania Press, Philadelphia, pp. 22–47

Niforou, C (2012) International Framework Agreements and industrial relations governance: global rhetoric versus local realities, *British Journal of Industrial Relations*, 50, pp. 352–73

Niforou, C (2014) Labour leverage in global value chains: the role of inter-dependencies and multi-level dynamics, *Journal of Business Ethics*, 130, pp. 301–11

Patriarka, M and Welz, C (2008) *European Works Councils in Practice: Key research findings*, European Foundation for the Improvement of Living and Working Conditions, Dublin

Pearson, R and Seyfang, G (2001) New hope or false dawn? Voluntary codes of conduct, labour regulation and social policy in a globalizing world, *Global Social Policy*, 1 (1), pp. 48–78

Ruggie, J G (2008) Protect, respect and remedy: a framework for business and human rights, *Innovations: Technology, Governance, Globalization*, 3, pp. 189–212

Senghaas-Knobloch, E (2004) Global economic structures and 'global governance' in labour regulation policy, artec-paper No. 113, ISSN 1613-4907, Universität Bremen,

Sullivan, J D (2009) *The moral compass of companies: business ethics and corporate governance as anti-corruption tools*, Global Corporate Governance Forum

Telefonica (2017) Business principles [online] https://www.telefonica.com/en/web/about_telefonica/strategy/business-principles

Telljohann, V (2005) The European Works Councils – a role beyond the EC Directive? *Transfer: European Review of Labour and Research*, 11 (1), pp. 81–96

Tørres, L and Gunnes, S (2003) Global framework agreements: a new tool for international labour, *Global Labour* [online] http://www.globallabour.info/en/globalframework.pdf

Trubec, D M, Mosher, J and Rothstein, J S (2000) Transnationalism in the regulation of labor relations, transnational regimes and transnational networks, *Law and Social Inquiry*, 25 (4), pp. 1187–211

UNI Global Union (nd) About us [online] http://uniglobalunion.org/sectors/icts/about-us

UNI Global Union (2015) UNI and Telefonica renew their global agreement [online] http://uniglobalunion.org/news/uni-and-telfonica-renew-their-global-agreement

Van Roozendaal, G (2002) *Trade Unions & Global Governance: The debate on a social clause*, Continuum, London

Waddington, J (2011) European works councils: the challenge for labour, *Industrial Relations Journal*, **42** (6), pp. 508–29

Xu, K and Li, W (2013) An ethical stakeholder approach to crisis communication: a case study of Foxconn's 2010 employee suicide crisis, *Journal of Business Ethics*, **117** (2), pp. 371–86

Yu, X (2008) Impacts of corporate code of conduct on labor standards: a case study of Reebok's athletic footwear supplier factory in China, *Journal of Business Ethics*, **81**, pp. 513–29

Yu, X (2015) Upholding labour standards through corporate social responsibility policies in China, *Global Social Policy*, **15** (2)

PART TWO
The functional areas of international HRM

07
International recruitment, selection and talent management

PETER FOSS

Learning outcomes

At the end of this chapter, you should be able to:

- understand the key processes associated with attracting, recruiting, selecting and retaining talent;

- gain a deeper understanding of the impact that employer and talent branding can have on attracting, selecting, managing and developing employees;

- identify and make informed decisions regarding the implementation of recruitment and selection processes;

- gain a practical appreciation of international talent management through the use of case studies.

Introduction

In our globalized world, organizational success depends on learning and performing better and faster than competitors. There are many ways that organizations can do this, such as through competition based on cost or quality. In knowledge-based organizations, one of the key factors that differentiates successful from unsuccessful firms is their people and talent, with talent being scarce and a competitive advantage. Although the notion of talent is not new, its application to the field of HRM and managing people is more recent. Cappelli (2008) stated that the purpose of talent management is to help a firm achieve its objectives, implying that talent management is a strategic process, having a number of interconnected activities. Using these observations, this chapter will examine the key areas of international talent management, recruitment and selection. This will be achieved by using the talent management anchor (see Figure 7.1) as a structure, including the following components:

1 strategy, culture and structure;

2 employer and talent brand;

3 diagnosing and planning;

4 acquiring and selecting;

5 managing; and

6 developing/retaining.

Greater focus will be placed on the first four elements of the talent anchor framework with the use of two case study examples.

Traditionally, HRM focused on its key functions or activities – resourcing, training and development, employee reward and employee relations. The more forward-thinking firms viewed HR activity strategically and aimed to integrate the HR functions with the strategy of the firm alongside the constraints of the external environment. However, other less strategically focused firms operationalized the HR functions more independently and as a consequence there was much less integration and coordination. Although viewing the role of people as a competitive advantage has long been recognized through the resource-based view of the firm (Barney, 1991), this recognition is not always mirrored in practice. There is the long-standing rhetoric that 'people are our most important assets', but frequently this is not always demonstrated in how some companies treat their employees, resulting in a tension between what is said and what is done.

Thus, some firms espouse having a soft approach to managing people that could include concern for their welfare through such activities as training and development, career planning, coaching and mentoring, although the reality may be much more of a hard and measurement-driven culture where there is lack of support for people demonstrated through concern for task achievement and the bottom line at any price (Truss et al, 1997).

One of talent management's primary assumptions is that people – especially those with the necessary talent, and those who are able and willing to perform at the highest level – can make a significant contribution to the competitive advantage of the firm. This implies that people with talent will be sought, nurtured and developed to form a partnership with the firm, especially if the company has a global presence (Scullion and Collings, 2010). Talent management is an investment in people, and as such requires adequate resourcing. This can be achieved more easily in large multinationals with 'deep pockets', yet small- to medium-sized firms (SMEs) need to resource and manage talent more efficiently. Although talent management aims to strategically integrate a range of HR-related activities, those of employer branding, recruitment and selection, development and retention remain central to its success, as will be highlighted in this chapter's two case studies examining talent management (National Instruments) and recruitment and selection (Skullcandy).

Defining talent

This discussion will begin by examining how talent is defined. A typical definition of talent is someone who has a natural inclination to do something well, without the need to be taught (Cambridge Advanced Learner's Dictionary, 2008). However, there are different viewpoints of talent ranging from natural talent (luck) to hard work (effort), yet, by contrast, there is evidence suggesting that deliberate practice and training triggers changes in the brain and provides the platform for people to do things that they normally could not do (Ericsson and Pool, 2016). Colvin (2008) sees deliberate practice as an activity to improve performance, and stretching individuals just beyond their current abilities is crucial to success.

Individuals, industries and organizations will view talent differently. Stahl et al (2012) found that there were two distinctive viewpoints on evaluating and managing talent. The differentiated (exclusive) approach distinguished employees between high (A players), average (B players) and below average (C players) performance in order to identify, develop and reward 'high potentials' and weed out those with low potential. Second, some firms believe that all their people are talented (inclusive) and used their top and lower levels of talent differently in order to bring greater value to the company. These two approaches can also be used together in a combined or hybrid approach that utilizes different career paths and development activities to make the most out of organizational talent differences. Availability and depth of resources in people can also determine what approach a firm takes. These same authors also found six core talent management principles that go beyond best practice and are aligned with their company strategy and culture:

1 alignment with strategy;
2 internal consistency;
3 cultural embeddedness;
4 management involvement;
5 balance of global and local needs;
6 employer branding through differentiation.

Consequently, Ross (2013) stated that definitions of talent are complex, often ambiguous, and can cause problems when it comes to determining whether someone is talented or not. In practice, each organization tends to define the talent required for a particular position through the person specification.

Talent management process

After reviewing how talent could be defined, the talent management process will now be explored. However talent is defined, it can be seen as focusing on those individuals who could make a difference to the performance of the organization and help to achieve its objectives. The CIPD (2016a) state that the aim of talent management is to attract, identify, develop, engage, retain and deploy people that an organization values and whom they believe can contribute to the firm either immediately or in the future. Lewis and Heckman (2006) reported three perspectives of talent management:

1 continuing to provide the traditional HR activities faster such as through the internet or across the entire organization;

2 management of succession pools through workforce and succession planning mostly with an internal focus;

3 talent is viewed as critical to the survival and success of the firm with a focus on performance pools of talent to draw on as needed alongside employee segmentation (as A, B and C levels), and the role of HR is to ensure everyone performs at a high level.

Although these perspectives need not be mutually exclusive, each of them differentially highlights the strategic need and business case for attracting, developing and retaining talent. This is especially relevant in the context of international business where a number of organizations may be competing for the same pool of talent, and wider external factors such as the economics of supply and demand for talent play a key role. Talent management needs to support the organization's strategy by effectively recruiting, deploying and managing people in order to achieve a competitive advantage. Without a talent mindset and focus from all levels, an organization can quickly fall behind its competitors. Consequently, organizations need to have an awareness of what elements would be the primary components of their talent management system and process.

There are a number of talent management frameworks, such as Phillips and Edwards (2008). However, the metaphor of an anchor of talent management will serve as the structure to this chapter. The rationale for this framework is that talent management can serve as a grounding, anchor or focal point for everything that the organization does – with people at its core, and all managers being responsible for its implementation. Key components of the talent anchor are shown below with the talent anchor framework following in Figure 7.1.

Figure 7.1   The talent anchor

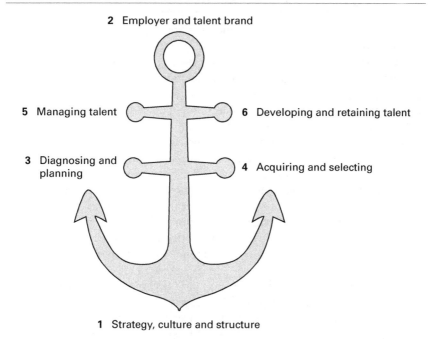

2 Employer and talent brand

5 Managing talent

6 Developing and retaining talent

3 Diagnosing and planning

4 Acquiring and selecting

1 Strategy, culture and structure

1 Strategy, culture and structure – basis for firm's talent management system.
2 Employer and talent brand – acts as a beacon to attract and retain talent.
3 Diagnosing and planning – talent diagnosis and planning process, and considers the three Cs: competency, capability and capacity.
4 Acquiring and selecting – process of acquiring and selecting talent.
5 Managing talent – improving performance across the organization.
6 Developing talent – engaging, developing and retaining talent for future career and leadership positions.

Thus, talent management is an ongoing process aimed at engaging employees for the long term, which joins together the goals of the organization with the performance goals of individuals. Firms need to analyse the need for talent and either develop those already in the firm or acquire others externally, as well as rewarding the best performers and laying the ground for succession planning. Trust, transparency and a continuous review of how talent is being managed is central to the process. Two case studies later in the chapter will provide examples of talent management and recruitment and selection processes.

Strategy, culture and structure

The first component of the talent anchor – strategy, structure and culture – will now be examined. Referring to the talent anchor framework above, talent management needs to be based on the organization's strategy, culture and structure, and integrated across functions and departments. As an example, a department store selling clothes based on a strategy of quality will put more emphasis and energy into publicizing and strengthening its brand reputation and promise along with acquiring talented salespeople with skills in satisfying and delighting customers, than a department store based on keeping costs to a minimum. Employer brand serves as a mechanism to attract external applicants as well as to retain current ones. Staying with this same example, a department store that focuses on quality will want their employees to have a different set of competencies than those for a low-cost operator. The former organization will want their employees to be able to engage and develop a rapport with customers in order to achieve customer satisfaction and loyalty, which tends to increase employee engagement and retention.

Culture and structure also influence how organizations manage talent. A culture that is more agile, flexible, diverse and open will typically attract and retain talent, as people have more freedom to express and develop their talent. These types of cultures tend to encourage knowledge sharing, creation and innovation, which can lead to greater competitive advantage along with the potential to enter new markets. Structure also has an influence on talent. Lawler (2008) contrasts structure-centric organizations (SCOs) with human capital-centric organizations (HCCOs) and states that while SCO firms are top-down hierarchies with tight job descriptions and person specifications and are slow in communication and decision making, HCCO firms are characterized by participative decision making, career focus, reward for performance, a sense of community, shared leadership and a commitment to talent management. Using a number of case examples, Lawler also makes the case that offering low wages is not the best option, as these types of companies have significantly higher turnover rates resulting in a loss of talent.

Employer and talent brand

After the role of strategy, culture and structure, the importance of the second component in the talent anchor – employer and talent brand – will now be examined. On the opposite side of the talent anchor framework from strategy, culture and structure is employer and talent brand. Although a firm's brand is developed internally in relation to its product and/or service as distinguished from its competitors, it is often the interface between the external and internal environments. Schumann and Sartain (2009) identified three distinct brand types:

1 **Customer brand** – aimed at influencing customers to purchase their product and/or service based on a brand promise.

2 **Employer brand** is what a company can offer its employees in exchange for their service.

3 **Talent brand** is the direction in which a company focuses its marketing activities in order to attract and retain employees through engagement.

Before any of us joins an organization, we want to know about the company's business, reputation, culture, values, conditions of employment and reward, along with what job security we can expect. Employer branding is focused on establishing and developing a reputation that is perceived as attractive to both current and potential employees in order to attract and retain talent. There is a widespread focus on improving company websites to enhance the user experience and promote the employer brand. Employers who are perceived by current and potential employees as a desirable place to work are often seen as an employer of choice; this is also referred to as employee value proposition (Armstrong, 2009) and can include good pay and flexible working. Employees can also act as customers in providing feedback to the company regarding how well the firm delivers on its brand promise. Thus, to what degree do employees continue to use the company's product and/or service and why?

According to *Fortune* (2016), the 10 best global companies to work for are as follows:

Table 7.1 Best 10 global companies to work for in 2016

Rank	Company	Headquarters
1	Google	USA
2	SAS Institute	USA
3	W.L. Gore and Associates	USA
4	Dell EMC	USA
5	Daimler Financial Services	Germany
6	NetApp	USA
7	Adecco	Switzerland
8	Autodesk	USA
9	Belcorp	Peru
10	Falabella	Chile

Reflective question

Identify three companies you would like to work for based on their employer or talent brand and why?

Particularly in an international context where some organizations may not be as well known as others, current employees can serve as the company's ambassadors for future employees. The organization's aim is for employees to be loyal to and promote the company brand. Whether a firm's reputation is positive or negative can be easily determined through social media. Some relevant questions for potential employees to ask could include: What do current employees say or feel about working for their employer? What are the results of the most recent engagement survey? What is the firm's reputation? What reward, development and career opportunities are available? In this context, the role of HR in acquiring and retaining talent has changed from one of purchasing to one of marketing.

Schumann and Sartain (2009) proposed that there have been significant changes recently in the drive for organizations to acquire and retain talent, which highlights a company's need to establish a talent brand. The most notable of these changes is the increased level of expectations of employers from Generation Y, who are very comfortable and engaged in the use of technology and social media as their preferred mode for interacting with peers and accessing information. Although this skill set can be a great asset to organizations, Generation Y also desire more immediate gratification, engagement and flexible working practices from their employers. A particularly good example of generational differences is from the movie *The Internship* (July 2013), where two older applicants compete for jobs at Google against applicants from Generation Y. The movie highlights strengths of the different generations as well as differences in expectations and skills of younger talent that companies need to address, even though it can conflict with the needs of older generations such as baby boomers. Brand loyalty on the part of employees goes a long way toward helping companies to achieve their goals as well as to attract the necessary talent.

Social media is a particularly important tool that can influence organizational reputations as well as attracting and retaining talent. Prior to the advent of social media, firms were more in control of what they disclosed into the public arena. Currently, a company can be either a hero or villain in an instant as a result of someone posting a video on social media. A useful example of negative publicity comes from the *San Diego Union Tribune* (Gomez, 2017), which reported the story of United Airlines' forceful removal of a passenger after a video of the event was posted across a range of social media sites worldwide. As a result of this posting, which was reportedly viewed up to 290 million times in China, United's stock dropped, prompting their CEO to apologize and promise urgent action to rectify how United handles overbooked planes in the future. Events such as this at United can cause significant damage to a company's brand image, employer brand and talent brand, highlighting the need for everyone in the firm to be a brand ambassador.

Diagnosing and planning

In the talent anchor, the four primary talent management activities are: diagnosing and planning for talent needs; acquiring and selecting talent; managing talent; and developing talent. There are additional activities embedded within each of these four activities. Now the role of employer and talent brand has been established, the third component of the talent anchor will be explored – diagnosing and planning. Diagnosing and planning an organization's talent needs is a critical, often quantitative activity that determines the firm's overall talent requirements. One of the key aspects of this activity is to evaluate how many current employees are ready or will develop sufficiently to be able to be promoted into more senior roles. For example, if an organization forecasts that it requires 75 staff in particular positions, and it estimates that 55 internal employees are able to move into these roles, then HR will need to acquire 20 applicants externally. Thus, diagnosis of talent needs, identifying the gaps that need to be filled and planning against resource considerations are the focus of this activity. Another consideration is the analytics that goes into deciding which are pivotal or talent-critical roles, as those require greater energy put into attracting and recruiting the required talent, which drives what Boudreau and Ramstead (2007: 4) call the 'talentship' evolution. Talentship's aim is to improve decisions that depend on human capital, and in turn organizational effectiveness. These authors pose questions based on an organization's strategy that address such issues as: finding the areas where talent can enable the firm to become better and different than their competitors; what pivotal talent programmes resources should be invested into where the biggest difference can be seen; and if a firm altered its goals, then how would this impact on organizational structures? One of the implications of this is that leaders and not just HR need to make decisions affecting talent acquisition, development and resourcing.

In order to develop or acquire talent, organizations need to differentiate between the three Cs – competencies, capability and capacity. A competency is an attitude, skill or knowledge that enables an employee to perform their job sufficiently, and identifies the organization's expectation about the level of employee performance (CIPD, 2016b). Furthermore, core competencies are the distinctive competencies not easily replicated that enable an organization to sustain its competitive advantage (Prahalad and Hamel, 1990). Many organizations design competency frameworks that define the competencies individuals need to possess. Capability is the ability of individual(s) to develop or improve upon the competencies that they already possess. Capacity is focused on how much of a particular skill set or role is sufficient – so the question of 'Do we have enough engineers?' is relevant here, and is often linked to available resources – so an organization may need more engineers, though they may or may not have sufficient resources to increase their capacity. To make the best use of talent, getting the right balance between present skill requirements (competencies), developing or stretching people into acquiring new skills (capability) and assessing whether the firm has sufficient strength in its key areas is an important diagnostic and planning activity.

One additional consideration is that all employees will have aspects of their skills and knowledge where they prefer to spend most of their time and energy, which is often referred to as a person's strengths or comfort zone. Although individuals and organizations recognize the need for employees to develop some of their less-preferred skills, and become involved in 'stretch assignments', they will typically be happier and more productive when engaged in their area of strength.

A good example of what happens when people are stretched beyond what they can comfortably do is provided by Peter and Hull (2009) and is known as the Peter Principle. This principle proposes that if people stay in an organization long enough, they will eventually be promoted into a job that they will not be able to perform sufficiently, and thereby will have reached their 'level of incompetence' (Peter and Hull: x). This is quite relevant today, as knowledge workers will frequently know more about their jobs than their managers – which was not always the case. Consequently, if an employee is seen as competent in what they do, then they may be promoted to the position of manager where some will be less competent, motivated, and committed than in their previous role, and could eventually leave the organization. There are numerous instances where a very competent performer, such as a programmer, has been promoted into a managerial position where he/she is ineffective. People can develop new skills, although extraneous factors such as anxiety and fear can prevent them from doing so effectively.

Reflective question

How would you react if you were promoted into a position that you did not have the required skills to perform?

Previously, reference was made to the inclusive (everyone has talent) and the exclusive (selective) approach to talent. Many organizations take the exclusive approach to talent where they identify and nurture a select group of talented individuals, who they expect will be the future leaders of the firm. Typically, this approach segments employees into such categories as A, B and C players. The notion of 'players' uses a sports metaphor with the assumption that everyone in the organization wants to move up the corporate ladder and eventually some of the B players will become A players. Although this upward movement will be accurate for many people, it is not universally true; some of those who want to do this allow their fears to prevent them from developing, and fail to achieve their personal goals. According to DeLong (2011) there will be many employees (B players) who are very happy in what they do and have no desire to move into a managerial position. They are often the people who know how to get things done in firms as well as how to navigate through the mire of organizational politics. One challenge for organizations is to recognize the different needs of employees and avoid pushing solid performers or B players up the career ladder when they are perfectly content in their present role, have an enormous influence on the firm's performance and have no desire to progress to the next step of the career ladder. Yet the more effective organizations will have a pool or database of qualified back-ups should one of their talented people leave – especially in talent-critical positions. Less effective organizations will not be able to respond so quickly.

Acquiring and selecting

After the diagnosing and planning process, the forth component of the talent anchor – acquiring and selecting – is now discussed. The acquisition and selection part of the talent anchor includes attracting or recruiting and selecting potential candidates. Price (2011) defined recruitment as 'attracting candidates prior to selection' (p. 547) and selection as 'a key element of employee resourcing in which successful applicants are evaluated and chosen by means of interviews and tests' (p. 548). The previous discussion on employer and talent brand addressed how a company's brand can be used as a recruitment tool. Many organizations will aim to fill as many vacancies as possible internally in order to engage and retain key employees. Some, though not all of the key reasons for recruiting external candidates include the following:

- the available opening may be an entry-level position;
- firms may not want, or are financially unable to invest a large amount of money into training and developing employees;
- there may not be a sufficient supply of local talent;
- the organization may want to bring in fresh ideas for some positions.

Whether focused on entry-level or selective senior positions, attracting people is an important activity for a number of reasons. First, for entry-level positions especially, if the person is a good fit with the organization and is an effective performer, then they could move into a leadership position. I once had a discussion with the head of global HR at an international bank who told me that they do not hire at entry level for just performing that particular role, but for future leadership potential that a person could offer the bank at a later time. Second, hiring someone will incur significant costs of both money and time, so it is important to make the right hiring decision. Bock (2015) wrote about insights at Google and stated: 'Hiring is the most important people function you have, and most of us aren't as good at it as we think. Refocusing your resources on hiring better will have a higher return than almost any training programme you can develop' (p. 67). He went on to suggest that if a firm has limited resources, then they must prioritize funds on recruiting and taking time in the hiring process to get the best people possible.

Cappelli (2008) proposed what he termed a 'talent on demand framework' (p. 77) based on supply chain and operations principles to address uncertainty in talent demand and supply. These four principles are:

- Principle 1: Make and buy to manage risk.
- Principle 2: Adapt to the uncertainty in talent demand.
- Principle 3: Improve the return on investment in developing employees.
- Principle 4: Preserve the investment by balancing employee–employer interests.

Bench strength, or how many back-ups an organization has for key positions, is a consideration and often a matter of financial resources. A good example of this is football teams – those teams with 'deep pockets' tend to have greater bench strength per position than those teams with fewer financial resources and a weaker brand. Decisions around how to adapt to the above risks are often determined by an organization's context such as industry, location etc. An example of this came from a recent interview (2017) I had with a manager of a large international financial institution located in London, who stated:

> The financial services industry in London is very competitive – frequently, there are 1,000 people applying for every position, so we rarely put money into developing people internally, and use external recruiters instead. If we do have the need for a special talent, then we tend to hire external consultants who are typically paid three times the going wage.

Whether a company operates locally or internationally, the process of attracting talent for external hires begins with diagnosis and planning, as previously discussed. After determining the talent required, a job analysis would look at the tasks and outputs that a job description and person specification are based upon, including key results areas. Some methods of job analysis are observation, work diaries, stakeholder interviews, expert panels and focus groups. A job description also specifies the comprehensive requirements of a job and where it is located within the organization structure. The job description is then used to compose a person specification which designates the personal characteristics required in order to perform the job effectively. A traditional personal classification system proposed by Roger (1952) used the following categories:

- physical make-up;
- attainments;
- general intelligence;
- special aptitudes;

- interests;
- disposition;
- circumstances of the job.

For example, if there was a job opening for a recent accounting graduate, an employer might expect them to have a presentable appearance and speech, have attained the necessary qualifications, be of at least average intelligence, have an aptitude for numbers, be interested in data and details, possess a calm disposition, and be able to adapt to the circumstances of the job.

One of the challenges in the recruitment and selection process is that if a company hires the right person for the job they want to fill today, then the job requirements may be outdated in a short period of time, which can constrain organizational flexibility. Price (2011) introduced an approach outlining three options for matching people with jobs, shown in Figure 7.2 below. Within the talent management approach, using a combination of these methods would enable a firm to fill a particular position as well as plan for the future.

Right person – who is the most suitable and qualified and able to do the job?

Culture fit – how can the firm reshape the job to enable the person to join the organization? Jobs can be altered if the person is seen as desirable.

Flexible person – who can the company find who is flexible and can adapt? This is a long-term orientation, grooming talent for the future.

Recruitment Methods

There are a range of recruitment methods available, and the choice of which methods to use can influence the number and quality of candidates applying for a position. Some of the more popular methods are:

Figure 7.2   Options for matching people and jobs

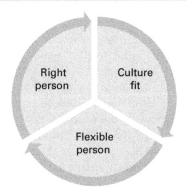

Adapted from Price (2011)

- employer branding;
- corporate website, internet;
- internal job board, including employee referral programmes;
- social media;
- national, local, international press, trade journals, radio and tv;
- external agencies such as job centres, employment agencies and headhunters.

Employer and talent branding is particularly important, and many organizations include the results of their annual employee surveys on the corporate website to attract candidates. One of the purposes of corporate websites is to promote their employer and talent brand. However, if the company is seen as an employer of choice, they will most likely encounter a large volume of applications, both solicited and unsolicited. Social media and e-recruitment also contribute to the quantity and quality of applications and shortlisting, as well as cost reduction. Broughton et al (2013) reported that 42 per cent of HR decision makers in an online panel indicated that they would make greater use of social media tools in the future, yet consideration needs to be given to verifying applicants' information, avoiding over-investing in social media and using it as part of a wider recruitment strategy.

One of the challenges in recruitment is who to shortlist. If the wrong decisions are made in shortlisting, then this will affect candidate quality. There is increased use of workforce analytics aimed at improving decision making in reaching and selecting the best candidates, managing performance and development. Collins (2013) discussed how analytics can prevent talent shortfalls by reducing knowledge loss as a result of turnover, identifying the types of jobs needed and where potential candidates would come from. These activities can transform HR into being a key business partner and contributor, yet the data does need to be relevant and valid.

Realistic job previews (O'Nell et al, 2001) aim to provide an accurate overview to potential hires about the company culture with positive and negative aspects of the job through use of job information, expectations, testimonies and questionnaires. This can also be a useful means for organizations to reduce turnover.

At the international level, if there is a shortage of local talent, then organizations would need to explore the global context in order to address the shortfall within legislative requirements. Minbaeva and Collings (2013) believe that global talent management (GTM) presents greater challenges than domestically, and discuss seven key myths that can inhibit its success. Some of these myths highlight the need for firms to take a strategic view and consider the importance of each position, its pivotal role, reduce performance variance, acknowledge that not all positions need to be filled by A players and that talent is not always mobile. A key implication discussed by these authors is that firms need to differentiate and focus on pivotal positions, resourcing them accordingly with a mixture of A, B and C players. Whether the acquisition and selection is at the local or international level, firms do need to review relevant information on application forms, CVs etc.

External recruiters will be used by some firms for such reasons as cost and efficiency savings, and SMEs may not have sufficient HR expertise within the firm. Use of external agencies has advantages as well as disadvantages, and for many firms, the ability to understand the organizational culture is a key aspect of the decision.

> **Reflective question**
>
> If you were recruitment manager at a medium-sized marketing firm, what recruitment methods would you use to attract external candidates, and why? Consider which methods you would give a higher priority to.

Selection process

Once candidates are recruited, the selection process begins. There are a number of available methods, and according to the CIPD survey (2015a) the most popular methods for selecting candidates are listed in Table 7.2 below.

Table 7.2 Methods used to select applicants (% of respondents)

Methods	Percentage
Interviews following contents of CV/application form	83%
Competency-based interviews	77%
Tests for specific skills	52%
General ability tests	47%
Literacy and/or numeracy tests	45%
Assessment centres	38%
Personality/aptitude questionnaires	36%
Group exercises (for example role-playing)	27%
Online tests (selection)	24%
Pre-interview references (academic or employment)	22%
Tools to enable self-selection	3%
Analytical algorithms to match people to roles	1%
Gamification	1%
Other	5%

SOURCE CIPD (2015a: 24), with the permission of the publisher, the Chartered Institute of Personnel and Development, London (www.cipd.co.uk).

From the above table, we see that interviews are the most-used selection method. Although interviews are popular, the quality of interviewers can vary greatly. Although most firms will use the interview as part of the selection process, the inclusion of other methods such as testing and assessment centres tends to give more power and confidence to the selection decision. As previously discussed, prior to selection, job analysis, job and person specification and screening will have been completed. There are four types of selection interview:

- Phone or video: used for initial discussion or with overseas candidates.
- Structured: standardized set of questions used to compare candidates using situational, behavioural or critical incident approaches.
- Semi-structured: a less structured and more open approach aimed at encouraging interviewees to talk more openly.
- Unstructured: questions are not preset, which allows for flexibility.

The above interviews can be conducted on an individual, panel or group basis with other candidates. There are benefits and drawbacks to each of these. Individual interviews are conducted by the same person, which would be consistent, though he/she could miss some important elements of the interviewees. Panel interviews are conducted by a group of people from the organization, including HR, management and employees, and can vary in size. The group interview includes several candidates at the same time and is interested in observing how candidates interact with one another to get an indication of how they would work with or lead others.

I know of a construction company that places a high priority on ensuring they get the right person for the job now and in the future. Whenever they have a job opening, all eight partners initially interview each candidate independently. If any one of the eight partners is not in favour of hiring any one of the candidates, then that candidate will not be hired. This approach guarantees total agreement. Even though it is a time-consuming process, it places great emphasis on getting the right person for the organization.

Testing

Psychometric testing can be a useful adjunct to the selection process. Analytics, as previously discussed, uses what is termed big data to increase the accuracy and effectiveness of recruitment, selection, management and development decisions. Some of the more useful types of test for selection include aptitude, ability, intelligence and personality. An aptitude test measures a person's potential to perform a task, such as numerical aptitude for bookkeeping. Ability tests measure those skills that have already been acquired, such as general, abstract reasoning, mechanical, manual dexterity and spatial ability. Personality questionnaires aim to quantify personality traits or types that are relevant to the job and person specification. However, Morgeson et al (2007) reported three concerns in using personality testing in selection:

1 there is low reported validity of personality tests in predicting job performance, with faking being a contributor;

2 the use of self-report personality tests needs to be reconsidered;

3 alternatives to self-report measures need to be found.

These concerns address previous debates around such issues as the degree to which personality is measurable, its stability over time and whether the measurement can be applied to different situations. A useful distinction needs to be made between personality and behaviour in that we all have personality preferences, although these need not be deterministic. Thus, we have the option to choose any range of behaviours in different situations. For example, introverts may act in an extroverted manner during an interview, but when hired may revert to their introverted preferences on the job, indicating that interviews are often a 'managed interaction' somewhat similar to a first date where first impressions are important, and need to be treated as such. Meinert (2015) stated that many personality tests are based on the five-factor model that uses openness, conscientiousness, extroversion, agreeableness and neuroticism. However, a new trend is emerging that matches applicants to jobs that would be most suitable to them through the use of neuroscience games and big data. Even though testing does have its criticisms, companies should consider using it as an aide in the selection decision.

I once conducted some psychometric testing for a trainer position. There were five people on the interview panel, and one of the panel members knew one candidate well. Testing was administered to the three candidates, and the candidate who was known by the panel member scored extremely low on working in a team, which was a key part of the job description and person specification. This panel member convinced the rest of the panel to ignore the test results and hire the candidate who he knew. After the candidate had worked for the company for one month, all of the panel members complained about this candidate's lack of teamworking skills.

An extension of individual psychometric testing is assessment centres, which offer a range of exercises provided to a group of candidates to determine their ability or potential for development. These are administered by trained assessors and can include such activities as in-tray, group, critical incident, case study, role play and work sample exercises. A good example of a recruitment and selection process is that used by Skullcandy, below.

CASE STUDY Recruitment and selection at Skullcandy

Skullcandy Inc, with its headquarters in Park City, Utah, United States is the parent company of the Skullcandy® and Astro Gaming® brands, with a music, sports, technology and creative culture. Skullcandy creates audio products for consumers with a fashion-focused lifestyle and sells its products through innovation in technologies and ideas, with leading-edge design, materialization and collaborations with up-and-coming musicians and athletes. Astro Gaming creates premium video gaming equipment for professional gamers, leagues, and gaming enthusiasts. Skullcandy and Astro Gaming products are sold and distributed through a variety of channels around the world from the company's global locations in Park City, San Francisco, Tokyo, Zurich, Mexico City and Shanghai, as well as through partners in some of the key culture, sports and gaming hubs globally.

In Skullcandy's Shenzhen, China subsidiary and all locations, their recruitment and selection goals for all positions are to:

- perform a professional, cost- and time-efficient recruitment process;
- conduct a transparent recruitment and evaluation to ensure that recruitment meets current and future talent and leader requirements;
- make a clear selection decision supported by strategy to communicate the selection offer to the desired talent individual or group.

There are six steps in their recruitment and selection process:

1 Preparation – the department supervisor meets with HR to discuss such topics as the person specification, job description, interview and evaluation form, time plan, and recruitment channel.

2 Recruitment channel – internal, referral, and external sources are all utilized. Internal hires comprise 40 per cent, with very few referrals, and external hires make up the remaining 60 per cent of all hires.

   – Internally, HR drafts the advertisement that is first available to all internal staff via e-mail and Wechat, where interested staff inform their supervisor prior to applying for the job.

   – Referral asks if any staff know of a relevant person that they could refer for the available opening; they need to complete an application and submit it to HR. If the applicant is hired, then a referral bonus is paid to the referring staff member after a successful probation.

   – Externally, the HR database, company and job search websites, Wechat and headhunters are utilized.

3 Screening – HR selects the appropriate candidates – internal and/or external based on agreed selection criteria set by the supervisor. The supervisor is included in screening CVs if needed for their technical expertise.

4 Verification call – prior to the interview, a phone call is made by HR to the candidates to verify their CV details, motivation, salary expectations, level of English language and any specific candidate concerns.

5 Interview – there are up to three levels at which interviews can take place: HR, supervisor and director levels. During the first interview, HR evaluates the candidate's CV, their personality, communication and teamwork aptitude along with their future plans, English and technical testing and salary discussion. The second interview is with the candidate's supervisor, who assesses their knowledge, job responsibilities and other relevant aspects. Interviews with the director – only for managerial candidates – address relevant questions pertaining to each candidate as well as their ability to fit into the organization and its culture. If, after any of these interviews the candidate is deemed to fall below Skullcandy's criteria, HR informs them by e-mail or phone. Phone is used if the candidate is acceptable but it may not be the right time to make them an offer and HR would like to save them in their database for future reference.

6 If Skullcandy wants to make an offer to the candidate, HR proceeds with a reference check by e-mail, mail or phone before the offer is extended. The reference checks are made with two former supervisors and an HR contact from previous positions.

7 Offer – HR makes an offer by phone or during the last interview. If the candidate accepts the offer, they are invited to sign the offer letter and provided with a welcome pack that includes the company policies and relevant forms.

Reflective questions

1 What would be the strengths and weaknesses of the recruitment and selection approach taken by Skullcandy?

2 What would be areas of improvement that you might recommend to Skullcandy's HR department?

This case study aptly demonstrates a clear recruitment and selection procedure with a logical progression from beginning to end. It identifies the recruitment channels of internal, external and referral along with the screening and interview process. It also describes their procedure for making an offer as well as maintaining candidates on a database if an offer is not made.

Selection decision considerations

Making selection decisions has many facets, although the primary concerns are around biases (CIPD, 2015b), with some listed below:

- affinity bias: tendency to like people similar to us;
- confirmation bias: tendency to look for information that confirms our impressions;
- groupthink: pressure to conform to perceived group consensus;
- halo and horns effect: tendency to ignore any characteristic of a person (either positive or negative) that contradicts our initial impression of them;
- status quo bias: desire to stick to the status quo.

Frequently, the more mature members of selection panels prefer to select candidates based on the status quo and perceived similarity, even when challenged by evidence and fairness considerations. An example of position or expert power influence is sometimes seen in SMEs and selection of international athletes.

An example of how *not* to make a selection decision follows here. A small oil and gas company in Singapore was recently taken over through a merger and acquisition. The current operation manager was not performing effectively, so was fired by the company. However, she complained to the board using a flood of tears, and was kept on in that position. In the meantime, a recruitment drive had subsequently hired someone else to fill her position. When it was discovered by the manager that the original job holder was still with the company they then moved the 'new' operations manager to the sales team. As a consequence, this small organization now had two people who were not performing!

Managing, developing and retaining

After an employee is on-boarded, they need to be managed, developed and retained, which are the fifth and sixth components of the talent anchor, and will be examined next. These two talent management processes are intertwined and aimed at managing and improving the performance of all employees, as well as developing those with potential in order to achieve the strategic aims of the company. Managing employees is focused on improving the performance of employees and can be done by way of immediate feedback. Additionally, performance management and appraisal is a more formal and structured way to assess performance, reward and development potential. Talented people are often attracted to high-performance cultures that challenge, engage, stretch and reward them. Performance appraisals are also useful in assessing the effectiveness of the recruitment and selection process – if employee performance is high, then recruitment and selection would be seen as effective, and the reverse would be true if employee performance is low.

One controversial approach to performance appraisal is forced distribution, as was applied at General Electric, aimed at revitalizing employees using a bell-shaped curve (Figure 7.3) that would typically yield 10 per cent above average, 80 per cent average, and 10 per cent below average ratings (Stewart, Gruys and Storm 2010). It was frequently used in sorting employee segmentation into A, B and C players to determine who would be promoted, developed, or fired (lowest 10 per cent). Its advantages are that employees are evaluated against the same criteria, they can promote a more open discussion based on feedback, and top performers can be identified. Its disadvantages are that employee performance may not fall into a normal bell-shaped curve, the categories may not accurately reflect employee performance, and it can be difficult to maintain morale when there is fear of being fired. Alternatively, graphic rating scales and critical incident methods can be used to appraise performance.

Figure 7.3 Forced distribution curve

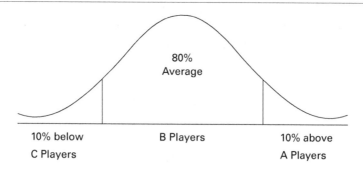

Performance appraisals identify potential leaders of the organization through talent pools that identify a group of potential successors to a range of leadership positions. The focus of succession planning is often on what is termed high potentials. Key drivers for succession planning include unexpected loss of key leaders, the need to reduce the cost of replacing employees, difficulty in finding talented replacements externally, poor bench strength, and the desire to fill positions from within to retain valued employees. Talent management programmes frequently invest significant resources into high potentials, though will also invest in those who show promise to become a high potential. The McKinsey–GE nine-box grid is a tool used to evaluate and plan successors based on two factors: performance and potential

(Ashton and Morton, 2005). A good example of talent management in action is the National Instruments case study below.

CASE STUDY Talent management at National Instruments

National Instruments (NI) empowers engineers and scientists with a software-centric platform that incorporates modular hardware and an expansive ecosystem. Customers can build high-performance systems within test, measurement and control that exceed requirements, quickly adapt to change and ultimately improve the world. Engineers and scientists at over 35,000 companies in over 95 countries use NI's platform and its revolutionary LabVIEW software to tackle the greatest engineering challenges of our time, from green energy to safer transportation and innovations in medical research.

NI began as a three-man operation in the garage of co-founder Dr James Truchard (Dr T). Today, it is a multinational corporation with more than 7,000 employees globally. When Dr T founded NI, he envisioned not just a company 'built to last' but a place where people would 'love their jobs'.

Over time, as the company has grown, it's become clear that an aligned, global talent management strategy is required to deliver on the company's original people vision. In 2016, NI unveiled its People Platform, which is how the company will attract, develop, reward and recognize its people through an aligned, optimized approach that includes philosophy, practices, behaviours and learning. The ultimate desired outcome of the platform is to engage and retain employees who are able to maximize their contribution to the business while achieving their own personal career growth goals.

One of the core components of the platform is a Global Talent Management Strategy including six core people management programmes that build upon one another throughout the year: goal-setting and performance reviews; engagement conversations; talent review (9-box); succession planning; career development planning; and compensation:

1 Talent review: an organizational perspective includes an analysis of what attitudes, skills and knowledge the firm needs, and what it currently has. Next, depth of the current bench strength, learning and development interventions, succession planning, and recruitment needs are considered.

2 Career development planning: an individual perspective asks questions as:
   - Where do I want to go?
   - How do I get there?
   - How can I grow and develop to achieve my goals?

3 Goal setting: individual, manager and organizational perspectives are linked to the overall purpose of ensuring that each individual's task and activities fit into and support the organizational strategy as cascaded down to department level. It also ensures that individuals have a shared understanding of how their own contributions fit into the overall strategy and performance of NI.

4 Engagement conversations: meaningful one-on-one dialogues between individuals and managers occur with the aim of understanding the motivations, challenges and opportunities of individuals in order to help both parties achieve their goals. This process also has the added benefit of building trust between employees and employer, thus strengthening the psychological contract, increasing individual engagement and organizational productivity.

5 Compensation: from the individual and organizational perspective, reward is seen as a de-motivator rather than a motivator, so the aim is to 'take it off the table' by rewarding those who make the most contribution and are necessary to retain in the future. The aim of this reward strategy is to have people performing effectively and being rewarded for doing so.

6 Performance reviews: undertaken using individual and managerial lens. The aim is for individuals to be aware of where they are in terms of current performance through feedback, to provide recognition and acknowledgement of their contributions, and to enable them to think about what needs to happen next.

The overall talent management process is frequent and ongoing, aimed at informing the organization about its overall bench strength and future readiness for any positions that will be required in the future and providing an opportunity for employees to understand growth opportunities within the company.

This case study clearly identifies core components of NI's global talent management (GTM) strategy. It is quite useful that talent review is put at the top of their list, as is career planning. At the outset, there is engagement with employees, which is a feature of the entire process. Their GTM strategy appears to be based more on a set of identifiable principles than best practice, which means they have chosen a strategy appropriate to the business.

Interestingly, they believe money is not a motivator and 'take it off the table'. This does not mean that they do not reward people well, but see other aspects of work such as engagement and career development as being more important.

Reflective questions

1 How thorough is NI's talent management process, and is anything missing?

2 For many people, money is seen as a motivator. What is your view on 'taking money off the table', and if you would make this suggestion, what might be the disadvantages of doing so?

Conclusions

Talent management is an integrated process that begins by alignment with a company's strategy, culture and structure. Company culture and organizational practice tend to reinforce one another. Successful talent management programmes tend to be based more on a set of integrated and tested principles that work within a particular company rather than following an externalized set of best practices – thus, the focus is more on appropriate rather than best practices for a particular company. The employer and talent brand is a strategic approach aimed at attracting, recruiting and retaining talented people. In order to achieve this, companies need to invest, engage and stretch people to reach a level of top performance. Acquiring and selecting people needs to have a balance between internal and external candidates in order to retain key talent. There are a range of selection methods, and firms do need to invest the required time, energy and money into getting the person that will be a good fit in terms of the culture, job, and development potential. Managing talent is a comprehensive activity that goes from on-boarding to performance management, whereas developing talent is aimed at assessing and developing career paths and leadership potential in order to retain talent and grow the organization. The talent anchor serves as a guide to this process for both local and international firms.

Key learning points

- Define what talent means, and recognize that talented people are a valued asset and competitive advantage.

- View talent management as a core activity where all managers are responsible for its success.

- Align strategy, culture and structure with talent management principles and practice.

- Clearly establish and promote the employer and talent brand to attract the best possible talent.

- Invest significant resources (time, energy and money) into acquiring and selecting talent.

- Once they are onboard, engage, value, challenge, reward, and develop talent.

- Promote a transparent and fair career, succession planning and development programme to retain key talent.

- Actively review your talent management process.

References

Ashton, C and Morton, L (2005) Managing talent for competitive advantage: taking a systematic approach to talent management, *Strategic HR Review*, 4 (5), pp. 28–31

Armstrong, M (2009) *Armstrong's Handbook of Human Resource Management Practice*, 11th edn, Kogan Page, London

Barney, J (1991) Firm resources and sustained competitive advantage, *Journal of Management*, 17 (1), pp. 99–120

Bock, L (2015) *Work Rules!* John Murray, London

Boudreau, J W and Ramstad, P M (2007) *Beyond HR: The new science of human capital*, Harvard Business School Publishing, Brighton, MA

Broughton, A et al (2013) The use of social media in the recruitment process, *ACAS* [online] http://www.acas.org.uk/media/pdf/0/b/The-use-of-social-media-in-the-recruitment-process.pdf

Cambridge Advanced Learner's Dictionary (2008) Cambridge University Press, Cambridge

Cappelli, P (2008) Talent Management for the Twenty-first Century, *Harvard Business Review,* March

CIPD (2015a) *Resourcing and Talent Planning*, survey report, CIPD, London

CIPD (2015b) *A Head for Hiring: The behavioural science of recruitment and selection*, Research Report, August, CIPD, London

CIPD (2016a) *Talent Management*, Factsheet, 23 August, CIPD, London

CIPD (2016b) *Competence and Competency Frameworks*, Factsheet, 1 July, CIPD, London

Collins, M (2013) Change your company with better HR analytics, *Harvard Business Review*, December

Colvin, G (2008) *Talent is Overrated*, Penguin, London

DeLong, T J (2011) *Flying Without a Net*, Harvard Business Review Press, Brighton, MA

Ericsson, A and Pool, R (2016) *Peak: How all of us can achieve extraordinary things*, Vintage, New York

Fortune (2016) The 25 best global companies to work for [online] https://www.fortune.com/2016/10/26/best-global-companies [accessed 10 June 2017]

Gomez, L (2017) What's next for United? CEO apologizes after stock falls, video goes viral in China, *San Diego Tribune* [online] http://www.sandiegouniontribune.com/opinion/the-conversation/sd-united-airlines-stock-falls-after-viral-video-uproar-20170411-htmlstory.html [accessed 01 May 2017]

Lawler, E E (2008) *Talent: Making people your competitive advantage*, Jossey-Bass, San Francisco

Lewis, R E and Heckman, R J (2006) Talent management: a critical review, *Human Resource Management Review*, **16** (2), June, pp. 139–54

Meinert, D (2015) What do personality tests really reveal? *SHRM* [online] https://www.shrm.org/hr-today/news/hr-magazine/pages/0615-personality-tests.aspx [accessed 14 May 2017]

Minbaeva, D and Collings, D G (2013), Seven myths of global talent management, *The International Journal of Human Resource Management*, **24** (90), pp. 1762–76

Morgeson, F P et al (2007) Reconsidering the use of personality tests in personnel selection decisions, *Personnel Psychology*, **60** (3), pp. 683–729

O'Nell, S et al (2001) *RJP Overview*, University of Minnesota, Institute on Community Integration, Research and Training Center on Community Living, Minneapolis

Peter, L J and Hull, R (2009) *The Peter Principle*, Harper Business, New York

Phillips, J J and Edwards, L (2008) *Managing Talent Retention: An ROI approach*, Pfeiffer, San Francisco

Prahalad, C K and Hamel, G (1990) The core competence of the corporation, *Harvard Business Review*, **68** (3), pp. 79–91

Price, A (2011) *Human Resource Management*, 4th edn, Centgage, Andover

Roger, A (1952) *The Seven-Point Plan*, National Institute for Industrial Psychology

Ross, S (2013) How definitions of talent suppress talent management, *Industrial and Commercial Training*, **45** (3), pp 166–70

Schumann, M and Sartain, L (2009) *Brand for Talent*, Wiley and Sons, San Francisco

Scullion, H and Collings, D G (2011) Global talent management, *Journal of World Business*, **45** (2), pp. 105–08

Stahl, G K et al (2012) Six principles of effective global talent management, *MIT Sloan Management Review*, Winter, **53** (2), pp. 25–32

Stewart, S M, Gruys, M L and Storm, M (2010) Forced distribution performance evaluation systems: advantages, disadvantages and keys to implementation, *Journal of Management and Organization*, **16** (1), pp. 168–79

Truss, C et al (1997) Soft and hard models of human resource management: a reappraisal, *Journal of Management Studies*, **34** (1), pp. 54–73

08

International staffing in multinational companies

JAMES BABA ABUGRE

Learning outcomes

At the end of this chapter, you should be able to:

- understand the staffing composition and practices in international business;

- appreciate the importance of cross-cultural training and development of expatriates;

- identify the different types of training programmes used by MNCs;

- understand how expatriates can succeed or fail in their adjustment in the subsidiaries;

- appreciate the lived experiences of expatriates' staffing successes in the subsidiaries through an empirical case study.

Introduction

In this chapter, we examine international staffing and staffing processes of multinational companies (MNCs) in international business in the face of globalization. As HR professionals manage cross-border businesses, they are required to understand the theory and practice of international human resource management (IHRM) in order to effectively apply the appropriate staffing processes to their subsidiary operations. As discussed in Chapter 4, multinational staff or employees who work outside their home countries are called expatriates. Therefore, in IHRM, expatriates are all employees who are transferred to a different country other than their own to work in the subsidiary MNC, and their role in international assignment is to establish a relationship between the MNC headquarters (HQ) and the MNC subsidiary in a distant location or country.

The empirical validation of this chapter uses a case study of interviews with senior expatriate executives from 17 MNC subsidiaries in Ghana. The case study provides significant major findings on staffing success and drivers of effective international staffing of MNCs and their subsidiary operations in complex environments.

As firms internationalize and expand globally into multiple countries, the major task that confronts their management processes is how to plan their workforce in these new foreign countries. The responsibility of ensuring that a capable workforce is engaged in the multinational operations of these companies can be termed international staffing. Thus, staffing in multinational corporations provides a narrative of how a global workforce is planned, including training the workforce to be capable and able to adjust to the global environment. International staffing describes the policies that MNCs use to ensure that the right personnel are available at the right time for international assignments. Accordingly, Briscoe, Schuler and Tarique (2012) describe staffing for MNCs as involving the hiring of employees at both the headquarters and the subsidiaries, as well as mobile employees who are hired in one locale and relocated to other subsidiary locales.

International staffing for MNCs requires more than choosing a person as an expatriate for an international assignment. Improper international staffing procedures can lead to multinational staffing pitfalls. Staffing pitfalls can arise when MNCs are merely looking for personnel with skills and experience rather than hiring candidates who are culturally adaptable to the subsidiary context and therefore truly capable of contributing to the higher performance of the MNC or its subsidiary. Hence, Hill (2007) asserts that international businesses must align their HRM functions to selecting individuals who not only possess the perceived skills required to perform specific jobs but who also 'fit' the prevailing culture of the firm. Consequently, Harzing, Pudelko and Reiche (2016) stress that international staffing plays a critical role in the global implementation strategy of MNCs. These global strategies include how international assignments can become valuable in effectuating knowledge flows from the MNC's headquarters to the subsidiaries in distant locations as a source of competitive advantage (Harzing, Pudelko and Reiche, 2016; Holtbrügge and Mohr, 2011). Extant literature provides clear evidence of the relationship between international staffing and subsidiary performance (Colakoglu and Caligiuri, 2008).

As a result, as MNCs expand globally, their HR managers are largely responsible for ensuring that subsidiary jobs and operations are staffed adequately through some different means or methods of recruitment.

Methods of recruitment

In staffing the MNC subsidiaries, HR managers apply three different methods of recruitment. The first recruitment method is to use the existing manpower supply of the MNC. This means some of the current staff at the MNC's headquarters are sent to the subsidiary as expatriates or home-country nationals. Second, the HR manager can suggest the use of local personnel or natives from the host subsidiary. These are often referred to as host-country nationals. The third and final method of international recruitment is the use of nationals from countries other than that of the headquarters or subsidiary. This cohort of employees are known as third-country nationals. Fundamentally, the task of international staffing is to assemble the right calibre of people who can effectively work as a team to realize the goals of the MNC abroad. Therefore, international staffing in MNCs is an important managerial function which determines the significance of human resource effectiveness in planning, organizing, directing and controlling the operations of international business. We will now consider the different types of international staffing used by MNCs in more detail.

Staffing composition and practices in international business/management

A critical feature of MNCs is the transfer of management expertise, knowledge and skills through human resource and recruitment practices across subsidiary operations; this is done through staffing processes and practices. Multinational corporations and their subsidiaries use a variety of staffing methods. These include ethnocentric, polycentric, regiocentric, and global approaches or geocentric staffing practices, depending on the primary strategic orientation of the MNC's internationalization choice (Deresky, 2008). Perlmutter (1969) originally identified the three standard staffing policies of MNCs as **ethnocentric, polycentric** and **geocentric** (see Table 8.1).

When MNCs discover that there is a high-pressure demand for global integration of staffing, they use parent-country nationals (PCNs) (ethnocentric staffing) rather than host-country nationals (HCNs) (polycentric staffing). When the pressure and demand for global integration of staffing is low then they use HCNs (polycentric staffing) rather than PCNs (ethnocentric staffing). Furthermore, MNCs that practise a global strategy are more likely to use an ethnocentric staffing approach, and the MNCs that practice a multi-domestic strategy use a polycentric approach. On the other hand,

MNCs that use or practice a transnational strategy adopt a mix of ethnocentric and polycentric approaches. Consequently, MNCs have since followed or adapted either one or all of these staffing practices (see Table 8.1 below for a detailed description and orientation of the staffing practices of MNCs).

This mode of staffing practices has subsequently been corroborated by some international business researchers (Caligiuri and Stroh, 1995; Deresky, 2008). Accordingly, MNCs pursuing ethnocentric staffing policy would typically appoint parent-country nationals (PCNs) to management positions in the subsidiaries. With geocentric staffing policy, MNCs would appoint persons from different nationalities, in most cases third-country nationals (TCNs), to positions in the subsidiaries, while polycentric staffing policy involves the use of host-country nationals (HCNs). While these three dimensions of staffing practices have been known and used over the years by MNCs globally, a fourth dimension, known as regiocentric staffing, was initiated by Deresky (2008). In this dimension, MNCs pursuing a regiocentric approach would typically recruit staff on a regional basis (or a regional block – say a subsidiary in an African country would appoint staff from other African countries). The regiocentric staffing method is able to create a specific combination of PCNs, HCNs, and TCNs based on the specific needs of the MNC or its production strategy (Deresky, 2008).

Table 8.1   Staffing practices and orientations of MNCs

Staffing type	Description	Orientation to subsidiary
Parent-Country National (PCN) (Ethnocentric staffing choice)	Reflects the belief in ownership and parochialism. Hence, MNCs believe in the superiority of home-country nationals as the supreme executives who can make a positive impact on the performance of the corporation.	Perlmutter originally described MNCs with a PNC focus as ethnocentric companies whose cultural assumptions are dominated by their home culture, and who try to apply this across their subsidiary operations. Hence, only home personnel are developed for key positions.
Host-Country National (HCN) (Polycentric staffing choice)	Reflects the belief in local and contextual cultures. This means people of local nationality are trained and developed for critical positions in their own country.	Polycentric MNCs encourage the variety of cultural contexts within which the subsidiaries operate. Subsidiaries are empowered on the matter of staffing.

(continued)

Table 8.1   *(Conitnued)*

Staffing type	Description	Orientation to subsidiary
Third-Country National (TCN) (Geocentric staffing choice)	Reflects the belief in pluralism and the responsiveness of multiple cultures working together. Hence, MNCs typically believe that top subsidiary executives can come from any country or region of the world and make a positive impact on the performance of the corporation, once they are developed for key positions.	MNCs with a geocentric focus adopt a global outlook in their subsidiary operations. HQ relies on its global manpower in the world, developed for key positions in the various subsidiaries everywhere in the world.
Regiocentric (PNC, HCN, TCN)	Regional people are developed to fill vacancies of key positions in any subsidiary in the region.	Regiocentric MNCs focus on a regional outlook which encompasses a cultural mix due to high interdependence on a regional posture.

Reflective question

Describe how each of the staffing practices in the table above could be suitable to a multinational company which has appointed you as a human resource manager.

Expatriates as multinational staffing

As discussed, when MNCs employ or transfer people to staff their subsidiaries abroad, these employees are called expatriates or international assignees. Thus, based on the nature of the international assignment, MNCs would select employees who have more understanding of international work experience. This is particularly significant given the growth of international businesses in the world. Thus, in the recruitment and selection of personnel to fill vacant positions for international assignment, selected staff are usually designated or described as expatriates.

A distinctive employment practice for managerial and technical assignments in foreign subsidiaries often requires the use of expatriates or transitional international assignees. Hence, the term expatriate refers to the process of international transfer of mostly PCNs and TCNs working in foreign subsidiaries of the MNCs for a defined period of time (Harzing, 2000). We can therefore define expatriates as employees who are transferred to a different country other than their own to work in the subsidiary MNC, and their role in the international assignment is foremost to establish a liaison between HQ and the subsidiary; this involves an enormous amount of social interaction through effective communication and knowledge sharing. As international transferees, expatriates provide socialization and informal communication relationships between MNC headquarters and subsidiary units (Macharzina and Wolf, 1996). Expatriates have become an important channel for the transmission of management practices from one country to another (usually from parent company (emerging economies) to subsidiaries/host countries (developing countries or in few cases another developed country).

Similarly, the transfer of management practices from one national context to another is an important consideration for managers in MNCs. Consequently, Harris and Holden (2001) have argued that expatriate managers have a considerable role to play as both interpreters and implementers of the HR and business strategy of the MNC. Expatriates also play an essential role as transmitters of culture, knowledge, skills and practices, and they often work as boundary spanners in the subsidiaries (Iles and Yolles, 2002). As managing executives from the MNC's HQ, the expatriates are accorded respect as HQ representatives in the host country because they coordinate between the HQ management team and the subsidiary team. HR management policies and practices in the form of administrative instructions and staffing strategies are so crucial for subsidiary operations, and therefore practising expatriates in the subsidiaries become the instruments for coordination and control in international business operations. The expatriates coordinate the management and administrative procedures between HQ and the subsidiary. Additionally, as HR systems and values are able to shape and influence the organizational culture and employees, the MNC's HQ try to transfer their HR strategies to the subsidiaries.

Strategic choices of MNCs' recruitment practices

The strategic choices of MNCs' recruitment practices deal with the different styles or approaches each MNC adopts in recruiting its staff for subsidiary operations. Bartlett and Ghoshal (1989) proposed four different strategic choices and dimensions that MNCs face in their international staffing practices: **global strategy, multi-domestic/national strategy, transnational strategy,** and **international strategy.** Each strategic choice determines the staffing practice that delivers the strategic goal and objective of the MNC. Thus, in the first place, a global strategic choice explains why overseas operations can be seen as a delivery pipeline to a unified global market serving a segmented market for the MNC, and therefore will require the use of PCNs, HCNs and TCNs. Second, a multi-domestic/national strategic choice may explain why overseas operations are perceived as appendages to a central domestic corporation and therefore will require the use of HCNs, TCNs and PCNs. Third, a transnational strategic choice explains why overseas operations are seen as a loosely coordinated network of relatively independent businesses and therefore will call for the use of HCNs and TCNs. Fourth, an international strategic choice explains why overseas operations are seen as portfolios of independent businesses and therefore will need the services of HCNs and TCNs. Thus, the four strategic choices underlying the strategy types of firms' internationalization and foreign direct investment are components of staffing orientations which provide a more theoretical understanding of staffing practices in MNCs.

Foreign direct investment (FDI) can basically be explained as the direct investment that occurs across national borders, ie when a firm from one country buys a controlling investment in a firm in another country or sets up a branch or subsidiary operation in another country (Dicken, 2003). FDI flows have potential benefits such as transfer of skills and know-how through expatriates who are working in foreign economies, particularly in developing countries. A common element of FDI is the operation of multi-national corporations (MNC), which accounts for around two-thirds of the world's foreign investment in the form of exports of goods and services (Dicken, 2003). In most cases, MNCs can make a significant contribution to export capabilities and export competitiveness in many developing countries.

Depending on the size of the MNC, there could be different forces operating relative to the use of staffing practices for international assignments. In most cases, bigger MNCs practise more use of HCNs. Additionally, they use international experience to blend their management team in the subsidiaries. Therefore, they are increasingly likely to move managers from the parent company or regional HQs as well as their foreign managers to assignments in countries other than their country of origin. On the other hand, most newly established subsidiaries which are yet to develop their international businesses will usually rely greatly on the experiences of expatriates from HQ, as MNCs trust their existing managers more than unknown foreign managers whom they perceive to be inexperienced. Hence, once staffing in the form of recruitment and selection has been determined and composed for the international assignment, the next staffing practice for the MNC is how training can be effected for the chosen assignees or expatriates. The basic training given to expatriates to enable them to work abroad is cross-cultural training, which equips them with knowledge of the essential practices of the assigned country.

Cross-cultural training and development of international assignees

International staffing deals with the recruitment and selection of specific personnel to fill vacant management positions in subsidiary MNCs in foreign countries. The selected candidates will normally have to undergo cross-cultural training in order to equip themselves with cultural knowledge of the foreign land they are being assigned to.

Cross-cultural training and development is a critical element of human resource practice for multinational operations. It is extremely important for MNCs' international staffing as it facilitates the development of essential skills required for global managers who are expected to sojourn to different countries and work with culturally diverse teams in order to perform effectively in the field of their assigned job (Pandey, 2012). When MNCs expand into global markets, they face an initial challenge of working together with culturally diverse employees (Cooper, Doucet and Pratt, 2007). These subsidiary firms must therefore address team dynamics that may occur in order to meet performance goals with team members who are physically dispersed as well as culturally diverse (Muethel and Hoegl, 2010). A major reason for the failure of MNCs in foreign assignments is a lack of cross-cultural competence, which is the ability of individuals to draw on a set of knowledge, skills and personal attributes in order to work successfully with people from different cultural backgrounds (Johnson, Lenartowicz and Apud, 2006). A clear example of such lack of competence is manifested in a northern Nigerian foreign-led institution where turnover of expatriate staff is high, with the given reason that foreign nationals 'can't stand it here' (Mugambi, 2012); this is simply because the foreign workers expect the local employees to behave exactly like them. Cultural differences, conflicts and misunderstandings are impeding the success of many international organizations around the world. Expatriates and nationals therefore need education on cross-cultural management in order to overcome cultural barriers in foreign subsidiaries (Senghaas, 2002).

Cross-cultural training is defined as 'the educative processes used to improve intercultural learning via the development of the cognitive, affective and behavioural competencies needed for successful interactions in diverse cultures' (Littrell et al, 2006: 356), while cross-cultural management can best be described as how employees communicate and manage relationships with co-workers and clients within their organizations in different cultural settings (Adler, 2002). Thus, cross-cultural management skills are considered essential for global managers of transnational corporations in order to deal with relationships within and outside the corporation. Adjusting to a new culture involves the gradual development of familiarity, comfort and proficiency regarding expected behaviour and the values and assumptions inherent in the new culture, which are different from the individual's native culture (Torbiorn, 1982). It is cross-cultural training that enables individuals to rapidly adjust to this new culture in order to effectively perform their new roles. Thus, the relationship between cross-cultural training and performance is a critical concern to MNCs. Black and Mendenhall (1990) examined the relationship between cross-cultural training and the performance of expatriates in multinational subsidiaries. They found that cross-cultural training of expatriates had significant impact on their (expatriates) work performance in the subsidiaries. Other studies have also found that negotiations between businessmen and women of different cultures often fail because of problems related to cross-cultural differences (Adler, 1997; Black, 1988; Tung, 1984) as the parties involved would normally find it difficult to understand each other. For example, according to Abugre (2016), when people from different cultures meet for the first time, because of the differences in their communicative behaviours, they may differ on substantive issues and therefore negatively influence each other due to mutual misunderstanding of their individual behaviours. Consequently, expatriates have to try to understand these observable and symbolic manifestations of the cultural differences of the local staff when they are working together in the various subsidiaries of MNCs (Abugre, 2016).

Unsuccessful cross-cultural interactions between international assignees and the local people in subsidiaries tend to be even more important when the costs of failure of the assignees or expatriates are high. Given the cost of these international assignments, MNCs are increasingly recognizing that they must take all steps necessary to promote foreign assignment success and to avert expatriate failure. Cross-cultural training is one of the critical processes in solving the cost problems of MNCs. It is cross-cultural training programmes instituted by MNCs that teach cross-cultural knowledge and awareness, critical for expatriates' work in foreign subsidiaries. Additionally, cross-cultural training and development facilitates the assignee's cross-cultural adjustment in the host country and hence minimizes any problems arising from the assignee's adjustment (Black and Mendenhall, 1990; Kealey and Protheroe, 1996). For example, O'Conner (2010: 196) found that US Army soldiers who had received cultural training were reported to have been more successful in their 'patrols', in their 'rebuilding projects' and also in 'regaining security in formerly hostile areas'. Cultural training refers to knowledge of the beliefs and values of a group of people that is essential for work. It equips the expatriate with the necessary tools and experiences that will enable them to be effective in the foreign land. Thus, for employees working in cross-cultural environments, improving their cultural intelligence and self-efficacy should lead to improved effectiveness in their overseas job assignments (Earley, Ang and Tang, 2006). Similarly, Lee and Sukoco (2010) found that cultural intelligence of expatriates had a significant and positive effect on both cultural adjustment and cultural effectiveness, which resulted in improved expatriate performance in foreign subsidiaries.

Hence, it appears that cross-cultural training can be advocated as a means of facilitating effective cross-cultural management and adjustment of international assignees in foreign subsidiaries. The next section will look at how cross-cultural training can be learnt or implemented through different approaches.

Cross-cultural training programmes

Many international business (IB) researchers have outlined a number of cross-cultural training programmes designed to improve expatriates' skills critical for performing effectively during international assignments. Major studies in cross-cultural training by Tung (1981; 1982), Brislin, Landis and Brand (1983), Mendenhall, Dunbar and Oddou (1987), and Black and Mendenhall (1989) have suggested the importance of training content for international assignees. Following these studies, training programmes have been designed to the commonly held taxonomy of the three learning domains (Yang, 2003). These classifications are **cognitive, experiential** and **affective**. A fourth programme content, **language training**, is added because of its importance and the fact that it affects all the first three learning domains. However, the methods used in teaching these learning domains can be classified into three major categories: presentation, hands-on, and group building (Noe, 2005). Presentation methods refer to training techniques in which trainees are passive recipients of information including facts, processes and problem-solving methods. Examples of presentation methods include lectures and audiovisual techniques. Hands-on methods refer to training processes in which the trainees are actively involved in learning, such as on-the-job training, self-directed learning, apprenticeship, simulations, case studies, business games, role play, and behaviour modelling. Group-building methods are designed to improve team or group effectiveness, and include action learning, adventure learning, coordination learning, cross training, experiential learning, guidelines, team leader training, and team training.

In practice, training activities in organizations utilize a wide variety of methods as teaching and learning aids, including lectures, video films, experiential exercises, cultural assimilators, and behaviour modification. Expatriate training requires skills and abilities that are highly demanding in the multicultural environment, and so the integration of these skills into the various training programmes is discussed in the subsequent sections which will now take a look at each category of training approach.

The cognitive approach

The cognitive approach is also known as the information-acquiring approach to cross-cultural training of expatriates. This approach has been supported globally and used by many MNCs, including training agencies, since the 1960s, but the method still remains a popular method of training today (Bhawuk and Brislin, 2000). The cognitive approach to cross-cultural training entails 'the learning of information or skills from a lecture-type orientation' (Mendenhall, Dunbar and Oddou, 1987: 339). It reflects the measurement of a person's capacity to learn or acquire skills that would enable them to do the right thing in a particular setting or environment. The basic assumption of the cognitive approach to cross-cultural training is that 'knowledge will increase empathy, and empathy will modify behaviour in such a way as to improve intercultural relationships' (Campbell, 1969: 3). Other IB researchers have christened it as 'area studies' (Tung, 1981), 'fact–orientation training' (Brislin, Landis and Brand,1983), 'information-giving approach' (Mendenhall, Dunbar and Oddou, 1987). 'Area studies', 'fact-orientation training', and 'information giving' basically explain the same ideas which include environmental briefing and culture-orientation programmes designed to provide trainees with information regarding the history, geography, religion, people, economy, and way of life of the target culture (Tung, 1981). However, Mendenhall, Dunbar and Oddou (1987) proposed that the skills needed for this cognitive approach to cross-cultural training are numerous, and therefore in-depth and comprehensive training programmes should be utilized. Consequently, Pandey (2012) suggests that popular movies, if appropriately selected for a specific cross-cultural training programme, could be very effective in achieving contextual learning objectives.

The experiential approach

The experiential approach to cross-cultural training and development was a reaction to the information-acquiring approach, which was criticized as inadequate to cross-cultural training. Experiential training, sometimes described as immersion, refers to 'techniques that provide realistic simulations or scenarios to the trainee, such as assessment centres, field simulations, etc' (Mendenhall, Dunbar and Oddou, 1987: 339). The experiential approach to cross-cultural training and development should focus on developing expatriates' interpersonal skills and increasing their awareness of self and others, particularly the local people (Yamazaki and Kayes, 2004). The experiential training and development can include interactional learning or field experience and cross-cultural social learning and adaptation.

In addition, the technique 'Learn by doing' appropriately describes the nature of experiential learning. Other methods such as look-see visits, role playing, intercultural workshops, and simulations are major techniques used in experiential learning (Kealey and Protheroe, 1996; Littrell and Salas, 2005).

Similarly, field experiences involve sending the candidate to the host country or to micro cultures nearby so that the candidate may experience the emotional stress of living and working within different cultures (Tung, 1981). Depending on the financial resources of the MNC and the accessibility of micro cultures, potential expatriates could be introduced to overseas assignments by living and working with members of micro cultures so that they can undergo this experience (Tung, 1981). On the other hand, the adapted social learning experience in cross-cultural training (Black and Mendenhall, 1990) suggests that the degree of novelty of new behaviours is significantly higher in the international context; hence, both domestic and international contexts of new work-related behaviours must be learnet in order to enhance the adaptability of the assignees.

The major benefits of experiential training to multinational corporations are that it helps their trainees to develop the skills necessary for effective performance, aids positive interaction with the locals in the subsidiaries and also improves trainees' cognitive skills in making the right and accurate predictions or attributions. Additionally, working together in the form of simulation and inter-cultural workshops can provide expatriates with better information about host culture and values. Overall, experiential training has been demonstrated to benefit trainees by assisting them to become more emotionally resilient, flexible and open to foreign cultures.

The affective approach

The affective dimension of training describes how the individual's personality traits and attitudes, which are sensitive to the affective processes of a culture, are learnt. The affective approach to cross-cultural training is defined as the 'learning of information or skills via techniques that raise affective responses on the part of the trainee, which results in cultural insights' (Mendenhall, Dunbar and Oddou, 1987: 339). Fiedler, Mitchell and Triandis (1971) proposed a cultural assimilator as a learning process that can affect an expatriate's ability to adjust. Similarly, Tung (1981) suggested a learning process known as sensitivity training where expatriates become aware of the values and behaviours of the local people in the subsidiary. Equally, Brislin, Landis and Brand (1983) advocated attribution training and cultural awareness of expatriates assigned to foreign subsidiaries. Hence, the affective approach to cross-cultural training facilitates the basic acquisition of values that prevail in the foreign culture which can affect the sensitivity of the assignee and align them to the context, thus enabling them to become adaptable to the new environment.

Foreign assignments require expatriates to be able to establish extensive contact with host-country nationals (Tung, 1981), which suggests that cultural assimilation training should be supplemented by language sensitivity and field training. Cross-cultural sensitivity training is designed to develop the attitudinal flexibility of the expatriate in order to create awareness and acceptance of the different behaviours encountered in the new culture (Tung, 1981). At the same time, the attribution training enables expatriate trainees to make isomorphic attribution and to be able to handle difficult situations in order to internalize the values and standards of the host country (Eschbach, Parker and Stoeberl, 2001; Littrell and Salas, 2005). Studies on cross-cultural training have shown that attribution training, especially the intercultural sensitizer or culture assimilator approaches, are effective in sensitizing trainees to cultural issues and assisting them to be more interpersonally effective in cross-cultural and intercultural encounters (Black and Mendenhall, 1990; Cushner and Landis, 1996; Kealey and Protheroe, 1996). Moreover, the intercultural sensitizer training facilitates interpersonal relations between people of different cultural backgrounds and eases their adjustment to the foreign culture, thereby improving work performance overseas (Cushner and Landis, 1996; Gudykunst, Guzley and Hammer, 1996).

Language training

Language is a very important instrument in the operations of international business (Babcock and Du-Babcock, 2001). Hence, Abugre (2016) argues that cross-cultural training must involve foreign language training because knowledge of the language of the host country is vital to successfully living and working in that country. In language training, the candidate is taught the language of the country to which they are assigned (Tung, 1981). As part of language acquisition, it is suggested that foreign languages movies should be used as learning tools in courses on cross-cultural management, cross-cultural communication or cultural studies (Pandey, 2012). This is because the linguistic skills and competency of the expatriate can be a key to expatriate adjustment and can also improve their effective negotiation skills in the foreign culture. Pre-departure language training facilitates the expatriates' cross-cultural adjustment and the development of their cross-cultural communication skills (Ko and Yang, 2011). As English is the language of the world business, it is quite possible to conduct business all over the world using the English language, but a willingness to communicate in the language of the host country, even if the expatriate is not fluent in it, can help build a healthy relationship with local employees and improve the expatriate's effectiveness (Hill, 2007). Thus, through language competency, MNC executives may be able to disseminate their strategies and policies and implement them effectively with little or no ambiguity in the operations of their foreign businesses.

Reflective questions

How do you see the importance of language training in cross-cultural management?

In reference to the different approaches to cross-cultural training suggested above, which one of them do you consider very effective? Give reasons for your choice.

Cross-cultural adjustment successes and failures of expatriates in the subsidiaries

The adjustment, success or failure of an expatriate in foreign assignment plays a key role in the effective operations of MNCs in international business. Consequently, expatriate adjustment has attracted a substantial amount of investigation and research publications (Black, 1990; Black,

Mendenhall and Oddou, 1991). This is because international HR continues to play a key role in MNCs' quest for foreign markets. As a result, the transferability of management practices from one national context to another calls for international assignments of expatriates. Literature on cross-cultural adjustment (Black, 1990; Caligiuri, 2000) describes adjustment as the degree of psychological well-being of an individual in relation to several aspects of the new environment that confront them. International assignment of an expatriate is very demanding due to the location of their work in an unfamiliar context, so adjustment can be considered as a means of reducing their stress levels so that they can live comfortably. In a study of American expatriate managers in Japan, Black (1988) describes the adjustment phenomenon as the perceived degree of psychological comfort and acquaintance an individual enjoys in working in a different culture. However, many writers on cross-cultural adjustment make a distinction between socio-cultural and psychological adjustment (Searle and Ward, 1990; Ward and Kennedy, 1996; Ward and Searle, 1991). Although the two concepts are interrelated, socio-cultural adjustment is related to the cultural and social norms of the host subsidiary and enables the expatriate to 'fit in' or efficiently interact with the community or members of the host culture (Ward and Kennedy, 1996). As a result, socio-cultural adjustment has been linked to the rudiments that promote and facilitate culture adaptation or learning and acquisition of social skills in the host culture (Searle and Ward, 1990). The concept of socio-cultural adjustment is based on cultural learning theory and calls for social behaviour and social skills that emphasize the attitudinal factors of the person (Black and Mendenhall, 1991). On the other hand, psychological adjustment refers to an individual's subjective well-being or satisfaction in their new cultural environment. Psychological adjustment is linked to an individual's emotional states and their cognitive and personality trait capacity (Ward and Kennedy, 1996). Consequently, in spite of preparation undertaken by expatriates for international assignment in a foreign country, their exposure to the culture will undeniably involve high levels of stress and uncertainty. Oberg (1960) describes this phenomenon as 'culture shock', which a lot of foreign assignees face now and then in the new cultural environment. The setting of a new host environment is definitely unfamiliar and creates socio-psychological uncertainty for the expatriate, which they would very much like to reduce.

Accordingly, for more than three decades, cross-cultural researchers have focused on finding the essential skills for expatriates' adjustment and success in their international assignments. The reason is that numerous international assignments have been prematurely terminated or have totally failed, creating excessive cost to MNCs. These failures result from the inability of expatriates to understand the complexities of cultural differences and consequently their failure to effectively manage across cultures (Branine, 2011). This high cost of expatriates' failure and adjustment has pushed most MNCs to reconsider their staffing and expatriation policies.

In an earlier investigation into expatriate adjustment, Black (1988) described three components of expatriate adjustments: (1) work adjustment, which encompasses supervision, responsibilities and performances; (2) relational adjustment, which includes communication with members of the host community; and (3) general or cultural adjustment, which includes living conditions in the host country. This has been consistently confirmed by many other researchers over the years (Black and Gregersen, 1991; Waxin, 2000). They sum up these factors as individual, organizational, and contextual variables. Individual factors include the individual's adjustability and prior international experience. Contextual factors consist of the length of time spent in the host country, the partner's social support and the organization's logistic support. Organizational factors include job-related variables (such as role clarity and role discretion), variables related to organizational social support (such as supervisory support, co-workers' support, and home-country organization support), differences in organizational culture between the home country organization and the host-country organization, and finally, cross-cultural preparation.

In a similar study, Black et al (1991) suggested that expatriates' adjustment involves two phases: anticipatory adjustment and in-country adjustment. They argue that anticipatory adjustment can have a positive impact on in-country adjustment, and that anticipatory adjustment of expatriates is positively influenced by cross-cultural training and their previous successful international assignment. Hence, they suggested that expatriates' anticipatory adjustment can be facilitated through the provision of cross-cultural training and using comprehensive selection materials during training.

Although a range of comprehensive assessments on expatriate adjustment have been useful in explaining some of the difficulties that impede expatriates' successful adjustment in foreign assignments, there still remain many things that are unclear about successful international staffing, expatriate cross-cultural training and expatriate adjustments. Consequently, this chapter employs an empirical examination of international staffing of MNCs, cross-cultural training of expatriates and expatriates' adjustment in complex environments to unearth valid and successful staffing practices of multinational corporations in international business.

CASE STUDY Cross-cultural staffing in Ghana

Data for this work was analysed using interviews of 21 senior executive expatriates working in 17 MNC subsidiaries in Ghana (see Table 8.2. for the biographical characteristics of the senior expatriate respondents used for the interview for this case study). Respondents for this study worked in a variety of MNCs from different industry segments. In all, 17 MNCs from the mining, communication, food and beverage, automobile, and policy industries participated in the study. The themes covered in the interviews included: importance of cross-cultural training; difficulties experienced by expatriates in Ghana; aspects of cross-cultural training; language competence; and expatriate and local staff teamwork. Information gathered from the interviews constitutes an essential aspect of this work and took into account a wide array of contextual factors inherent in MNC staffing policies and cross-cultural training of expatriates in MNCs. In addition, the potential impact of organizational-level control on the role of training in the staffing of MNCs was a key determinant to the objectives of this work. Hence, participants for the interview were mainly very senior-level expatriate executives in MNCs in Ghana. The empirical data was accessed through the experiences and interactions narrated by all participants and recorded using a semi-structured interview guide. Results and findings of the work are presented in the subsequent paragraphs.

Staffing strategies of MNCs

Findings from the interviews indicate that staffing strategies of MNCs generally emanate from the headquarters or parent company of the firm. All expatriate staff, be they PCN, TCN or regiocentric, are recruited and sent to the various subsidiaries. However, there are two groups of local staff (HCNs) that are usually recruited for subsidiary operations by the HR department in the local subsidiary country. The first group of local employees constitutes the basic level or miscellaneous employees recruited and trained in the local subsidiaries by the HR department when vacancies exist. Their names are then sent to headquarters for documentation. The second group, which usually constitutes senior executive positions, are also recruited in the subsidiary but with recommendation or authorization from headquarters.

Table 8.2 Characteristics of respondents

Label of MNC	Interviewee's position	Nationality and staffing policy type
Company 1	Vice-President HRM	TNC
Company 1	Vice-President Transformation	TCN Regiocentric type
Company 2	Group Director HRM	PCN
Company 3	Director HRM & Operations	PCN
Company 4	Vice-President HRM	PCN
Company 4	Regional Manager HR	PCN
Company 5	Director of Finance and Admin	PCN

(continued)

Table 8.2 *(Continued)*

Label of MNC	Interviewee's position	Nationality and staffing policy type
Company 6	Plant Manager	TCN Regiocentric type
Company 7	Managing Director	PCN
Company 8	General Manager	TCN
Company 9	Regional Policy Advisor	TCN Regiocentric type
Company 9	Regional Economist	TCN Regiocentric type
Company 10	Business Operations Manager	TCN
Company 11	Senior Manager	TCN
Company 12	Reg. Commercial Manager	PCN
Company 13	Head of Credit	PCN
Company 14	Head of Business Support	TCN
Company 15	Head of Fixed Income Trading	TCN
Company 15	Senior Operations officer	TCN
Company 16	Brands Manager	TCN
Company 17	Managing Director	PCN

Reflective question

Why do you think higher executive positions in the subsidiaries are dominated by parent-country nationals (PCNs) and third-country nationals (TCNs)?

Cross-cultural training as a driver of expatriates' general adjustment

Stories of individual expatriates in the interview demonstrated that cross-cultural training of expatriates is very instrumental in the operations of international business as it helps expatriates to build rapport with local staff and improves expatriates' effectiveness, thereby facilitating their general adjustment. All interviewees strongly agreed that cross-cultural training is the basis of expatriates' ability to fully understand the local subsidiary environment as regards the culture of the people around them. The findings showed that cross-cultural training of an expatriate allows better communication, better teamwork, and consequently working better with local staff, leading to healthy adjustment of the assignee. This is articulated strongly by a respondent:

An advantage of cross-cultural training for expatriates is that you are able to read and interpret the messages of the local environment. So you have a better understanding of everything: the economy, the client, who deals with what, how it works, even the business environment. When you understand how the society is organized, it helps you to avoid mistakes, thereby enhancing your general adjustment in the subsidiary environment.

Cross-cultural training as a solution to successful cross-cultural assignment of expatriates

Another theme explored in this chapter is the extent to which cross-cultural training helps to minimize any negative work behaviour by an expatriate in a foreign subsidiary. Given the strategic importance of global assignments, an unproductive expatriate may be injurious to the MNC's expectations in a host country (Gregersen and Black, 1990). For this reason, cross-cultural training has been shown to improve the cultural effectiveness of international assignees. This has largely been supported by results of this study. What is really significant is for expatriates to understand the application of the English language in the local context. Additionally, expatriates need to have training in host-country cultural values in order to improve their relationships not only with their local colleagues in the companies but within the local communities where they reside, which will give them an extra advantage in their work. An expatriate should understand and appreciate some amount of the local culture where they find specific differences so that they can adapt to that behaviour. This is brilliantly explained by one of the respondents:

> I think all expatriates should be subjected to cross-cultural training and understanding of local behaviours. I've gone to countries before where we had this cultural training class and it was very effective because you didn't spend weeks or months trying to figure out why I'm being less productive at work than I think I ought to be, and why am I so frustrated every day, or even how come I don't understand why people do things the way they do.

Some of the interviewees showed that cross-cultural training is a human capital issue essential for fast-moving consumer goods industries; it is crucial for their knowledge and development, which in turn facilitates their efficiency in service delivery. Thus, expatriates in these industries must understand not only the local staff, but the whole culture of the business set-up in the host country. Expatriates in the sales business and those in the field succeed if they can learn aspects of the local language usage through cross-cultural training in communication behaviour, and this can be effective when post-arrival training is arranged for them. This is highlighted by one of the interviewees:

In fact, before I came to Ghana, I did go on a short programme to familiarize myself with some of the customs and also to expand on the language and geography and so forth pertaining to Ghana. Although I had been on two previous expatriate assignments, it's the first time I did something like this, and I found it enormously beneficial and this has contributed to the success of my work here.

Cross-cultural training as the basis for understanding the local environment and contextual behaviours

The interviews showed that there are obvious differences in work behaviour between local subsidiary workers and the expatriates. The differences in behaviours at work became an initial problem for most expatriates to accept, especially as they became conscious of the unrelated behaviours of the local employees working in the subsidiaries. There are generally differences in points of references, expectations and approaches to work. Indeed, despite expatriates' general satisfaction with their current assignment, several respondents expressed a feeling of dissatisfaction with the work behaviour of the local employees during official work hours. More specifically, there seemed to be different approaches concerning how local employees perceive time management, the use of local indigenous languages during work while expatriates were left speculating what was being said, the collectivist nature of the employees – accepting family visits during official work hours– and the indirectness of local employees in communication. All these behaviours affect communication and work and leave the expatriates to speculate on the actions of the local people. Thus, cross-cultural awareness training will offset most of these differences in work conduct and educate expatriates more on local employees' work behaviour. This helps the expatriate to better understand the local environment and contextual behaviours of the people.

Cross-cultural training as a response to globalization

International business has grown out of the globalization of countries, and describes the interconnection of countries. It is a drift towards opening up foreign markets and the expansion of international trade and investment. Through globalization, we have moved from being a world of national differences in policy regulations, culture and business systems to a world in which barriers to cross-border trade and investment are rapidly declining, hence the proliferation of MNCs and the seeking of more and newer markets in foreign cultures. Consequently, there is a great deal of multiculturalism, and even countries that are close to each other have many different ethnic groups with different behaviours and customs. As a result of multiculturalism and the benefits of globalization, expatriates have to understand the diversity of the national conditions; not only do they have to appreciate that they are guests in the country and abide by its traditions, cultures and customs, they also need to understand the mindset of the local people in the subsidiary MNC. Thus, appropriate cross-cultural skills that facilitate more effective contact among different people from different national and cultural backgrounds is the solution to effective globalization.

Cross-cultural training in language as a facilitator to expatriates' language competence in the subsidiary

Language, tone, and accent are essential aspects of identifying and recognizing a culture. Therefore, understanding, expectations and appreciation of the subsidiary culture, and particularly complex subsidiary cultures like those in Africa and Asia which embrace a multiplicity of local languages and accents, means expatriates must be able to embrace these differences and adjust to them. The field results indicated the problem many expatriates have with language and understanding the accents of the local employees. The interviews showed that people's accents can be different even though they may be speaking the same English language; these different accents and tones can result in both expatriates and local staff failing to understand each other properly. Thus, even though English is the language of business in the greater part of the world, there are different ways of speaking and understanding the English language, including issues of foreign accents, and also the problem of local staff tending to speak in their local languages in the presence of expatriates. Thus, cross-cultural training in language will facilitate expatriates' understanding of the local language and communication style of the subsidiary, thereby enhancing their language competence.

Reflective exercise

In the light of the case study findings, outline the importance to international staffing of each of the six themes emanating from the interviews.

Conclusions

This chapter has chronicled the staffing processes of multinational companies including empirical narratives of staffing and cross-cultural training of expatriates in foreign subsidiaries. The findings indicated largely that cross-cultural training plays a critical role in making it possible for expatriates to work well in foreign subsidiaries. The chapter presented the staffing strategies of MNCs and outlined the role of PCNs, HCNs and TCNs in the recruitment and selection processes for international assignments. It also proposed two modes of recruitment for local employees in the subsidiaries: those on the lower echelon who are recruited locally by management, and higher-level executives who are appointed locally, but are recommended and authorized by the MNC's HQ.

Empirical findings from this chapter indicate the significance of cross-cultural training of expatriates in the successful globalization of trade and the general adjustment of international assignees. The chapter thus advocates cross-cultural training as an effective foundation for international staffing of multinational corporations seeking foreign markets in distant environments.

Key learning points

- Communication problems are one of the key reasons for the failure of international assignments.

- It is therefore important for potential international assignees to be carefully vetted and trained prior to their appointment abroad.

- Cross-cultural training and prior immersion in the host country are both crucial determinants of the likelihood of expatriate failure.

References

Abugre, J B (2016) The role of cross-cultural communication in management practices of multinational companies in Sub-Saharan Africa, in *Sustainable Management Development in Africa: Building capabilities to serve African organizations*, eds H H Kazeroony, Y Du Plessis and B B Puplampu, Routledge, New York, pp. 123–40

Adler, N J (1997) *International Dimensions of Organizational Behavior*, South-Western College Publishing, Ohio

Adler, N (2002) *International Dimensions of Organizational Behavior*, 4th edn, South-Western College Publishing, Ohio

Babcock, R D and Du-Babcock, B (2001) Language-based communication zones in international business communication, *Journal of Business Communication*, **38**, pp. 372–412

Bartlett, C A and Ghoshal, S (1989) *Managing Across Borders: The transnational solution*, Harvard Business School Press, Boston

Bhawuk, D P S and Brislin, R W (2000) Cross-cultural training: a review, *Applied Psychology: An International Review*, **49** (1), pp. 162–91

Black, J S (1988) Work role transitions: a study of American expatriate managers in Japan, *Journal of International Business Studies*, **19** (2), 277–94

Black, J S (1990) Locus of control, social support, stress, and adjustment in international transfers, *Asia Pacific Journal of Management*, **7**, pp. 1–29

Black, J S and Gregersen, H B (1991) Antecedents to cross-cultural adjustment for expatriates in Pacific Rim assignments, *Human Relations*, **44** (5), pp. 497–515

Black, J S and Mendenhall, M (1989) A practical but theory-based framework for selecting cross-cultural training methods, *Human Resource Management*, **28** (4), pp. 511–39

Black, J S and Mendenhall, M (1990) Cross-cultural training effectiveness: a review and a theoretical framework for future research, *Academy of Management Review*, **15** (1), pp. 113–36

Black, J S. and Mendenhall, M (1991) The U-curve adjustment hypothesis revisited: a review and theoretical framework, *Journal of International Business Studies*, **22** (2), pp. 225–47

Black, J S, Mendenhall, M and Oddou, G (1991) Toward a comprehensive model of international adjustment: an integration of multiple theoretical perspectives, *Academy of Management Review*, **16** (2), pp. 291–317

Branine, M (2011) *Managing Across Cultures: Concept, policies and practices*, Sage, London

Briscoe, D, Schuler, R and Tarique, I (2012) *International Human Resource Management: Policies and practices for multinational enterprises*, 4th edn, Routledge, London

Brislin, R W, Landis, D and Brand, M E (1983) Conceptualizations of intercultural behaviour and training, in *Handbook of Intercultural Training, Vol.1, Education and Training*, eds D Landis and R W Brislin, Society for Intercultural Education, Training and Research, Washington, DC

Caligiuri, P (2000) Selecting expatriates for personality characteristics: a moderating effect of personality on the relationship between host national contact and cross-cultural adjustment, *Management International Review*, **40** (1), pp. 61–80

Caligiuri, P M and Stroh, L K (1995) Multinational corporation management strategies and international human resources practices: bringing IHRM to the bottom line, *International Journal of Human Resource Management*, **6** (3), pp. 494–507

Campbell, R D (1969) *United States Military Training for Cross-Cultural Interaction*, Matrix Corp, Alexandria, VA

Colakoglu, S and Caligiuri, P (2008) Cultural distance, expatriate staffing and subsidiary performance: the case of US subsidiaries of multinational corporations, *The International Journal of Human Resource Management*, **19** (2), pp. 223–39

Cooper, D, Doucet, L and Pratt, M (2007) Understanding 'appropriateness' in multinational organizations, *Journal of Organizational Behavior*, **28**, pp. 303–25

Cushner, K and Landis, D (1996) The intercultural sensitizer, in *Handbook of Intercultural Training*, 2nd edn, eds D Landis and R S Bhagat, Sage, Thousand Oaks, CA

Deresky, H (2008) *International Management: Managing across borders and cultures, text and cases*, 6th edn, Pearson Prentice-Hall, USA

Dicken, P (2003) *Global Shift: Reshaping the global economic map in the 21st century*, Sage Publications

Earley, P C, Ang, S and Tan, J S (2006) *CQ: Developing Cultural Intelligence at Work*, Stanford University Press, Stanford, CA

Eschbach, D M, Parker, G M and Stoeberl, P A (2001) American repatriate employees' retrospective assessments of the effects of cross-cultural training on their adaptation to international assignments, *International Journal of Human Resource Management*, **12** (2), pp. 270–87

Fiedler, F E, Mitchell, T and Triandis, H C (1971) The culture assimilator: an approach to cross-cultural training, *Journal of Applied Psychology*, **55** (2), p. 95

Gregersen, H B and Black, J S (1990) A multifaceted approach to expatriate retention in international assignments, *Group and Organizational Studies*, **15** (4), pp. 461–85

Gudykunst, W B, Guzley, R M and Hammer, M R (1996) Designing intercultural training, in *Handbook of Intercultural Training*, 2nd edn, eds D Landis and R S Bhagat, Sage, Thousand Oaks, CA

Harris, H and Holden, L (2001) Between autonomy and control: expatriate managers and strategic IHRM in SMEs, *Thunderbird International Business Review*, **43** (1), pp. 77–100

Harzing, A W K (2000) An empirical test and extension of the Bartlett and Ghoshal typology of multinational companies, *Journal of International Business Studies*, **31** (1), pp. 101–20

Harzing, A W, Pudelko, M and Reiche, B S (2016) The bridging role of expatriates and inpatriates in knowledge transfer in multinational corporations, *Human Resource Management*, **55** (4), pp. 679–95

Hill, C W (2007) *International Business: Competing in the global market place*, 6th edn, McGraw-Hill, New York

Holtbrügge, D and Mohr, A T (2011) Subsidiary interdependencies and international human resource management practices in German MNCs, *Management International Review*, **51** (1), pp. 93–115

Iles, P and Yolles, M (2002) International joint ventures, HRM, and viable knowledge migration, *International Journal of Human Resource Management*, **13** (4), pp. 624–41

Johnson, J P, Lenartowicz, T and Apud, S (2006) Cross-cultural competence in international business: toward a definition and a model, *Journal of International Business Studies*, **37** (4), pp. 525–43

Kealey, D J and Protheroe, D R (1996) The effectiveness of cross-cultural training for expatriates: an assessment of the literature on the issue, *International Journal of Intercultural Relations*, **20** (2), pp. 141–65

Ko, H C and Yang, M L (2011) The effects of cross-cultural training on expatriate assignments, *Intercultural Communication Studies* **XX** (1), pp. 158–74.

Lee, L-Y and Sukoco, B M (2010) The effects of cultural intelligence on expatriate performance: the moderating effects of international experience, *The International Journal of Human Resource Management*, **21** (7), pp. 963–81

Littrell, L N and Salas, E (2005) A review of cross-cultural training: best practices, guidelines, and research needs, *Human Resource Development Review*, **4**, pp. 305–34

Littrell, L N et al (2006) Expatriate assignments: a neglected issue of 25 years of cross-cultural training research, *Human Resource Development Review*, **5** (3), pp. 355–58

Macharzina, K and Wolf, J (1996) Internationales führungskräfte-management- zukunftsherausforderung erfolgsorientierter unternehmensführun, in *Handbuch Internationales Führungskräfte-Management,* eds K Macharzina and J Wolf, Raabe Verlag, pp. 3–14

Mendenhall, M E, Dunbar, E and Oddou, G R (1987) Expatriate selection, training and career-pathing: a review and critique, *Human Resource Management*, **26** (3), pp. 331–45

Muethel, M and Hoegl, M (2010) Cultural and societal influences on shared leadership in globally dispersed teams, *Journal of International Management,* **16** (3), pp. 234–46

Mugambi, H M (2012) I can't stand it here: expatriate experiences in northern Nigeria, in *Communicating Across Cultures*, ed E Christopher, Palgrave Macmillan. London, pp. 149–55

Noe, R A (2005) Employee Training and Development, 3rd edn, Irwin/McGraw-Hill

Oberg, K (1960) Cultural shock: adjustment to new cultural environments, *Practical Anthropology*, 7, pp. 177–82

O'Conner, R A (2010) The fatal errors of cross-cultural communication in United States troops in Iraq, *The International Journal of Diversity in Organizations, Communities and Nations*, **96** (6), pp. 187–200

Pandey, S (2012) Using popular movies in teaching cross-cultural management, *European Journal of Training and Development,* **36** (2) pp. 329–50

Perlmutter, H V (1969) The tortuous evolution of the multinational corporation, *Columbia Journal of World Business*, **4** (1), pp. 9–18

Searle, W and Ward, C (1990) The prediction of psychological and sociocultural adjustment during cross-cultural transitions, *International Journal of Intercultural Relations*, **14** (4), pp. 449–64

Senghaas, D (2002) *The Clash Within Civilizations: Coming to terms with cultural conflicts*, Routledge, London

Torbiorn, I (1982) *Living Abroad: Personal adjustment and personnel policy in the overseas setting*, Wiley, New York

Tung, R L (1981) Selection and training of personnel for overseas assignments, *Columbia Journal of World Business*, **16** (1), pp. 68–78

Tung, R (1982) Selecting and training procedures of U.S., European, and Japanese multinational corporations, *California Management Review*, **25** (1), pp. 57–71

Tung, R (1984) *Key to Japan's Economic Strength: Human power*, Lexington Books, Lexington, MA

Ward, C and Kennedy, A (1996) Crossing cultures: the relationship between psychological and socio-cultural dimensions of cross-cultural adjustment, in *Asian Contributions to Cross-cultural Psychology*, eds J Pandey, D Sinha and D P S Bhawuk, Sage, New Delhi

Ward, C and Searle, W (1991) The impact of value discrepancies and cultural identity on psychological and socio-cultural adjustment of sojourners, *International Journal of Intercultural Relations*, **15** (2), pp. 209–25

Waxin, M F (2000) *L'adaptation des cadres expatries en Inde: ses déterminants et l'effet de la culture d'origine*, Thèse de Doctorat, IAE Aix-en-Provence, Aix-en-Provence

Yamazaki, Y and Kayes, C D (2004) An experiential approach to cross-cultural learning: a review and integration of competencies for successful expatriate adaptation, *Academy of Management Learning & Education*, **3** (4), pp. 362–79

Yang, B (2003) Toward a holistic theory of knowledge and adult learning, *Human Resource Development Review*, **2**, pp. 106–29

09
International reward

DANIEL WINTERSBERGER

> ### Learning outcomes
>
> At the end of this chapter, you should be able to:
>
> - identify the key factors (performance, seniority, cost of living, strategic relevance) to be taken into consideration when making decisions on compensation;
> - understand the importance of equity (both procedural and distributive) in pay setting;
> - understand some of the key methods (such as job evaluation) for determining reward;
> - understand some of the key theories of motivation that underpin the link between reward and performance and to critically evaluate the applicability of these theories across different national and cultural contexts;
> - understand the complexities associated with managing 'total reward' in organizations and beyond, across national, cultural and institutional contexts.

Introduction

In this chapter we examine reward from an international perspective. By doing so, we first introduce the issues associated with rewarding people in organizations, followed by an examination of some of the complexities we might encounter when rewarding people in different national, cultural and institutional contexts. We will cover relevant theories of motivation, some of which might explain the ways in which we attitudinally and behaviourally respond to different rewards under different circumstances. In this context, the chapter will highlight that reward is about more than just money, and that organizations are increasingly foregrounding intrinsic rewards that are related to the job itself (such as making tasks more interesting and giving employees greater autonomy). Finally, we will look at a non-monetary reward (flexibility and working from home) in more depth, critically evaluating the evidence of its benefits to organizations and employees, and its applicability in different cultural contexts, including in the US, the UK and China. While flexibility is well established in knowledge-intensive sectors in the UK and US, attempts to attract and retain employees and their commitment are a more recent (though increasingly significant) phenomenon in rapidly emerging economies such as China. Therefore, it is pertinent that we look at the issues around implementation of non-monetary benefits such as flexibility in countries where firms do not have a long-established tradition of offering such rewards, or where such benefits traditionally have low significance for employees.

Managing pay

Before delving head first into the ways in which we determine people's pay levels, let us dispel a very stubborn myth, namely that labour rates (wages paid out to individual workers) are the same thing as overall labour costs (overall costs of the workforce relative to output). In an influential article published in the *Harvard Business Review*, Jeffrey Pfeffer (1997) argued that the two are separate and that the assumption that we can cut labour costs by cutting labour rates, though widespread, is flawed; low labour rates (ie low wages) might actually increase labour costs. In fact, while lowering wages may lead to labour cost reduction in the short term, it often becomes more expensive in the long term due to the costs associated with a poorly committed workforce. It goes without saying that low pay leads to poor employee morale and job satisfaction and therefore also poorer performance, ultimately potentially costing the organization more due to low efficiency (Brown and Nolan, 1988). Moreover, dissatisfied workers don't tend to stay with their organization if there are alternatives in the labour market and the cost of employees leaving due to low pay can be significant for an organization. For example, the cost of turnover can exceed 100 per cent of the payroll cost of the vacated position (Bryant and Allen, 2013).

CASE STUDY   Market-leading compensation at a low-cost airline:
the case of Southwest

Southwest Airlines (SWA), launched in 1967 in Dallas, Texas, is an American low-cost airline (LCA) and is often seen as the epitome of the low-cost model which many years later was to be emulated by European LCAs such as Ryanair and easyJet as well as LCAs in emerging economies, such as IndiGo and Spicejet (India) and Azul (Brazil). The low-cost model entails the cutting of costly intermediaries such as travel agents for booking as well as the harnessing of economies of scale in maintenance through the operation of a relatively uniform aircraft fleet (Doganis, 2006). Of course, the model also entails working its assets (aircraft and staff) particularly efficiently. With its focus on short-haul domestic American flights, the airline emphasizes short aircraft turnaround times on the ground (sometimes as short as 25 minutes) in order to maximize flying time. Somewhat counter-intuitively, however, SWA also pays industry-leading salaries to their captains and flight attendants (Gittell, 2003). Despite paying their cabin crew some $10,000 per year more in base salary than competitors (Gittell, 2003), they have long had significantly lower unit costs than any competitor airline in the United States (Pfeffer, 1997). They achieve lower operating costs despite higher wages through a workforce that is highly committed, prepared to work flexibly and able to use discretionary effort to solve any problems for the airline as they emerge (Gittell, 2003). This example lends some support to Pfeffer's (1997) claim that one of the most stubborn myths in reward management is that labour rates are directly equivalent to labour costs. It is important to keep this in mind in the following section, where we discuss the ways in which we determine how much to pay people.

Determining pay levels

What factors do we need to take into consideration when determining people's pay levels? You may have your own thoughts on this issue, perhaps thinking about your own preferences, expectations and values. In the following section, we examine four key factors often cited by managers when prompted to speak about the criteria they find significant in determining people's pay levels, namely 'market' rates, cost of living, employee strategic relevance and performance, as well as seniority.

'Market' rates

A survey conducted in 2015 by the UK Chartered Institute of Personnel and Development with HR and reward managers across the UK found that the 'market' rates were one of the most important factors taken into consideration in compensation decisions (CIPD, 2015). Matching competitor salaries (the 'market' rate) is a common approach taken, though sometimes organizations may want to attempt to exceed competitor salaries in order to source the best talent in the labour market or to elicit high degrees of employee loyalty and commitment to the organization. Allen and Meyer (1990) discern three dimensions of organizational commitment. First, an 'affective' dimension of commitment entails an emotional bond between an employee and their employing organization. Such emotional bonds may occur as a result of a particularly strong identification with an organization and its values. Second, a normative dimension of organizational commitment entails a sense of moral obligation whereby an individual employee may perceive that he or she owes the company something (their discretionary effort, creativity, loyalty etc) in return for what the company offers them. Finally, Allen and Meyer (1990) discern a 'continuance' dimension of commitment, which entails a more rational evaluation of the costs and benefits associated with leaving the firm or remaining. It is quite clear that organizations that pay above competitor (perhaps market-leading) salaries are likely to develop high levels of continuance commitment amongst their workforce. Some, however, may go beyond a mere rational evaluation (cost and benefit) of their rewards versus their input (effort, skills, expertise, time etc) into the job and perhaps feel a more moral obligation towards their organization if they are paid significantly more than what competitors would offer them; they may even develop an emotional bond with their employer as a result (McFarlin and Sweeney, 1992). This is more likely to happen when they are offered a better overall compensation package not only in terms of base pay levels (salary) but also in the form of other, less quantifiable rewards, which we will look at in more depth in this chapter.

Cost of living

Another factor that certainly requires some attention in international compensation decisions is **cost of living**. Each year, the Economist Intelligence Unit (EIU) publishes a global 'cost of living survey' within which they rank around 130 global cities (usually cities within which there is substantial economic activity from abroad) based on their cost of living for 'expatriates' and 'business travellers', ie those who are not locally recruited but assigned or posted to the city by their current employer in their home country. The most expensive cities in the ranking in 2015, in descending order, were:

1 Singapore;
2 Zurich;

3 Hong Kong;

4 Geneva;

5 London;

6 New York;

7 Copenhagen;

8 Seoul;

9 Los Angeles;

10 Tokyo;

11 Shanghai (joint 10th with Tokyo).

Source: Economist Intelligence Unit (2017)

The low end of the ranking is dominated by several South Asian cities, notably Chennai, Karachi, Mumbai and Bangalore, as well as one African city, Lusaka, the capital of Zambia, which has been bottom of the list since 2015 following the devaluation of the local currency by falling copper prices (Economist Intelligence Unit, 2017).

Such rankings are often taken into consideration in international reward as they provide global HR and/or reward managers with (seemingly) objective criteria on which to weight living cost allowances for international assignees. The advantage of the *Economist* index in this context is that it specifically focuses on living costs for those not permanently living in the host country, thus potentially not having access to state-provided services such as healthcare, schooling and education for children. Take for example Singapore and Copenhagen, two cities in the top 10 globally in terms of living costs according to the *Economist*. While they may well be very expensive cities for non-residents, the same cannot necessarily be said for citizens/ permanent residents within these countries, given the provision of free, high-quality public healthcare as well as public-sector accommodation, neither of which would be available for international assignees, who would have to provide their own healthcare insurance and pay private-sector accommodation fees. Some large organizations such as the United Nations carry out their own benchmarking when it comes to living costs and thereby can factor in certain amenities (such as UN-provided schooling for staff family members) which would not be provided to other international assignees.

Internal benchmarking (ie assigning weightings to cities in terms of living costs for international assignees) is one aspect of international reward and living costs to take into consideration for large organizations such as the United Nations. However, even beyond international assignments, living costs arguably play a crucial role in international reward. Organizations in cities with high living costs (such as London) are reporting increased difficulty in recruiting talented individuals. In London, the Confederation of British Industry (CBI) has recently gone so far as to speak of a looming job crisis (Burn-Callander, 2015). Almost 60 per cent of managers in London-based businesses surveyed by the CBI in 2015 conceded that they have significant difficulty filling positions, particularly in lower-wage and entry-level jobs. The average house price in London is 12 times the average salary, compared to a ratio of 7.6 to 1 for the UK as a whole (ONS, 2017a), and one side effect of this is that low and middle earners increasingly seek more affordable housing that is more on the periphery, further away from work, leading to long commuting times. This is already reported as a major issue in the Bay Area around San Francisco (Rauber, 2016), where various tech giants such as Google and Facebook have their headquarters. Not surprisingly, there is strong evidence that long commuting times adversely affect employee wellbeing and job satisfaction (Blanchflower and Oswald 1999). Using large-scale data on commuting times and overall life satisfaction, the UK Office for National Statistics (ONS) found that every 10 minutes of additional commuting time is associated with a 2 per cent decrease in general life satisfaction (ONS, 2014). Thus, long commutes are likely to adversely affect employee job performance as well as employee retention in the long term. They are also likely to be a deterrent for prospective applicants who may be put off by a potential employer as a result. High living costs can therefore be a major disadvantage for employers outside of traditional high-wage industries such as investment banking when it comes to recruiting skilled graduates.

One response of private-sector employers in cities with high living costs is a so-called 'living cost allowance'. This usually takes the form of a higher salary than one would receive in other cities with lower living costs and commute times, which aims to cover the additional cost of working in that city. In the case of London, this has come to be known as a 'London weighting'. Recent data from the Labour Research Department (LRD) reveals that the London weighting in the private sector typically ranges between £2,000 and £4,500 PA, with employers such as Nationwide Building Society and Tata Steel offering around £4,550 and £4,350 respectively for employees based in inner-London locations (Labour Research Department, 2013). However, despite such weightings, organizations in areas with high living costs continue to struggle with recruitment (Burn-Callander, 2015) and the aforementioned issues around lengthy commuting times and poor employee morale. It is for this reason that when discussing global reward, we look beyond mere base pay and living cost allowances towards other benefits such as flexible working and telecommuting, which may mitigate these pressures. These practices will be examined in more depth later in this chapter.

Employee performance and strategic relevance

Beyond cost of living, other factors often taken into consideration when making compensation decisions include the **strategic relevance** and **performance** of individual employees. Strategic relevance is a complex criterion. An individual employee may possess high levels of strategic relevance for the organization by virtue of possessing high-level skills that are fairly rare in the labour market. For example, in the United States, recent increases in training requirements (time and costs) for pilots has increasingly deterred young people from pursuing a career in this industry, leading to a pilot shortage. This has particularly affected regional carriers, many of which have recently seen themselves having to significantly increase the starting salaries of new first officers, by as much as 12 per cent in some cases (Carey, 2016). As a commercial passenger plane (for the time being at least) cannot be flown without a flight crew, pilots, by virtue of their indispensable skills and qualifications, hold what has been referred to as high levels of 'structural' bargaining power (Wright, 2000). In other words, their key function in airline operations makes them indispensable and hence they are able to command significantly higher salaries than, for example, those working in functions for which such costly and complex training is not required, such as baggage and cargo handling. While structural power tends to be associated with formal qualifications and skill levels, this is not necessarily the case. A long-serving member of staff in a menial function may have substantial degrees of structural power as a result of the extensive tacit knowledge they have built up over their long service for the company. Tacit knowledge and skills are implicit in the sense that they can't be simply transferred (eg through a training programme or a policy manual from one person to another) but are built over time (Polanyi, 1966) and on the job. Therefore, it is not surprising that **seniority** (ie employee job tenure) is a further key factor often mentioned by HR professionals as important in the context of determining employee pay levels.

Seniority

World-over, seniority is indeed a key factor to take into consideration with compensation decisions, but the magnitude of this varies geographically based on some of the cultural factors highlighted in Chapter 2. For example, Japan, in scoring highly on collectivism as well as long-term orientation in Hofstede's framework, is likely to be associated with employers valuing loyalty to the organization. Not surprisingly, therefore, (until recently at least) Japan has been associated with substantial pay differentials in organizations based on employee age and seniority (Clark and Ogawa, 1992). Pay progression was slow but steady, and moreover, employees generally joined companies in entry-level positions at a young age, working until retirement (Suzuki, Kubo and Ogura, 2011). This generated a strong disincentive for employees to leave the company to take up work at a competitor that generally only recruited at entry level, or at least on a lower pay grade. Recently, however, large Japanese companies such as Toyota, Hitachi and Panasonic have made headlines as they seem to be departing from the tried-and-tested system of offering significant reward for long-term job tenure (seniority-based pay). This is consistent with Prime Minister Shinzo Abe's attempts to reform the Japanese labour market, part of which involves attempts to increase the appeal of entry-level jobs and boost the spending power of young people (Inagaki, 2015). Similarly, in the Korean context (a country long characterized by a similar emphasis on seniority), Bae (1997) observed a shift to more performance-driven payment schemes.

This section has examined several factors (market rates, cost of living, strategic relevance, performance and seniority) that firms may take into consideration when making compensation decisions, and some of the cross-national and cross-cultural differences in terms of the importance ascribed to each of these variables. Regardless of the relative importance of these factors in different cultural contexts, HR and reward managers need to take care that their choices do not adversely affect employee notions of fairness and, as a result, their motivation to perform. In the next section, we therefore examine some of the relevant theories that influence our perception of fairness in compensation, and look at some of the practices (such as job evaluation) that companies use to determine reward as transparently and fairly as possible.

Equity in compensation

Reward practice in contemporary work organizations is arguably heavily influenced by several underpinning theories of motivation. For example, Maslow's Hierarchy of Needs (more on this later) stipulates that people's needs at work are both intrinsic (ie related to the job itself), and extrinsic (what material rewards they get in compensation for their effort at work). In the context of fairness in compensation, an influential contribution has been made by the so-called 'equity theory' (Adams and Freedman, 1976). Put crudely, the theory outlines the fairly obvious notion that we assess what we put into a job against what we get out of it. However, when it comes to evaluating our inputs, things become a bit more complicated. While we may think primarily about the time we spend working or perhaps our work effort, there is a lot more an employer needs to consider when they decide how much to pay someone. While employee performance is a fairly obvious criterion, it is also a problematic one. For one thing, we only know about potential rather than actual performance prior to appointing someone and determining their pay grade and pay level. We may make inferences based on their performance in the selection process, previous experience and educational credentials, but such predictions may often be wrong. Moreover, not all aspects of performance can readily be quantified. In traditional routine and repetitive jobs, a form of output-based payment system as proposed by Frederick Winslow Taylor under his 'principles of scientific management' (Taylor, 1911) may work fine, as output (in the form of units produced, telephone calls made, products sold etc) can clearly be quantified. However, not many jobs have such clear, unambiguously quantifiable output metrics. Take for example the performance of a doctor or nurse. While some aspects of performance (speed, efficiency) may be amenable to quantification, this may coerce people to sacrifice other, equally important aspects of performance such as the quality of patient care. Overall, therefore, it is important to pay people not only commensurate with their performance, but also, as far as possible, commensurate with their perceptions of what they feel that they *deserve*, given their skills and effort.

Employee notions of fairness may be determined by two dimensions of equity: distributive and procedural. First, **distributive equity** is about what we get in comparison to others. We may compare our own salary to that earned by others in similar job functions within the organization (internal equity) or perhaps also to key reference groups which may not be within the same job category or organization (external equity). Distributive equity is fairly simple insofar as we will be dissatisfied if we feel that we are being left short changed compared to others with similar or inferior qualifications, work experience and performance. However, we also need to consider a second dimension of equity. While distributive equity is about what we get compared to others, **procedural equity** is about the extent to which we feel that the process by which our reward is determined is fair and transparent. In other words, while distributive equity is about what we get in comparison to others, procedural equity is about why we get what we get.

Achieving procedural equity is not always easy, but a starting point is to work on increasing the transparency of the pay determination process. A process named 'job evaluation' is often mentioned as a good way to objectively determine pay levels.

Non-analytical job evaluation

Traditionally, **non-analytical job evaluation** techniques were used. Jobs were evaluated overall and compared to other jobs in terms of their strategic relevance to the organization. However, such a crude way of ranking jobs does not really succeed in eradicating subjectivity, nor does it necessarily increase procedural equity insofar as the key criteria on which the jobs have been ranked are not transparent to those affected (Armstrong and Baron, 2003: 3) and may lead to discrimination against jobs which traditionally don't enjoy high status and where there is often little objective basis on which to determine the relative worth of different jobs.

Analytical job evaluation

In order to overcome the biases associated with non-analytical job evaluation and to bring more objectivity into pay and pay grade determination, organizations operating with pay scales/pay grades often turn to analytical processes of job evaluation. Such processes usually involve some type of 'points-based' system on the basis of which different job demands are weighted. Points for each job demand (multiplied by the weighting where applicable) are then added up and the total number of points can be used to determine the grade of a job. Below is an example of a points-based system as part of an analytical job evaluation scheme for employees within the UK National Health Service (NHS). In the 'Level 1' column, you can find the respective weightings for each variable (ie how significant it is perceived to be by the NHS). For example, the criterion 'knowledge training and experience'

(16) has the highest weighting, whereas levels of 'physical effort' (3) appear to be considered less significant. As a result, one can conclude that greater priority is placed on hard skills and formal qualifications (eg a degree in medicine) than on weighting jobs by the amount of effort required. Seniority is to some extent rewarded by the different grades (horizontal rows).

Reflective question

To what extent do you believe that the above points-based system used by the UK NHS meets employee preference for procedural equity? Do you agree with the weightings of the different job demands? If not, why?

Table 9.1   Analytic job evaluation in the UK National Health Service (NHS)

Factor	Level 1	2	3	4	5	6	7	8
1 Communication and relationship skills	5	12	21	32	45	60		
2 Knowledge, training and experience	16	36	60	88	120	156	196	240
3 Analytical skills	6	15	27	42	60			
4 Planning and organisation skills	6	15	27	42	60			
5 Physical skills	6	15	27	42	60			
6 Responsibility – patient/ client care	4	9	15	22	30	39	49	60
7 Responsibility – policy and service	5	12	21	32	45	60		
8 Responsibility –finance and physical	5	12	21	32	45	60		
9 Responsibility –staff/HR/ leadership/training	5	12	21	32	45	60		
10 Responsibility – information resource	4	9	16	24	34	46	60	
11 Responsibility – research and development	5	12	21	32	45	60		
12 Freedom to act	5	12	21	32	45	60		
13 Physical effort	3	7	12	18	25			
14 Mental effort	3	7	12	18	25			
15 Emotional effort	5	11	18	25				
16 Working conditions	3	7	12	18	25			

SOURCE NHS (2013:73)

Job evaluation schemes using points-based systems certainly lead to higher levels of transparency for employees interested in knowing why they get what they get. However, they do not necessarily make the process of pay determination more objective. Take for example the weightings used by the NHS in their points-based system above. Why is 'emotional effort' weighted at less than a third of the value of knowledge, training and experience? Perhaps to answer this question we need to revisit the concept of strategic relevance, discussed earlier. While the provision of good patient care argu- ably requires substantial degrees of empathy and people skills, emotional skills in their own right are 'soft skills' which do not require formal qualifi- cations. In contrast, to become a surgeon, for example, requires many years of tertiary education and on-job experience. Similar to the aforementioned example of airline pilots, medical professionals (doctors and nurses) by virtue of the formal qualifications (higher education, further training and on-job experience) required to be licensed practitioners, command signifi- cantly higher wages than those working in healthcare with fewer formal qualifications. Strategic relevance therefore seems to be a key factor for the NHS when it comes to pay determination. As a result of the adversarial rela- tionship between the UK health secretary, Jeremy Hunt (Conservatives), and the professional association of doctors (a conflict revolving, amongst other factors, to a great extent around pay for newly trained doctors) there is significant evidence of and public concern about UK doctors moving abroad for better pay, potentially leading to a shortage of doctors in the UK (Smith, 2016). In other words, doctors, by virtue of holding high levels of 'struc- tural' bargaining power (Wright, 2000), have the potential to command higher salaries than, say, unskilled workers, perhaps explaining why the NHS weights 'knowledge, training and experience' significantly heavier in their points-based job evaluation than emotional effort. The question then becomes whether such pay determination mechanisms are in fact more objective than, for example, non-analytic job evaluation. Someone has to determine how much to weight the different job demands, and this process in its own right is highly subjective.

Reward beyond pay

So far in this chapter we have looked at reward mainly in the context of pay and pay determination. However, reward is increasingly about more than just money, as work organizations, particularly in advanced indus- trial economies with good public healthcare and social security systems, are recognizing that people are increasingly driven to perform by non- monetary factors. Even in countries where contextual factors (availability of public healthcare and social security systems) are not so favourable, such as the United States, companies are increasingly finding it difficult to motivate their higher-earning staff with monetary benefits. Take the exam- ple of Google. It is well known that the company offers their high-calibre technical staff in its California headquarters reward commensurate with their skills, ability and experience. Despite the generous pay levels offered by Google, there is far more coverage both by themselves and outsiders of the intrinsic benefits of working there, such as working in a fun and engaging environment with interesting people and simply doing things that matter while encountering continuous opportunities for self-development through training (Google, 2017).

Beyond performance-based pay

This is due to profound changes to the nature of work, where people work and how they work. Labour markets around the globe have been profoundly transformed, first by an industrial revolution, leading to a shift from employment in agriculture to employment in manufacturing, and more recently by a shift away from manufacturing towards services as the dominant sector. In the UK, for example, more than 80 per cent of jobs are in services (ONS, 2017b). While the profound economic restructuring from manufacturing to services now dates back four or even five decades, emerging economies such as China, India and Brazil are still in the midst of this transition. In 2016, China's service sector for the first time contributed more than 50 per cent to overall GDP levels, and the government aims to get this up to 80 per cent over the coming decade (Hsu, 2017). The service sector is very broad, encompassing industries such as transport, cleaning, IT, sales, auditing and many more. Put simply, the service sector includes all industries where nothing tangible is produced, although it also encompasses the restaurant industry, where something tangible (a meal) is very much produced, but the service provision that goes with the meal is a significant part of the final 'product'. Owing to Taylor's (1911) scientific management and Fordism, jobs in manufacturing were, for much of the 20th century, quite predictable, routine and repetitive, and a person's output could clearly be quantified in terms of units produced; the greater the work effort (and perhaps to some extent dexterity), the greater the output. This is quite well reflected in a well-known anecdote found in Taylor's *Principles of Scientific Management*, where the author, then owner of an iron-processing plant, asks one of his workers (named 'Schmidt') whether he would be prepared to significantly increase his rate of loading iron onto a truck for a similarly significant increase in pay commensurate with performance:

> Schmidt … what I want to find out is whether you are a high-priced man or one of these cheap fellows here. What I want to find out is whether you want to earn $1.85 a day or whether you are satisfied with $1.15, just the same as all those cheap fellows are getting (Taylor, 1911: 11).

One of the key principles of the piece-rate system under scientific management was that workers carried out the tasks precisely as directed by industrial engineers, as these modes of operation were the scientifically derived most efficient way to work, minimizing process loss and risk of injury. Control within such standardized environments was simply output based, and as tasks were relatively narrow (such as loading iron onto a truck all day), output could clearly be quantified. It might be argued that in contemporary work environments, output as such is not always clearly quantifiable. A management consultant, for example, may receive a bonus for quantifiable metrics such as delivering projects on time and under budget, but many aspects of performance (such as how he or she interacts with clients and colleagues) cannot objectively be quantified, let alone constantly observed. As a result, it might be argued that reward in a contemporary work organization can no longer be simply viewed as pay for performance, but instead as pay for work ethic, attitude and many other non-quantifiable factors. While an employment contract will clearly specify wages and working hours, expected effort at work, attitude and performance cannot always be defined in advance. Worker capacity to perform is therefore 'indeterminate' insofar as 'the precise amount of effort to be extracted cannot be "fixed" before the engagement of workers … for purposeful … action' (Smith, 2006: 389). In other words, expected effort and performance at work is continuously being renegotiated and more complex aspects of performance (emotional displays, empathy, teamworking etc) are not amenable to quantification under performance-based payment schemes.

A further weakness of performance-based payment schemes is that pay does not always lead to better performance. In an influential book, Pink (2009) explores some of the key flaws of payment by results, highlighting that often such schemes have the unanticipated effect of actually impeding successful employee performance. Drawing on fairly large-scale evidence (experiments entailing tasks and rewards with several thousand participants, replicated in various countries, including the United States and India), Pink argues that high monetary stakes often lead to high levels of pressure, stressing employees and therefore stifling their creative potential. As a result, Pink argues, money acts as a good motivator only for simple, manual repetitive tasks (such as in the aforementioned example of loading iron onto a truck). In contrast, where a task requires critical thinking, creativity and improvisation, money actually leads to worse performance, as evidenced by the aforementioned experiments (Pink, 2009).

When put into context with some relevant theories of motivation, these findings are not at all surprising. Abraham Maslow, an American psychologist, developed one of the most influential 'content' theories of motivation. In other words, he looked at what motivates us at work and found that money (and the things we can buy with it such as food and shelter) is only a very basic need that does not lead to increased satisfaction and motivation, but the deficiency of it leads to dissatisfaction. In contrast, higher-order needs such as autonomy and self-actualization actually lead to motivation (Maslow, 1943). This is somewhat consistent with another influential content theory of motivation, namely that of American psychologist Frederick Herzberg, who differentiated between so-called 'hygiene' and 'motivational' factors as sources of satisfaction and dissatisfaction (Herzberg, Mausner and Snyderman, 1959). While 'hygiene' factors encompass material rewards such as pay, 'motivational' factors cover various intrinsic rewards such as autonomy and interesting work. Herzberg and colleagues argued that insufficient employer attention to hygiene factors (for example when pay levels are set too low) will lead to employee dissatisfaction and demotivation but no matter how well an employer addresses these factors (for example by paying very high salaries), these hygiene factors can never lead to satisfaction. Instead, motivational factors (or higher-order needs in Maslow's terms) are those factors that lead to satisfaction, but they can only do so once the hygiene factors have been met. This is somewhat consistent with Maslow's argument that lower-order (material) needs have to be addressed to prevent dissatisfaction, followed by higher-order needs (such as self-actualization and autonomy) in order to make an employee satisfied with their job.

From theories of motivation to practical implications: total reward in organizations

In practice, the aforementioned theories of motivation can be linked with the growing influence of 'total reward'. This is defined as 'a strategy whereby employers bring together both **intrinsic** and **extrinsic** rewards. These can add up to a total value of everything staff receive as a result of working from their employer' (Employee Benefits, 2017). Extrinsic rewards are usually monetary in nature, and are often seen as 'tangible' rewards given in return for work. The term extrinsic denotes the fact that the reward is external to the work itself. Examples of extrinsic rewards include bonuses, company cars, laptops and any other benefits, generally with a quantifiable value. In contrast, intrinsic rewards are more directly related to the job itself and as such include aspects such as autonomy (freedom) and flexibility on the job, as well as interesting tasks at work more generally. It is clear from the above examples of extrinsic and intrinsic rewards that while the value of extrinsic rewards can generally be objectively and unambiguously quantified in monetary terms, it is a lot more difficult to exactly define the value of intrinsic rewards (such as flexibility and autonomy); these types of rewards are likely to be valued to a different extent by different people, but it is of utmost importance for employers, in building an appealing employer brand for prospective applications, to ensure that any intrinsic rewards associated with the job are mentioned. The following framework, developed by the Hay Group (now part of Korn Ferry), a global management consultancy firm, exemplifies the different quantifiable and non-quantifiable rewards an employer may offer, highlighting the distinction between extrinsic and intrinsic rewards. As you can see in Figure 9.1, they include so-called 'engagement factors' associated with the nature of the work itself (quality) as well as contextual factors such as work–life balance and opportunities for development within the roles as key intrinsic factors an employer needs to add to the equation when laying out to employees the rewards they offer for a particular job.

Figure 9.1 The Hay Group Total Reward Framework

		Engagement factors	
Intrinsic *Elements that contribute to internal value or motivation*	• Quality of work • Work-life balance • Inspiration and values • Enabling environment • Growth and opportunity		Total reward
Extrinsic *All the things we can assign a monetary value to*	• Tangible benefits, eg cars, professional memberships, discounts	Active benefits	Total remuneration
	• Retirement • Health and welfare • Holidays	Passive benefits	
	• Stock and equity • Performance shares	Long-term rewards and incentives	Total direct compensation
	• Annual incentives • Bonus and split awards	Short-term variables	Total cash
	• Base salary • Hourly wage	Base cash	

CASE STUDY   Flexibility as a reward with mutual benefits at BT
Group PLC

This chapter has already highlighted cost of living as a key factor influencing compensation decisions. London is one of the world cities consistently in the top 10 of rankings of the most expensive cities to live in. Preceding sections have made mention of cost of living allowances, or 'London weightings' in the case of the British capital. However, such weightings often merely encourage people to take the job with the company, but in practice do very little to cut commuting times and cost. In fact, they often merely compensate for the increased costs of commuting. An annual travel card for the greater London area (Transport for London Zones 1–9) cost a whopping £3,104 in 2017, according to Transport for London). This creates a very strong disincentive to commute to work in London, especially for people living in the suburbs or even, as is increasingly common, commuting in from other regions of the UK.

The BT group, a holding company owning British Telecommunications with headquarters in London, has demonstrated recognition of this issue by implementing a policy that is somewhat more original than a London weighting. BT recognized that employee morale was suffering as a result of long commuting times. Reduced morale led to lower productivity, performance, absenteeism and turnover. A lengthy commute, especially in a crowded train, is often a strong disincentive to go to work, and as a result, sick leave had become an issue. Turnover was also a key issue the organization faced and at least part of the blame seemed to be attributable to long commuting times. Apart from London weightings (already given to the workforce), BT was left with two options in an attempt to increase productivity and reduce absenteeism and turnover. The first option (often taken by firms) would have been to leave London. For example, Deutsche Bank has recently moved thousands of back-office functions to UK's second city, Birmingham, where living costs are significantly cheaper (Brown, 2014).

BT, however, chose an alternative option to moving substantial parts of their operation outside the capital. The organization has opted instead for what they refer to as 'homeshoring' by offering staff the opportunity to work from home when they want to. BT still provides office facilities, but rather than fixed workstations, BT has implemented a system of 'hot desking' where work stations can be booked in advance.

Flexible working and working from home are a form of reward with benefits to both employees and employers. On the employer side, one of the key benefits of telecommuting is that this type of reward is not expensive. There are no additional payroll/equipment costs, unlike with many other, mainly extrinsic rewards. In fact, flexible working and telecommuting can save the employer money. BT, for example, report that around 15,000 of their workforce of around 80,000 have opted for home working, saving the company around £80 million per year due to being able to cut down on office space and provision of facilities (work stations) for these employees.

On the BT employee side, those with an opportunity to work flexibly often speak of increased quality of living due to cutting down on commuting time, having more time for leisure, better health, lower stress levels and an increased discretion on when to work, having the ability to pick their own more productive times for work. This is somewhat consistent with broader empirical evidence from a range of industrial and national contexts, where home working is linked with greater employee job satisfaction, loyalty and productivity (Bloom 2014; Baruch, 2000).

However, this is not to detract from some of the potential pitfalls (both on the employer and employee sides) associated with working from home. From an employee perspective, the high levels of autonomy and freedom associated with working from home are not desired by everyone. Some prefer structure to their day and an office-based environment. For this reason, BT was probably doing the right thing by rolling out the home-working scheme on a voluntary basis. Some feel lonely at home and feel that they are missing out on important insider information disseminated in informal meetings during and after work.

There is also evidence that flexible working may lead to the unanticipated consequence of increased stress as the lack of structure associated with a typical 9–5 office- or factory-based job makes it very difficult for home workers to differentiate between work and leisure time (Kelliher and Anderson, 2010). This is particularly a problem with home workers as their place of living also becomes their place of work. What is often found is that those receiving the 'reward' of working from home often feel a sense of obligation to work harder than they would in the office as a means to show that they can be trusted with this privilege. Kelliher and Anderson (2010) refer to this as intensification as reciprocation or exchange. This can be linked with the concept of normative commitment (Allen and Meyer, 1990) discussed earlier in the chapter. Self-consciousness and normative control may therefore be a powerful mechanism for extending managerial control to the home of employees with minimal supervision required. Nonetheless, evidence of the psychological benefits of home working is still very strong (Baruch, 2000) and some form of flexibility (either in the form of working from home or flexitime) tends to be part of most organizations' total reward packages.

Reflective exercise

The preceding section has laid out evidence of some of the employer-level benefits of working from home. While the evidence (employee loyalty, commitment, productivity and cost savings on travel and office space as well as reduction in sick days) is fairly compelling, not all employers are unequivocally convinced of the benefits of flexible working. Marissa Mayer, CEO of Yahoo!, has recently made headlines by abolishing home working (in 2013), arguing that 'speed and quality' can be lost when working from home (Carlson, 2013). In a leaked copy of a memo from HR, employees were told: 'We need to be one Yahoo!, and that starts with physically being together.' The memo went on to argue that 'Some of the best decisions and insights come from hallway and cafeteria discussions, meeting new people, and impromptu team meetings' (Cohan, 2013), highlighting the importance of informal collaboration, the type which tends to only occur when people spontaneously meet in a common workplace.

Questions

1 Critically evaluate the benefits and drawbacks of working from home from an organizational and employee perspective.

2 To what extent would you agree with Marissa Mayer's arguments in favour of banning home working at Yahoo!?

3 Reflect on your own preferences. Where do you get work done better and more productively?

Reward across cultural and institutional contexts

Much of the literature on reward management is written from a western perspective, as are all the theories of motivation we discussed previously in this chapter. As such, reward management, informed by theories of motivation devised solely by European and North American psychologists, is often a fairly ethnocentric endeavour. In Chapter 2, we looked at some of the key cultural frameworks (eg Hofstede's cultural orientations and the World Values Survey) which may impact on IHRM operations across different national contexts. Reward is an area of IHRM that is likely to be affected by cultural factors. Take for example Hofstede's cultural dimensions of individualism and collectivism. In societies scoring high on individualism (such as the UK and US), we might expect employees to prefer performance-based bonuses to be paid on an individual basis, whereas in more collectivist-oriented societies (such as Japan and China) we may expect people to be more comfortable with having a significant proportion of their bonus based on organizational or group performance. Beyond individualism–collectivism, it has been shown that 'power distance' is a potentially even more significant determinant of differences in reward practices across different cultural contexts (Fischer and Smith, 2003). As mentioned in previous chapters, high levels of power distance are generally associated with a higher tolerance of inequality amongst members of a society. As a result, it may be expected that pay differentials within organizations might be higher in countries with high levels of power distance. This in turn might be re-enforced where levels of individualism are high, but research has also shown that individualistic societies value meritocracy in reward decisions (Steers, Sanchez-Runde and Nardon, 2010). It is perhaps not a coincidence that the traditional notion of the American dream (underpinned by the assumption that anyone can get rich through hard work) stems from one of the countries scoring highest on Hofstede's individualism score.

Beyond culture, there are other, more proximate institutional factors impacting on reward across different contexts. For example, mechanisms of pay determination might be influenced by different employee voice mechanisms across different national contexts. In Germany, where pay bargaining happens at sectoral level between employers' associations and unions (see Chapter 5), organizations need to ensure that they pay their staff at least the salary specified in the collective agreement (ie the terms and conditions set out by unions and employers' associations at industry level). In the Japanese context, the 'nenko' system of rewarding seniority and loyalty to the company through slow but steady promotion based on job tenure may no longer be as influential as it once was (see Chapter 5), but nonetheless still needs to be considered, for example in areas such as employee share ownership programmes (Geng, Yoshikawa and Colpan, 2015).

Pay ratios (ie the earnings of the highest earners relative to the earnings of the lowest earners) within organizations also differ greatly between countries. The United States has become renowned for particularly strong disparities between worker and executive pay levels. This is supported by the ratio of CEO pay to ordinary worker pay in listed private companies, which stood at a staggering 354:1 in 2014, contrasted sharply by the somewhat more 'moderate' ratio of 36:1 in Austria (Statista, 2015). Executive pay in absolute terms (David Cote, CEO of Honeywell, received over US $55 million in total compensation in 2015 (Forbes, 2016)) and relative terms (see executive pay ratio) have caused widespread outrage. In an influential *New York Times* article, economist Paul Krugman even spoke of an 'outrage constraint' on the side of public and shareholders that is likely to restrict executive pay ratios rising to even more extreme proportion in the United States, but argues that executives of large organizations are becoming increasingly creative in 'camouflaging' increases in executive pay. For example, this could be through increasing the proportion of the pay package comprising stock options which are always given to CEOs at market price, meaning that they receive a generous reward package regardless of company performance (Krugman, 2002).

Despite cultural factors arguably still playing a key role in shaping people's reward preference, there is also some evidence of increasingly homogenous reward packages around the globe, especially in organizations operating in more internationalized environments. In the next case study, we examine the issues and challenges around the implementation of flexible working as an intangible benefit in a large Chinese travel agency. China is an apt context in which to look at these challenges, as the country scores high on survival values and relatively low on self-expression values (see Chapter 2) and therefore we would expect fairly negative attitudes (or at least employee reservation) towards such benefits which cannot be assigned a monetary value.

CASE STUDY Home working and employee performance in China

CTrip, a Chinese travel agency with revenues of around US $1.2 billion in 2014 and around 30,000 employees, recently partnered up with several economists for an experiment in which they wanted to systematically measure the impact of working from home on employee morale, wellbeing and performance (Bloom et al, 2014). Several call centre employees who volunteered to take part in the experiment were randomly selected to work from home or in the office for a period of nine months. The result after nine months was that home working overall led to a 13 per cent increase in performance (measured in the form of productivity, number of calls taken and quality of the work). Moreover, the experiment found that those working from home tended to spend more time working during their shift due to taking fewer breaks. Call centre operatives were able to process calls faster, reportedly due to being in a quieter environment at home. While this provides strong evidence in support of the employer-level benefits of home working, there are also implications for employees to be considered. Home workers in this experiment, in general, reported improved job satisfaction, and it is not surprising, therefore, that the turnover rate (due to employee resignation) fell amongst those working from home. As a result of these benefits, CTrip rolled out the home-working option to their remaining workforce and over half of their employees took the option. Surprisingly, however, half of those originally randomly selected to work from home opted to return to the office upon completion of the nine-month experiment.

Reflective questions

1 Why do you think that more than half the employees who worked from home during the experiment preferred to return to working in the office again?

2 What role, if any, do you think cultural factors may have played in shaping their attitudes to home working?

3 What could the company have done differently?

CASE STUDY Total reward at Unilever

Based on an interview with Keith Williams, head of global reward at Unilever (World at Work, 2013).

Unilever is represented in over 100 countries globally, and in 2010 set out to devise an integrated global total reward system on the basis of which the company aimed to be able to evaluate the relative value of each benefit provided in different countries in order to ensure that staff were remunerated fairly in the different countries. Obviously, one key factor to consider in this context is of course cost of living; however, Unilever took their total reward system a lot further.

A key issue faced by Unilever in their total reward benchmarking exercise has been the great variety of workers (156,000 in total around the globe) and their various backgrounds ranging from the chief executive to manufacturing workers and even those employed in primary sectors such as tea picking (World at Work, 2013). Unilever were very keen not only to collate the absolute figures (in terms of salary earned in each job category by country), but also how people felt about their overall reward package. To this end, they distributed a 'rate my reward survey' prior to developing their total reward system. Unilever also wanted to ensure that the total reward system could provide real-time information about the current cost of their global workforce at any point in time. Of course, this has to take into consideration fluctuation in currency values and exchange rates which can be substantial over fairly short periods of time (take for example the 30 per cent slump in the British pound to euro exchange rate following the vote to leave the EU).

Another factor to be taken into consideration is ancillary labour costs associated for example with social security and/or healthcare benefits which in some countries can be significantly more substantial (a greater proportion of overall payroll costs) than in others. Scandinavian countries such as Norway have some of the highest social security costs in the world, and it is probably not a coincidence that companies such as Norwegian Air International have turned to 'flags of convenience' (see Chapter 13) as a means to source their staff from other countries in order to circumvent high labour costs associated with social security benefits. Unilever want to ensure that they can accurately benchmark their full labour costs across contexts with different taxation systems as well as different customs and practices. For example, in India, Unilever are working in a joint venture with Unilever Hindustan. The situation is complicated in India, as any increase in salary within their joint venture will require supplementary payments such as an increase in housing allowance. The total reward system therefore allows Unilever not only to find out the current cost of their global workforce, but can also predict labour costs for future scenarios – eg a pay increase in certain countries.

The benefits of implementing such a system are also clear from an employee perspective. Employees can see the extra value of benefits they get beyond their pay cheque and additionally, through the 'rate my reward survey' they feel that they have a voice in articulating their satisfaction and dissatisfaction with particular aspects of the reward package.

Reflective questions

1 Think about your own country of origin. What might be the key challenges faced by organizations that try to benchmark and quantify the relative values of different intrinsic and extrinsic rewards they offer their workforce?

2 What do you think about the 'rate my reward' survey used by Unilever? Do you see any potential constraints on the organization's ability to act on the feedback received by their workforce?

Conclusions

In this chapter we have considered reward as a complicated area of IHRM due to the complexities and subjectivities associated with determining pay levels for individuals in organizations. We looked at some of the factors (performance, cost of living, strategic relevance, seniority) that organizations often have to take into consideration when deciding how much to pay people in domestic as well as overseas appointments. We then considered some of the ways in which organizations, through methods such as benchmarking and analytical job evaluation, attempt to make the process of pay determination more transparent in order to meet employee desires for procedural equity, while remaining aware of the still inherently subjective nature of such methods. We have also considered some of the relevant theories of motivation which may account for our attitudinal and behavioural responses to different types of reward, and have highlighted the increasing importance of intrinsic rewards as sources of motivation and the growing uptake amongst organizations of 'total reward'. In the context of total reward, we have focused on the impact of flexible working on employee wellbeing, motivation and performance in different national and cultural contexts.

Key learning points

- Reward is not just about money but should incorporate other intangible 'intrinsic' rewards.
- Preferences regarding different rewards are likely to be contingent on cultural values.
- Reward managers working across borders need to be sensitive to national differences in pay bargaining.

References

Adams, J S and Freedman, S (1976) Equity theory revisited: comments and annotated bibliography, *Advances in Experimental Social Psychology*, **9**, pp. 43–90

Allen, N J and Meyer, J P (1990) The measurement and antecedents of affective, continuance and normative commitment to the organization, *Journal of Occupational and Organizational Psychology*, **63** (1), pp. 1–18

Armstrong, M and Baron, A (2003) *Job Evaluation*, Kogan Page

Bae, J (1997) Beyond seniority-based systems: a paradigm shift in Korean HRM? *Asia Pacific Business Review*, **3** (4), pp. 82–110

Baruch, Y (2000) Teleworking: benefits and pitfalls as perceived by professionals and managers, *New technology, Work and Employment*, **15** (1), pp. 34–49

Blanchflower, D G and Oswald, A J (1999) Well-being, insecurity and the decline of American job satisfaction, *NBER working paper 7487*

Bloom, N (2014) To raise productivity, let more employees work from home, *Harvard Business Review*, **92** (1/2), pp. 28–29

Bloom, N et al (2014) Does working from home work? Evidence from a Chinese experiment, *The Quarterly Journal of Economics*, **130** (1), pp. 165–218

Brown, G (2014) Eyes on Birmingham as Deutsche Bank Expands, *Birmingham Post* [online] http://www.birminghampost.co.uk/business/business-news/eyes-banking-world-birmingham-deutsche-7366789

Brown, W and Nolan, P (1988) Wages and labour productivity: the contribution of industrial relations research to the understanding of pay determination, *British Journal of Industrial Relations*, **26** (3), pp. 339–61

Bryant, P C and Allen, D G (2013) Compensation, benefits and employee turnover: HR strategies for retaining top talent, *Compensation and Benefits Review*, **45** (3), pp. 171–75

Burn-Callander, R (2015) Jobs crisis looming as entry-level workers driven out of London by soaring rents, *Telegraph*, [online] http://www.telegraph.co.uk/finance/jobs/11850805/Jobs-crisis-looming-as-entry-level-workers-driven-out-of-London-by-soaring-rents.html [accessed 19 October 2014]

Carey, S (2016) Pilot shortage prompts regional airlines to boost starting wages, *Wall Street Journal*, [online] https://www.wsj.com/articles/pilot-shortage-prompts-regional-airlines-to-boost-starting-wages-1478473042

Carlson, N (2013) Why Marissa Mayer told remote employees to work in an office ... or quit, *Business Insider* [online] http://www.businessinsider.com/why-marissa-mayer-told-remote-employees-to-work-in-an-office-or-quit-2013-2?IR=T

CIPD (2015) Reward management 2014–15 [online] https://www.cipd.co.uk/knowledge/strategy/reward/surveys

Clark, R L and Ogawa, N (1992) Employment tenure and earnings profiles in Japan and the United States: comment, *The American Economic Review*, **82** (1), pp. 336–45

Cohan, P (2013) 4 reasons why Marissa Mayer's 'no at home work policy is an epic fail', *Forbes* [online] https://www.forbes.com/sites/petercohan/2013/02/26/4-reasons-marissa-mayers-no-at-home-work-policy-is-an-epic-fail/#393e820f2246

Doganis, R (2006) *The Airline Business*, Psychology Press

Economist Intelligence Unit (2017) Worldwide cost of living report [online] https://www.eiu.com/public/topical_report.aspx?campaignid=WCOL2017

Employee Benefits (2017) Total reward factsheet [online] https://www.employeebenefits.co.uk/total-reward/

Fischer, R and Smith, P B (2003) Reward allocation and culture: a meta-analysis, *Journal of cross-cultural psychology*, **34** (3), pp. 251–68

Forbes (2016) 10 highest paid CEOs, *Forbes* [online] https://www.forbes.com/pictures/eggh45jef/david-cote-of-honeywell/#456d68e31b97

Geng, X, Yoshikawa, T and Colpan, A M (2015) Leveraging foreign institutional logic in the adoption of stock option pay among Japanese firms, *Strategic Management Journal*, **37** (7), pp. 1472–92

Gittell, J H (2003) *The Southwest Airlines Way*, McGraw-Hill

Google (2017) How we care for Googlers [online] https://careers.google.com/how-we-care-for-googlers/ [accessed 30 June 2017]

Herzberg, F, Mausner, B and Snyderman, B B (1959) *The Motivation to Work*, 2nd edn, John Wiley, New York

Hsu, S (2017) China takes another step towards a service economy, *Forbes* [online] https://www.forbes.com/sites/sarahsu/2017/02/21/china-takes-another-step-towards-a-service-economy/#162660c928c1

Inagaki, K (2015) Japan inc shuns seniority in favour of merit-based pay, *Financial Times* [online] https://www.ft.com/content/87586772-a600-11e4-abe9-00144feab7de#comments [accessed 30 April 2017]

Kelliher, C and Anderson, D (2010) Doing more with less? Flexible working practices and the intensification of work, *Human Relations*, **63** (1), pp. 83–106

Krugman, P (2002) The outrage constraint, *New York Times* [online] http://www.nytimes.com/2002/08/23/opinion/the-outrage-constraint.html

Labour Research Department (2013) Workplace Report June 2013: supplements aim to help staff working in and around capital http://www.lrdpublications.org.uk/publications.php?pub=WR&iss=1667&id=id136938

Maslow, A H (1943) A theory of human motivation, *Psychological Review*, **50** (4), p. 370

McFarlin, D B and Sweeney, P D (1992) Distributive and procedural justice as predictors of satisfaction with personal and organizational outcomes, *Academy of Management Journal*, **35** (3), pp. 626–37

NHS (2013) *Job Evaluation Handbook* [online] http://www.nhsemployers.
org/~/media/Employers/Publications/NHS_Job_Evaluation_Handbook.
pdf [accessed 30 April 2017]

ONS (2014) Commuting and Personal Wellbeing 2014 Report,
National Archives [online] http://webarchive.nationalarchives.gov.
uk/20160105231823/http://www.ons.gov.uk/ons/rel/wellbeing/
measuring-national-well-being/commuting-and-personal-well-
being–2014/art-commuting-and-personal-well-being.html

ONS (2017a) Housing Affordability Report, *ONS* [online] https://www.
ons.gov.uk/peoplepopulationandcommunity/housing/bulletins/housingaf
fordabilityinenglandandwales/1997to2016

ONS (2017b) Dataset 'Employment by Industry', *ONS* [online]
https://www.ons.gov.uk/employmentandlabourmarket/peoplein
work/employmentandemployeetypes/datasets/employmentby
industryemp13

Pfeffer, J (1997) Six dangerous myths about pay, *Harvard Business
Review*, **76** (3), pp. 109–19

Pink, D (2009) *Drive: The surprising truth about what motivates us*,
Riverhead Books, New York

Polanyi, M (1966) *The Tacit Dimension*, Doubleday, Garden City, NY

Rauber, C (2016) Is a 21-county 'megaregion' the answer to the Bay Area's
housing and commuting woes? *San Francisco Business Times* [online]
http://www.bizjournals.com/sanfrancisco/news/2016/06/30/bay-area-
commute-housing-costs-megaregion.html

Smith, C (2006) The double indeterminacy of labour power: labour effort
and labour mobility, *Work, Employment and Society*, **20** (2),
pp. 389–402

Smith, J (2016) Australia curbs flow of disgruntled junior doctors,
Financial Times [online] https://www.ft.com/content/38513e9a-a029-
11e6-86d5-4e36b35c3550

Statista (2015) Ratio between CEOs and average workers in world
in 2014, by country, *Statista* [online] https://www.statista.com/
statistics/424159/pay-gap-between-ceos-and-average-workers-in-
world-by-country/

Steers, R M, Sanchez-Runde, C J and Nardon, L (2010) *Management
Across Cultures: Challenges and strategies*, Cambridge University Press

Suzuki, H, Kubo, K and Ogura, K (2011) Employment relations in Japan,
in *International and Comparative Employment Relations: Globalisation
and change*, eds G J Bamber, R D Lansbury and N Wailes, Sage
Publications

Taylor (1911), F W *The Principles of Scientific Management*, Harper, New York

World at Work (2013) Creating a global total rewards system at Unilever (video interview), World at Work [online] https://www.worldatwork. org/adimComment?id=73908 [accessed 30 June 2017]

Wright, E O (2000) Working-class power, capitalist-class interests, and class compromise, *American Journal of Sociology*, **105** (4), pp. 957–1002

10
International training and workforce skills

DANIEL WINTERSBERGER

Learning outcomes

At the end of this chapter, you should be able to:

- understand and evaluate the potential impact of national institutional factors on workplace-level training and development:
  - specifically, to understand the relevance of 'varieties of capitalism' for national training and development infrastructure and training at workplace level;
- understand how training and development schemes can be implemented at organizational level – eg apprenticeships;
- understand some of the key disincentives to train and the potential business case for workplace investment into training and development regardless of institutional context.

Introduction

This chapter is about differences in training practices and infrastructure between different national cultural and institutional contexts. It is not primarily about the training of staff within MNCs. The issue of training in MNCs was covered in Chapter 8 on international staffing, which encompasses topics such as cross-cultural training, the development of international assignees, and specifically, cross-cultural training programmes for expatriates. In this chapter, we will look at some of the differences in workforce skills development between different countries, and examine in more depth what this means for potential employers within these markets.

Before discussing the differences in national training infrastructure and workforce skills development, it is important to familiarize ourselves with some key concepts and frameworks. In Chapter 5, we discussed how different 'varieties of capitalism' (Hall and Soskice, 2001) may impact on HRM in different national contexts. To reiterate briefly, the varieties of capitalism framework of Hall and Soskice differentiates between liberal and coordinated market economies and explains differences in areas such as corporate governance, employee voice and indeed also training and development between firms in coordinated and liberal market economies respectively. In this chapter we will examine what implications the two 'ideal types' of capitalism (on the one hand, liberal market economies such as the UK and US, and on the other hand, coordinated market economies such as Japan and Germany) have for training and development and workforce skills development both within and beyond the organization. We will examine the role of national vocational education and training (VET) infrastructure and how differences between countries shape what sort of skills an employer (for example a multinational aiming to set up a subsidiary) may expect to find in different countries. When we look at workforce skills, knowledge and expertise, it is important to distinguish between skills and knowledge that are specific to a particular organization (for example the ability to use the store management software of McDonald's is specific to McDonald's and can't be meaningfully applied elsewhere) versus those skills that are likely to be 'transferable' to other organizations or even professional contexts. Examples of transferable skills include soft skills such as problem solving, creativity, teamworking, general computer literacy as well as cross-cultural competence and language skills. We will examine how different institutional factors within countries lead to different 'skill equilibria' (low skill versus high skill) in different countries, and how such equilibria impact on the relative comparative advantage of firms in different industries in such countries.

Global labour market developments and their impact on workplace-level training

It was not until the 1920s (ie very recently in the context of human civilization) that fewer people worked in agriculture than in services and manufacturing in advanced industrial economies such as the UK and US. It was in the 1920s, the heyday of the 'industrial revolution' in the UK, that more people were employed in the secondary sector (manufacturing) than in the primary sector (extracting and agriculture). With increasing mechanization, however, by the 1950s, fewer were being employed in manu-facturing than in the tertiary sector (services – encompassing all 'interactive', ie customer-facing work, including retail, hospitality, transport and also consulting and financial services). Since then, employment in both manu-facturing and agriculture has plummeted in comparison to employment in services. In the UK, for example, the service sector currently accounts for over 80 per cent of employment (ONS, 2017b). Similar figures are found the US (Bamber et al, 2015) and other global advanced industrial economies. In Singapore, currently 73 per cent of the population is employed in services (Ministry of Manpower, Singapore, 2017). In emerging economies such as India, the employment rate in services (as percentage of total employment) is significantly lower. In India, for example, employment in services accounts for only 27 per cent of total employment (World Bank, 2017). This is also due to the large informal sector in the Indian economy and the fact that many rural communities still rely on agriculture, but the trend over recent years has been a rapid expansion of the service sectors as a growing middle class is converted from producers to consumers of goods and services and as western firms outsource key functions such as IT and call centres to India. So we can conclude with some degree of certainty that many countries in the world are gravitating towards a dominance of employment in services. The 'factory' of the 21st century is found in the form of call centres and other centres of mass service delivery.

Reflective exercise

Reflect for a minute on the profound transformations of the global labour markets (shift from agriculture and manufacturing to employment in services). What do you think the impact of this has been on workforce skills and the skills required by employers?

Shift from hard to soft skills

What sort of skills do service providers require from their workforce? The 'service sector' encompasses a broad range of industries, spanning diverse sectors such as retail, hospitality, sales, as well as IT and management consulting. Beyond breaking the service sector down by trade as we have done above, it is perhaps also useful to distinguish between low-skill and high-skill service work. The former might include jobs in sectors with low barriers to entry for applicants (in terms of training requirements) such as retail and casual hospitality work, whereas the latter might include those jobs for which more formal qualifications as well as work experience might be required, such as a senior consultant in IT. Moreover, we need to consider the nature of the work. What most service-sector jobs have in common is that those working within these jobs deal predominantly with people rather than inanimate objects and factors of production as they would working on an assembly line in manufacturing, for example. This places distinctive skills requirements on them, and it is likely that those employed in services require on a day-to-day basis a higher degree of soft skills than perhaps they would need in a fairly standardized assembly line job in manufacturing. In high-end service work, advanced technical or product knowledge may be required. Take for example the case of pharmaceutical sales, where often salespeople are trained to a high level and receive a lot of knowledge about the products they are selling. Service work can also be distinguished on the extent to which interactions with customers are high or low volume. A check-in operator working for an agency that provides ground handling services to airlines is likely to have a high volume of daily interactions with customers. In contrast, a high-end private banker may meet only a couple of clients per day, yet the margins associated with the transaction of each interaction may be very significant for their employer.

What all these jobs have in common, though – high margin and low margin, high skill and low skill as well as high volume and low volume – is that they all to some degree require soft skills such as customer service and communication. This is not to argue that such skill requirements are absent in manufacturing sectors. In fact, new forms of work organization and a 'Japanization' of the global manufacturing industry (see Chapter 12) have led to increased task complexity, worker autonomy and importance of interaction, teamworking and problem solving. However, the general absence of a 'tangible' product (ie a physical product) in services makes the human factor and the 'soft skills' more important. While tangible, inanimate factors of production 'behave' fairly predictably, things become more complicated in the provision of an intangible service and therefore those working in the service sector, particularly the more interactive side of service work (eg cabin crew, call centre operatives, receptionists etc) need to have the ability and emotional intelligence to adapt to the needs of different clients/customers/passengers/patients etc. As a result of the profound shift in employment from manufacturing to services, it is not surprising that the priority of organization-level training has also shifted from 'hard' technical knowledge to more 'soft' skills (Laker and Powell, 2011).

While some advanced industrial economies (UK and US) have rates of employment in services of 80 per cent or more, not all comparable countries have had their labour markets transformed to the same extent. In Japan and Germany, for example, the service sector accounts for 'only' 70 per cent of overall employment; it is 68 per cent in South Korea and 71 per cent in the Eurozone overall (World Bank, 2017). Most of the aforementioned countries (with the exception of South Korea) have industrialized at broadly the same time and all of them are at a similarly advanced stage of industrialization, so we would assume that mechanization in manufacturing has progressed to a similar extent as in the UK and US. As a consequence, we might assume that countries such as the UK and US have weaker manufacturing sectors and stronger service sectors than, for example, Germany and Japan, who in turn are likely to have a greater comparative advantage in manufacturing but a disadvantage in services in comparison to the UK. Indeed, it is the case that Germany and Japan have become renowned for their strong manufacturing sectors, whereas the UK and the US have become well known for their strong service economy, including sectors such as banking, finance and high-end consulting. This point is further supported when we look at the relative contribution of manufacturing to overall GDP levels.

Table 10.1 The contribution of the manufacturing sector to GDP

Country	Manufacturing sector (% of GDP)
UK	10
US	12
Eurozone	16
Japan	18
Germany	23
South Korea	30

SOURCE World Bank (2017)

So why is there a stronger manufacturing sector in countries such as South Korea, Germany and Japan and a stronger service sector in the US and UK? A very strong reason is likely to lie in the fact that all of these countries are fairly strong 'ideal types' of different 'varieties of capitalism' (Hall and Soskice, 2001). The varieties of capitalism (VoC) framework has been covered in more depth in Chapter 5, so in this chapter we only apply it to the issue of training and workforce skills.

The 'deficit' view of training in liberal market economies

Liberal market economies (LMEs) are primarily characterized by an economic government policy that is more business friendly and tends to have a 'laissez faire' approach to regulation. This can similarly be applied to workforce skills development. Unlike coordinated market economies (CMEs), there is little government intervention in the form of minimum standards and incentives for training (or penalization for lack thereof) at workplace level in comparison to CMEs. Governments in LMEs such as the UK and the US therefore pursue a more 'voluntarist' approach to training and development insofar as firms are encouraged rather than coerced into providing vocational education and training (Upchurch, 1997). Inter-firm relationships in LMEs are generally more competitive than in CMEs and therefore organizations, well aware of the threat of a competitor company 'poaching' their well-trained workers, are often reluctant training providers.

CASE STUDY The 'deficit' view of training at a liberal market economy low-cost airline – Ryanair

Ryanair is an Irish low-fare airline (LFA) which has rapidly transformed short-haul air travel in Europe by offering significantly lower fares than competitors for over a decade. The airline's CEO, Michael O'Leary, has long been infamous for his abrasive approach in dealing with customers, but has also become notorious for his highly adversarial employment relations policies (O'Sullivan and Gunnigle, 2009). With regard to training and development, Ryanair, consistent with an LFA operating from a liberal market economy, pursues a very 'hard' (Legge, 1995) variant of HRM (Boyd, 2001). Cabin crew are not directly recruited by Ryanair but instead sourced from agencies; Ryanair therefore does not offer any in-house training but has passed the responsibility for training new cabin crew recruits to the legal standard to agencies. Potential cabin crew recruits pay the respective agencies their training costs (nearly £2,000) up front and the remainder in instalments in their first year working for the airline and remain on probation in their first year. Those who are rejected during their probationary period are still pursued for training costs (Pate and Beaumont, 2006).

Beyond the fear of poaching, there exists a further key disincentive to train in LMEs. Decision making within large firms in LMEs is more shareholder driven due to the lower proportion of 'patient' capital (eg bank loans) as found in CMEs (see Chapter 5). The lack of patient capital (and resulting pressure for short-term shareholder value maximization) creates a strong disincentive to train. First, training is costly (Bartel, 2000). With regard to training costs, we need to consider not only the cost of the training programme itself (training staff, equipment, facilities etc), but also the lost working time and productivity of employees during their training programme. Another 'weakness' of training from the perspective of shareholders is that, while it may be beneficial to the firm in the long term (increase in employee morale, productivity and retention – more on these benefits later), it is certainly costly in the short term, and often the payback horizon (return on investment) of training is longer than the investment horizon of outsider shareholders who are looking for more short-term maximization of their share value. Then there is the issue of actually measuring the benefits of training. While cost is clearly quantifiable (work days lost, staff and equipment costs), the benefits of training are actually very difficult (probably impossible) to measure. Moreover, because the benefits of training in the form of improved employee morale, performance and retention accrue steadily over a period of time, it is very difficult for HR managers to make training programmes palatable to investors and the management board.

In order to make the benefits of training more quantifiable, some have turned to measuring 'transfer of training' (Garavaglia, 1993; Saks, Salas and Lewis, 2014) as a proxy of how beneficial a specific training programme is to the organization. By transfer of training we mean the extent to which trainees (ie those being trained) are able to apply the knowledge, skills and expertise they acquire in the training programme to practice in their organization. However, similarly this can't always be reliably measured, and organizations often rely on employee 'self-reporting' (ie self-completed questionnaires) on the extent to which they feel that the training they received is useful and relevant to their job. Of course, such a measure is very crude because employees themselves may not always know how relevant their training is to their job until much later in their career, and self-reporting is usually done upon completion of the training.

A final disincentive for LME employers to train their workforce can be found in the fact that the voluntarist approach to training in LMEs has generated a system where young people, well aware of employers as reluctant training providers, are more likely to enter higher education in an attempt to develop their skills and to have a stronger bargaining position in a competitive labour market. 'Educational attainment' is a benchmark used by the Organization for Economic Cooperation and Development (OECD) as a measure of what percentage of the population has tertiary education. The European country with the lowest rate of tertiary education amongst 25–34-year-olds within their population is Germany, with just under 30 per cent of people in this age group having completed higher education. In contrast, significantly higher educational attainment rates can be found in liberal market economies such as the US (46.5 per cent) and the UK (49.2 per cent) (OECD, 2017a). What does this mean for employers in LMEs? First, they are able to source from a wider pool of graduates with high levels of 'general' skills. In contrast to 'firm-specific' skills and 'tacit knowledge' (more on this later), general skills are transferable between firms and are generally softer in nature than, for example, skills acquired through an apprenticeship. More general and soft skills (as acquired through university education, for example) in turn are likely to be useful for jobs in service work, and the service industry, as discussed earlier, is a more significant contributor to the economy and tends to be stronger in liberal market economies. In a sense, therefore, there is 'institutional complementarity' (Amable, 2000) in LMEs between a fairly market-based approach to training (young people 'buy' their training by entering higher education), the generalist skills acquired as part of higher education and the comparative advantage LMEs such as the UK and US seem to have in services which in turn require more general and soft skills.

We can conclude that there are three, somewhat interrelated disincentives to train in LMEs. First, shareholder demand for short-term returns on investment, second, the 'laissez faire' government approach towards training and development (minimal regulation and intervention) has allowed firms to 'free ride' and draw on a ready supply of highly skilled graduates. This second disincentive indirectly leads to a third and final disincentive. In very voluntarist legal systems (with minimal sanctioning of firms that are reluctant training providers) there is a strong fear that competitors may save on training costs of their own workforce and recruit well-trained and highly skilled employees from other companies – the 'fear of poaching' discussed previously.

Training in coordinated market economies

Consistent with one of the key features of coordinated market economies (high levels of state regulation and involvement in the market), governments in CMEs take a more regulatory and less voluntarist approach towards training provision at organizational level. First, there is more rigid enforcement of minimum standards in terms of content of firm training programmes. Second, higher training levies (a compulsory percentage of payroll employers have to pay into a pot that funds national vocational training) ensure overall higher levels of vocational training. Vocational training, in contrast to higher education, tends to be more firm specific by its very nature, where around half or more of a trainee's time is spent working in a company, with the remainder spent in national vocational education and training colleges which in turn are partly funded by training levies.

A key feature of continental European coordinated market economies such as Germany and Denmark is the 'dual' system of interest representation when it comes to training. This system involves all 'social partners' (including trade unions and employers as well as the state) in the planning and implementation of vocational education and training programmes. Involvement of employers ensures that training provided by national colleges meets the practical needs of business, while involvement of government and trade unions ensures that training provided within companies is of a high standard and meets the skills requirements of the wider economy. **Union involvement in particular** secures skills for employability rather than job- or company-specific skills. This contributes to the need for companies to adapt and innovate. It can be said, therefore, that this system ensures that training meets the needs of employers and employees alike. Moreover, the role of **governments** and **social institutions** in supporting investment in training and the economic performance of companies is essential for this system to work. Particularly in Denmark, there is a legacy of collaborative unions and workplace learning programmes are centrally set and determined to ensure high standards and consistency, while generous state subsidies ensure a high uptake amongst firms and apprentices (Grugulis, 2013: 181).

The apprenticeship route

In contrast to university education, skills knowledge and expertise gained through 'vocational' training, by definition, are less general and tend to be more practical and niche specific. For example, the German conglomerate and largest manufacturing and electronics company in Europe, Siemens, offers an array of pathways as part of their vocational training, offering apprenticeships specializing in various day-to-day jobs such as electrical engineering, production engineering, as well as clerical roles in both office and factory environments (Siemens, 2017). As apprentices are paid (albeit very little) by the organizations in which they are trained, this route has proven very popular in Germany and other continental European CMEs such as Austria, where around half the population opts for the apprenticeship route. Beyond being paid while formally still in training, another advantage that attracts apprentices to the model is the very early clarity of career paths and relatively stable career progression that ensues upon completion of the apprenticeship. Employers, well aware that they have spent substantial amounts of time and money on training their apprentices, are highly likely to hang onto them upon completion of their training, usually in a fairly secure and well-paid job. In Germany and Austria, around 40 per cent of middle-school graduates (aged around 16) opt for continuing their education as part of an apprenticeship. A broad range of options exists both in manufacturing and services. In Austria, around 250 trades can be learnt as part of an apprenticeship and the content of training for each of these trades is continuously revised by the state (Ministry of Education) in consultation with the employers' association (Chamber of Commerce) as well as trade unions, in order to ensure that the content of training meets the needs of all parties. Around 60–80 per cent of the time is spent working in the firm, while 20–40 per cent is spent in schools and colleges where apprentices learn the relevant theory for their trade. Apprentices are paid around 500–800 euros per calendar month to cover basic living costs, and graduate after three years with a certificate confirming that they are a 'master' of their trade. It is clear from this example why many young people in CMEs find apprenticeships desirable. The time is split well between practical, hands-on tasks (in the company) and classroom time to learn relevant theory. Then there is the prospect of being paid a wage from a very young age, despite formally still being in education.

Beyond benefits to the employee, it can be said that employers also benefit from offering apprenticeships. For one thing, they ensure that those who complete the apprenticeship (assuming they will remain with their company, as is often the case) have developed high levels of tacit knowledge and job-specific skills. By tacit knowledge (Polanyi, 1962) we understand the type of knowledge that can't easily be 'codified' (ie imparted to someone by talking them through the process or writing a policy manual) and therefore is best learnt by 'doing', ie working on the job. Because apprentices start their programme at as young as 16 years old and continue for around three years, spending substantial amounts of time in the organization, they gain not only knowledge but also skills. The French language usefully distinguishes between the two verbs: 'connaître' (to be acquainted with or aware of something) and 'savoir' (to actually know how to do something).

Varieties of capitalism and workforce skills development

Recapping on the VoC framework, its significance and the comparative advantage firms in CMEs tend to have in manufacturing (as opposed to services in LMEs), we may see institutional complementarity here in the same way, as having a large proportion of university graduates holding general skills works well in the more service-based economies of LMEs. Apprentices complete their training with high levels of firm-specific skills, tacit knowledge and substantial hands-on experience in a particular segment (eg electrical engineering) within one organization. As such, they certainly hold superior firm-specific knowledge than would a university graduate, but are likely to have spent less time developing other softer and more general skills such as intercultural competence, language and presentation skills.

Apprenticeships are complementary with the higher degrees of employment protection and job security in CMEs such as Japan, Germany and South Korea; where job security is good, people are more inclined to develop firm-specific and tacit knowledge rather than general skills as would be obtained from university. LMEs such as the UK and the US generally have a lower 'employment protection legislation' (EPL) index (OECD, 2017b), meaning that it is easier for employers to get rid of their workforce. Fairly high EPL indices are generally found in CMEs, especially Germany. Overall, it appears therefore that there is strong complementarity in LMEs. Because firms are reluctant training providers, young people opt for more transferable and generalist skills from university which in turn are more useful for a more service-based economy. In CMEs, where employment protection is stronger, more young people choose to go down the vocational education and training (VET) path, which in turn is useful in a more manufacturing-driven economy as is typical for CMEs.

State-managed vocational training and the Taiwanese economic miracle

Taiwan is a good example of how a manufacturing- and export-driven economy has been strengthened by substantial degrees of state intervention in the area of vocational training. Much of Taiwan's staggering economic growth over the last 50 years or so can in one way or another be attributed to the establishment of and continued government investment into vocational education and training. Going back to the late 1950s, a time when more than half of employment in Taiwan was still in agriculture, there was a strong labour shortage, and the government instructed technical colleges to 'use applied science in order to train technical manpower' (ICDF, 2017). This goal was reformulated in 1976 (a period of extremely fast economic growth for Taiwan) to 'teaching applied science **and technology** to train professional personnel with practical skills' (ICDF, 2017 – emphasis added). While in the 1950s, colleges and vocational schools served the purpose of training people for the agricultural sector, this changed in the mid-1960s to 1970s, when demand from the growing manufacturing sector rose for people with practical technical skills, and as a result, from the mid-1960s, the government started rapidly developing higher technical vocational education (ICDF, 2017).

As the significant manufacturing output also required clerical and commercial skills (such as sales, marketing and accounting), the government pushed the establishment of 'commercial vocational schools' in the 1970s. The next big shift came in the 1990s, when the rapid emergence of IT substantially altered the industrial structure. New technologies called for higher-level skills, and as a result of an increasing number of vocational students wanting to pursue higher education, the government allowed technical colleges to convert themselves into 'institutes of technology' (ICDF, 2017). It is arguably due to the substantial degrees of government intervention and participation in the planning of the national VET infrastructure that Taiwan has achieved levels of employment and productivity which are still today the envy of many advanced industrial economies. By proactively intervening in the VET infrastructure, the government has ensured that the skills graduates bring into the labour market exactly meet the skills requirements of the employers but also in the long term allow employers to adapt their technology and production processes to meet competitive productivity levels. In the case of Taiwan, where state intervention in VET went as far as the government determining the content of curricula and even textbooks (Chen, 2002), such strong degrees of central governmental coordination have certainly driven a very productive manufacturing- and export-driven economy and ensured that the country has managed the transition to higher value-added production without any meaningful skills shortage.

Signs of change in LMEs?

So far, this chapter has examined the way in which the socio-political and economic context shapes workforce skill development both at organizational and national level, how quite different skill equilibria (general skills through higher education versus firm-specific skills and tacit knowledge through vocational training) result from these contextual differences, and how these different skill equilibria support the basis of LME (services) and CME (manufacturing) competitive advantage. It is worth noting, however, that there are signs of change in both LMEs and CMEs. In the UK, for example, over the past few years there has been increasing awareness of issues around a lack of 'middle-range' skills (see for example Unwin, 2004) in the workforce and that there is increasing polarization between high and low skills. On the one extreme, unskilled people are finding it increasingly difficult to get employment, while on the other hand, well-trained graduates in the right field and with good work experience are in strong demand and command high salaries. Between the extreme cases of an unskilled worker and a highly skilled graduate, there is a lack of those that hold vocational skills acquired via hands-on training as part of an apprenticeship. Especially in the UK, there has been a lack of trained plumbers (West, 2015) and electricians as well as those from other craft trades (Unwin, 2004) over the past decade, in part as a result of too few apprenticeships being offered by companies, and in part due to reluctance amongst young people to go for the vocational route. Underpinning this widespread reluctance to undergo vocational training are perhaps to some extent the public perceptions of the relative value of vocational training. In the UK, vocational training was long viewed as a route for the 'less able' and less committed pupils to stay in education longer (Unwin, 2004) and as a result, there is a strong disparity between those that enter higher education and those that 'settle for' vocational training.

But there are signs that this is increasingly changing in LMEs. In 2012, the European Commission established the 'Rethinking Education' initiative across all EU member states. This was set up to 'reform education systems across the EU so as to meet growing demand for higher skills levels and reduce unemployment' (European Commission, 2012). One of the key objectives of this initiative is to promote apprenticeships across the EU. Within the UK, the then-chancellor of the exchequer (finance minister) George Osborne promised the UK 3 million new apprenticeships by 2020 and announced that the onus of skills funding was to shift from government to the private sector via an increase to apprenticeship levies. The situation in 2017 is that all UK companies with a payroll cost of over £3 million per year have to pay 0.5 per cent of any payroll cost in excess of £3 million into a pot to fund vocational education and training. Other LMEs also increasingly use an apprenticeship levy to ensure the private sector plays their part in skills funding. Singapore, for example, now has a modest (0.25 per cent of gross salary) 'skills development levy' in place.

The business case for training and development

It is not only governments which increasingly appear to try to coerce employers to provide more and better training to their employees (via the aggressive top-down measure of training levies). Employers themselves are increasingly recognizing the significance of the 'business case' for training. UK employers, for example, are indeed responding to increasing incentives to hire apprentices as they are starting to see the benefits. Apprentices make for a much lower payroll cost than ordinary workers, and although they are not yet fully trained and spend significant amounts of time in colleges, they often make up this fact through high levels of commitment to the organization (Ryan, 1998). Linking this with different dimensions of commitment, as discussed in Chapter 9, we can probably see why apprentices are generally more loyal to their employer, more proactive and prepared to expend discretionary effort (Ryan, 1998). First, the fact that an apprenticeship is a programme (usually three years in duration) means that apprentices are likely to hold high levels of 'continuance' commitment (Allen and Meyer, 1990) towards their employing organization. This is because they are well aware of the implications of terminating their apprenticeship before completion. It is likely that apprentices will also have high levels of affective commitment towards their organization. Signing up for an intensive three-year programme with hard work and lots of learning outside of regular hours requires at least some degree of certainty that the vocational route and company they have chosen appeals to them, and people who enjoy what they do inherently have higher levels of commitment (Porter et al, 1974). Another benefit of enabling young people to enter the company via the apprenticeship route is that it ensures the skills they acquire are relevant to the business, and although some of the training offered as part of vocational training is indeed transferable, apprentices do build substantial amounts of firm-specific tacit knowledge through learning by doing on the job.

CASE STUDY National training infrastructure and competitive advantage in biscuit manufacturing

This case study is based on Mason, Van Ark and Wagner (1994).

In order to better understand the role of national training infrastructure and government policy in determining company practice, it is helpful to do an inter-country comparison of practice within a particular industry. This is exactly what Mason and colleagues did in the context of food processing (specifically biscuit manufacturing) in four European countries: the UK, the Netherlands, France and Germany. The manufacturing systems were systematically compared on the basis of factors such as workforce skills, technology and productivity levels. The authors of the study chose food processing because, as an example of 'light manufacturing', it presents an industry within which the UK traditionally had a smaller productivity gap in comparison to other branches of manufacturing such as automotive. Moreover, food processing plants in the UK were traditionally significantly larger than in other European economies, and so it might be expected that in the context chosen for this study, productivity levels in the UK might be higher than in other countries.

The study found that the sampled plants within all three continental European countries had a higher proportion of 'vocationally qualified' staff within their workforce in comparison to the British plants, where workforce skills appeared to be more polarized between 'unskilled' workers (those with neither a degree nor vocational qualifications), and highly skilled workers (those with a university degree in their field). In the German plants, the majority of workers came from apprenticeships in bakery, and most of the supervisory staff had advanced training and certificates as 'masters' of their trade. This advanced training was in the area of production technology as well as logistical and managerial functions, equipping them to support the production process (eg machine maintenance) and also to proactively improve it. In contrast, in the British plants, there were only very few process workers and hardly any of the supervisors had vocational qualifications.

The authors found that production technology and systems reflected the differences in workforce background. UK plants drew on a very high degree of advanced technology to mechanize, automate and standardize the production process, while the production processes in the continental European plants were less standardized and more manual/craft skills were required from the workforce (Mason et al, 1994). Moreover, the study found that the workforce background, via the aforementioned difference in production mechanisms, also had an impact on the way in which the firms competed. German and French plants focused more on small and medium-sized batch production and a higher degree of product customization and quality rather than price. Inevitably, such an emphasis on customization leaves less scope for trial runs and requires higher degrees of adaptation and improvisation. In contrast, British plants focused more on standardized mass production and an emphasis on economies of scale as a means to compete on the basis of price. Both these competitive approaches appear to be consistent with workforce skills. An emphasis on customization and quality requires skilled craft workers, able to draw on their tacit knowledge (in areas such as dough making and adaptation of machinery) as well as the ability to work in a functionally flexible manner and to continuously solve problems. The UK model, in contrast, requires a small group of highly skilled workers (graduate engineers perhaps) to set up and standardize production processes and unskilled (hence cheaper) workers to follow these standardized routines. It might appear that both these production processes generate their own benefits and have their own downsides. Perhaps we might assume that the British method is more efficient, hence leading to greater efficiency, and that the German method works well under the assumption that their products are sufficiently differentiated for the market to pay a premium for them.

However, the study found that not only the quality but also the productivity was higher in those plants (Netherlands, France and Germany) where the workforce comprised skilled workers. The authors have a simple explanation on this based on their observations. Machine (and hence production process) downtime was overall longer and a more significant impediment to the production in the British plants. This was attributed to the fact that in the continental plants, supervisors with advanced vocational qualifications were able not only to perform routine machine maintenance but also to repair machines temporarily until new machinery was bought or existing machinery was repaired by experts. As a result, the stoppages in the production process were not as long as in the British plants where companies often had to wait for skilled technicians to come in. The emerging productivity advantages in the continental plants in turn further facilitated the emphasis (especially in the German plant) on product quality, product extensions and customization. Smoother production processes allow them to spend more time on experimenting with new ideas, for example biscuit fillings.

Reflective questions

1 Recap on the differences between skills development in LMEs and CMEs. To what extent do you think this case supports this argument?

2 What does this case tell us about the link between workforce skills, production processes, productivity and sources of competitive advantage?

3 Why do you think the authors chose biscuit manufacturing as a representative industry in which to explore inter-country differences?

4 To what extent do you believe that findings from this study are representative of other industries both in manufacturing and services?

5 To what extent do you believe that German companies could compete on cheap mass production and UK companies on customized higher-end products? Explain your answer with reference to national training systems and the likely competitive strategy taken by firms under these circumstances.

Conclusions

In this chapter we have examined the role played by national institutional factors and the resulting training infrastructure (legal constraints etc) in shaping a nation's workforce skills development systems and the impact such systems have on employers, their production systems and technology. By comparing ideal types of liberal and coordinated market economies, the chapter has highlighted the strong and significant 'disincentives' for employers to train their workforce. These disincentives include a fairly 'voluntarist' governmental policy on workforce skills development, and the resulting employer fear of having well-trained workers 'poached' by competitors. We have also examined the way in which employer reluctance as training providers has led to a polarization of the labour force in LMEs between those with high-level general skills on the one hand and a large proportion of unskilled workers on the other. We then looked at the case of biscuit manufacturing to explore how the broader societal issues around workforce skills might be linked with production systems and technology, highlighting that LME firms in manufacturing often compete on the basis of price and fairly standardized goods, whereas firms in CMEs often compete on the basis of higher product quality and customization – a strategy facilitated by having a workforce which, to a large extent, has been vocationally trained.

Key learning points

- National-level training infrastructure and systems of workforce skills development are likely to differ between national contexts.

- These differences are likely to be rooted in institutional factors such as legislation on minimum standards for training as well as the nature of inter-firm relations.

- In liberal market economies, there is a stronger disincentive for employers to train because:

  - laxer legislation on training means that fear of competitors (as reluctant training providers) poaching highly skilled workers is greater;

  - inter-firm relations in liberal market economies are more arm's length, with less inter-firm collaboration.

- As a result, coordinated market economies have a more robust system of workplace vocational education and training, leading to a lower number of people with university degrees and more people with middle-range vocational skills.

- The service economy is therefore stronger in liberal market economies, while the manufacturing sector is comparably more dominant in coordinated market economies.

References

Amable, B (2000) Institutional complementarity and diversity of social systems of innovation and production, *Review of International Political Economy*, 7 (4), pp. 645–87

Allen, N J and Meyer, J P (1990) The measurement and antecedents of affective, continuance and normative commitment to the organization, *Journal of Occupational and Organizational Psychology*, 63 (1), pp. 1–18

Bamber, G J, Lansbury, R D and Wailes, N (2015) *International and Comparative Employment Relations: National regulation, global changes*, Allen & Unwin

Bartel, A P (2000) Measuring the employer's return on investments in training: evidence from the literature, *Industrial Relations*, 39 (3), pp. 502–24

Boyd, C (2001) HRM in the airline industry: strategies and outcomes, *Personnel Review*, 30 (4), pp. 438–53

Chen, J J (2002) Reforming textbooks, reshaping school knowledge: Taiwan's textbook deregulation in the 1990s, *Pedagogy, Culture & Society*, 10 (1), pp. 39–72

European Commission (2012) Rethinking Education [online] http://ec.europa.eu/education/policy/multilingualism/rethinking-education_en

Garavaglia, P L (1993) How to ensure transfer of training, *Training & Development*, 47 (10), pp. 63–69

Grugulis, I (2013). Employment in service and the service sector, in *Managing Services: Challenges and innovation*, eds K Haynes and I Grugulis, Oxford University Press

Hall, P A and Soskice, D, eds (2001) *Varieties of Capitalism: The institutional foundations of comparative advantage*, Oxford University Press

ICDF, 2017 Sharing Taiwan's experience in technical and vocational education and training [online] http://www.icdf.org.tw/ct.asp?xItem=40484&ctNode=29877&mp=2

Laker, D R and Powell, J L (2011) The differences between hard and soft skills and their relative impact on training transfer, *Human Resource Development Quarterly*, **22** (1), pp. 111–22

Legge, K (1995) What is human resource management? In *Human Resource Management: Rhetorics and realities*, ed K Legge, Macmillan Education UK, pp. 62–95

Mason, G, Van Ark, B and Wagner, K (1994) Productivity, product quality and workforce skills: food processing in four European countries, *National Institute Economic Review*, **147** (1), pp. 62–83

Ministry of Manpower, Singapore (2017) Labour market statistical information [online] http://stats.mom.gov.sg/Pages/Employment-Summary-Table.aspx

OECD (2017a) Population with Tertiary Education, *OECD Data* [online] https://data.oecd.org/eduatt/population-with-tertiary-education.htm

OECD (2017b) Indicators of employment protection. http://www.oecd.org/els/emp/oecdindicatorsofemploymentprotection.htm

ONS (2017b) Dataset 'Employment by Industry', *ONS* [online] https://www.ons.gov.uk/employmentandlabourmarket/peopleinwork/employmentandemployeetypes/datasets/employmentbyindustryemp13

O'Sullivan, M and Gunnigle, P (2009) 'Bearing All the Hallmarks of Oppression': union avoidance in Europe's largest low-cost airline, *Labor Studies Journal*, **34** (2), pp. 252–70

Pate, J M and Beaumont, P B (2006) The European low-cost airline industry: the interplay of business strategy and human resources, *European Management Journal*, **24** (5), pp. 322–29

Polanyi, M (1962) Tacit knowing: its bearing on some problems of philosophy, *Reviews of modern physics*, **34** (4), p. 601

Porter, L W et al (1974) Organizational commitment, job satisfaction, and turnover among psychiatric technicians, *Journal of Applied Psychology*, **59** (5), p. 603

Ryan, P (1998) Is apprenticeship better? A review of the economic evidence, *Journal of Vocational Education & Training*, **50** (2), pp. 289–325

Saks, A M, Salas, E and Lewis, P (2014) The transfer of training, *International Journal of Training and Development*, **18** (2), pp. 81–83

Siemens (2017) Overview of apprenticeships offered (in German) [online] http://w5.siemens.com/web/at/de/corporate/portal/jobs_karriere/lehrlinge/pages/lehrlinge.aspx

Unwin, L (2004) Growing beans with Thoreau: rescuing skills and vocational education from the UK's deficit approach, *Oxford Review of Education*, **30** (1), pp. 147–60

Upchurch, M (1997) 'Social partnerships', the market and trade-union involvement in training: Britain and Germany compared, *Journal of European Social Policy*, **7** (3), 191–208

West, K (2015) UK needs plumbers, builders and engineers as skill crisis hits economy, *Guardian* [online] https://www.theguardian.com/business/2015/feb/10/uk-plumbers-builders-engineers-skill-crisis-economy

World Bank (2017) Employment in services as % of total employment [online] http://data.worldbank.org/indicator/SL.SRV.EMPL.ZS?end=2010&locations=IN&start=2010

11
International employee relations

GERAINT HARVEY

Learning outcomes

At the end of this chapter you should understand:

- what employee relations is;

- how workers add value to the firm (human capital);

- how and why the firm seeks to secure maximum value from the worker (labour process) and how the worker might resist (labour power);

- different ways of seeing the firm (frames of reference);

- why management offer workers a degree of influence in the firm and what affects their decision to do so; and finally,

- how globalization has affected employee relations.

Introduction

The purpose of this chapter is to introduce you to the theory and practice of *employee relations*. The chapter begins by introducing employee relations in the contemporary business environment – one in which the notion of an employment relationship (between a firm and the worker it employs) is being increasingly eroded by commercial relationships (between a firm and the worker it contracts for a specific amount of work). Employee relations is relevant for all workers within a firm and is essentially about the way in which management encourages workers to meet the objectives of the firm. The chapter covers a number of scholarly concepts, identified in the Learning Outcomes above, and considers the application of employee relations in the international context of civil aviation.

What are the dimensions of employee relations?

In the UK, the term employee relations has increasingly replaced 'industrial relations' because of the association between the latter and a manufacturing sector that has been in decline in the UK for many years (see Edwards, 2003). The study of employee relations is relevant both for those who are employed (be that full-time, part-time or zero-hours contractors) and those whose status in the gig economy is ambiguous. Under this system, workers are hired for a specific gig as an independent contractor 'working only to complete a particular task or for defined time and with no more connection with their employer than there might be between a consumer and a particular brand of soap or potato chips' (Friedman, 2014: 171). Employee relations is likewise relevant for those who are only nominally self-employed, ie those working under conditions of false self-employment (Davis, 2015) or bogus self-employment. Common characteristics of bogus self-employment include the absence of worker control over the price of their labour (ie tendering), working time and work routine. It is a system whereby 'workers are improperly engaged on a self-employed basis in order to evade the tax and insurance costs of direct employment' (Behling and Harvey, 2015: 970). Consequently, the term 'worker' is used instead of 'employee'.

Employee relations is a broad concept that encompasses all aspects of the relationship between the employer (represented by management) and the worker. It remains a 'central feature of organizational life' (Blyton and Turnbull, 2004: 3) because of its importance both to the organization and to the individual worker. Employee relations is then 'about people: people interacting with one another, pursuing objectives, reaching agreements, engaging in co-operative and conflictual behaviour' (Blyton and Turnbull, 2004: 7). We return to each of these in due course, but to begin with, the employment relationship comprises two components: *market relations* and *managerial relations* (Edwards, 2003: 8). The former, market relations, refers to the price of labour and so workers might participate in determining wages, hours of work, holidays and pension entitlement and so on. The latter, managerial relations, refers to the amount of work carried out within working hours, the tasks to be covered in that time and the penalties to be imposed for failure to meet one's obligations. It is this latter component that covers what and how much work is done, which is the more problematic as it encapsulates aspects that are fluid, 'open-ended and uncertain', subject to interpretation and open to continual negotiation.

Reflective question

What is the difference between market relations and managerial relations?

Let's proceed by exploring worker potential and how the worker might contribute to the competitive advantage of the firm, or in other words, how they may add value.

Human capital

The value of the worker might be understood according to dimensions of human capital defined as 'knowledge, skills and energies and, underpinning these ... physical and emotional health, intellectual capabilities, personality and motivations' (Boxall, 2014: 579). It is possible to extricate four dimensions of human capital.

Intellectual Capital

First, *intellectual capital* is often used interchangeably with human capital. Intellectual capital refers to the knowledge, skills and abilities possessed by workers as they relate to the technical functioning of one's work, or the 'cognitive complexity and the capacity to learn, together with the tacit and explicit knowledge, skills and expertise an individual builds over time' (Gratton and Ghoshal, 2003: 3). Explicit knowledge refers to knowledge that can be codified and articulated easily, whereas tacit knowledge is intuitive and difficult for a worker to explain how they came by it (Polanyi, 1962). Intellectual capital is linked with *emotion capital*.

Emotion capital

Whereas the intellectual capital refers to the potential for a worker to carry out a task with *technical* efficacy, *emotion capital* refers to the potential for a worker to carry out a task with *affective* efficacy. Emotion capital is the potential for the worker to engage in emotional labour (Hochschild, 1983; see also Bolton and Boyd, 2003) or the management of facial and bodily display to meet the expectations of customers, for example.

Physical capital

Physical capital is a concept developed by Bourdieu (1984) which links the individual's aesthetic to their social class. However, it has been used by others (see for example Harvey, Vachhani and Williams, 2014) to indicate the potential for the employee to benefit the firm through their aesthetic labour, for example their physical attractiveness, how they dress etc (see for example Witz, Warhurst and Nickson, 2003; Warhurst and Nickson, 2009).

Social capital

Finally, *social capital* is distinctive from the other dimensions because it refers to one's potential to be effective as a consequence of one's social network. Social capital is 'the sum of resources, actual or virtual, that accrue to an individual or a group by virtue of possessing a durable network' (Bourdieu and Wacquant, 1992: 1190), or to offer the more succinct synopsis, 'who one knows, and how well one knows them' (Gratton and Ghoshal, 2003: 3). See Burt (2001) for a more elaborate discussion.

The labour process and labour power

Why is this discussion of human capital relevant to a chapter on employee relations? First, it demonstrates the various ways in which the worker might add value to the firm, or from another perspective, the range of things that might be commodified through a broadened labour process. The labour process, as articulated by Braverman (1974), refers to the way in which work is degraded and intensified within the capitalist system that drives firms to exchange their produce for a price greater than the cost of production. To generate a price greater than the cost of production, management invariably seek production cost reduction that often involves reducing relative labour costs, ie increasing productivity (work intensification), and/or reducing absolute labour costs, ie paying less for labour (degradation). For more on the labour process, see Thompson (1989).

Reflective question

What is the labour process? Why might firms within the capitalist system degrade and intensify work?

Second, the brief discussion of human capital highlights the importance of potential. Management select workers on the basis of their human capital as presented during the selection process, eg what qualifications and experience the worker has (intellectual capital), how the worker behaves during the interview/how they respond to questions (emotion capital), who the worker has worked with previously (social capital) and how they appear at interview (physical capital). However, no firm can extract human capital and there is no guarantee of the extent to which the worker will utilize their human capital to benefit the firm.

Reflective question

With reference to the four dimensions discussed above, in what ways and to what extent are workers able to limit their use of human capital?

The indeterminacy of labour power (see for example Smith, 2006) is the term used to describe the absence of guaranteed effort on the part of the worker. Workers are able to impose sanctions on the firm by withholding their labour power.

The disruptive capacity of labour power

Workers can disrupt the production, distribution and/or the exchange of goods and services (Batstone, 1988) via i) strike action, whereby workers withdraw their labour for a period of time, or ii) what has been referred to as 'ca'canny', whereby workers restrict the quantity and quality of work (Dubois, 1979: 45). Workers who have a high degree of human capital have the skills that are in demand and can therefore more effectively disrupt the processes of production, distribution and/or the exchange of goods and services. The disruptive ability of workers might be due to a shortage of skills in the labour market, so that employees cannot readily be replaced (Batstone, 1988) and/or the location of workers within workplace operations, whereby their skills are central to operations. The disruptive capacity of workers based on their importance to the firm's operations is known as structural power (Wright, 2000; see also Harvey and Turnbull, 2012a; Donaghey et al, 2014).

Reflective question

In what ways can labour power be used against the firm?

Asymmetry of power in the employment relationship

The balance of power between management and worker (or labour) is fundamental to our understanding of employee relations and to suggest that workers have the upper hand in the employment relationship is absurd. An asymmetry of power exists (Blyton and Turnbull, 2004: 41) but management is certainly the dominant actor in the employment relationship. Workers depend upon the firm for an income far more than the firm depends upon any individual worker – or as the well-known idiom has it:

'no one is indispensable', even the most structurally significant worker. It is in the interests of the worker for the firm to succeed so that it persists as an employer. Moreover, the success of the firm means that it is in a better position to reward staff and meet demands for improved terms and conditions (although it has been argued that better financial performance enables the firm to better withstand the disruptive capacity of labour power and therefore more inclined to resist the demands of workers: see Martin (1992: 29–30)). At this level, there is a commonality of interest between management and the worker in the sense that both want the firm to succeed and neither want the firm to fail. Commonality of interests brings us neatly onto the 'frames of reference' (Fox, 1974).

Frames of reference and structured antagonism

Fox identifies three frames of reference, two of which are considered here. Fundamental to the unitary frame of reference is commonality of interests between management and worker and the belief that the firm is comprised of workers motivated to act in the economic interests of the firm. According to this frame of reference the interests of workers and of management are fundamentally aligned so that the natural state of the workplace should be one of harmony. Conflict in the workplace is considered to be abnormal, indicative either of a failure on the part of management to manage effectively or that there are deviant individuals in the workforce. Conflict, it is argued, can and should be eliminated by competent managers. Whereas the unitary frame of reference is the more common within HRM scholarship, pluralism dominates the field of employee relations. The pluralist frame of reference accepts the basic commonality of interest as set out above, but holds that there are nonetheless myriad interests that motivate members of the firm. A difference of interests is most stark between the management and the worker. Consequently, conflict between these groups is inevitable (Fox, 1974).

The consequent tensions in the employment relationship are at the heart of what Edwards (1990) refers to as a 'structured antagonism'. For instance, the interests of workers are served both by cooperating with management in order to meet the economic goals of the firm, or as Burawoy and Wright (1990: 256) put it, 'workers have positive interests in the profitability and survival of the firms for which they work' in order to keep their job because 'unemployment represents a cost to workers', and by resisting management in order to meet their own economic interests/challenge their exploitation. Management, on the other hand, at once and the same time seek to control workers and also to harness their creativity (intellectual capital). Control in the form of rules is problematic because of the nature of and response to rules. Rules can be either formal or informal. Informal rules can emerge unintentionally and often serve to undermine management prerogative; for example, a single instance of goodwill might generate a 'custom and practice rule', whereby 'managements may unwittingly allow one-off concessions to grow into established expectations' if 'workers have the power to insist that the expectations are honoured' (see Edwards, 2003: 14). Formal rules, on the other hand, set out conditions that can be used against management in certain circumstances, as in the case of *work to rule* whereby workers adhere strictly to rules set out by management to the detriment of efficiency. In short, control invites resistance and so worker consent is necessary.

Organizational commitment has proven highly influential as an alternative to control and a more optimal means of securing worker effort (Walton, 1985). Commitment has become the dominant focus of studies within mainstream HRM literature, so much so that warnings have been issued about the psychologization of employee relations; that research omits the broader socio-legal context of the employment relationship and focuses solely on management practice and the attitudinal response of employees (see Godard, 2014).

Degree of influence

Consent has traditionally been sought via participation, ie offering workers the opportunity to participate in the decision-making processes that govern the employment relationship. The degree of worker influence (Marchington et al, 1992; Marchington and Suter, 2013) is affected by various factors and stakeholders. For example, the degree of worker influence waxes and wanes in correlation with management need for consent (and compliance) (see Ramsay, 1977).

Degree of worker influence and the state

The state and the trade union also play a role in the degree of worker influence. The state exerts influence over the employment relationship by setting minimum and maximum thresholds in terms of wages (national minimum wage) and hours of work, for example. The state also indirectly influences the employment relationship through its relationship with trade unions, offering them a more conducive environment in exchange for moderation in negotiation, for example the UK social contract of the 1970s (Edwards, 2003: 10). The impact of the state on the degree of worker influence is manifested in its support for a certain type of employee relations, such as partnership (discussed below) and in legislation that strengthens or erodes the negotiating position of the trade union. For example, the Employment Relations Act of 1999 introduced by New Labour provided a statutory procedure for union recognition in organizations employing 21 or more workers, while the Conservative government introduced the Trade Union Act of 2016 that increased both the minimum turnout for strike action to be lawful and the notice given to employers for strike action (from 7 to 14 days). The different role played by the state in employee relations in various national contexts has been covered in detail by Bamber et al (2011) and Frege and Kelly (2013).

It should be noted that labour can apply pressure on the state so that it supports the degree of worker influence. The political influence of labour is perhaps best understood in its ability to mobilize public opinion in support of its aims. However, labour power and public opinion have a 'perverse' relationship whereby public support increases when there is a legislative/state environment that favours management over labour, such as during the years of the Thatcher government in the UK (1979–92) and the Reagan administration in the US (1981–89), and declines in an environment where the legislative/state environment creates more conducive conditions for labour (Martin, 1992: 44–45). One final point on public opinion concerns the way in which trade unions have attempted to enhance their degree of influence by 'demonstrating the complementarity of workers' and consumers' interests' (Heery, 1993: 288), thereby winning the support of customers. In its most 'ambitious' form, trade unions have 'mounted broad-based campaigns which have been designed to articulate producer and consumer opposition to government or management policy' (Heery, 1993).

Degree of worker influence and the trade union

Second, the trade union and its ability to organize effective collective action also contributes to the degree of worker influence. The trade union, as an association of wage earners for the purpose of maintaining or improving conditions of working life, is 'independent of the employers with which it negotiates or seeks to negotiate' (Farnham and Pimlott, 1995: 105–06) and represents the interests of its members. It should be noted that trade unions have had a duality of purpose, both in representing members ('vested interests') and wielding a 'sword of justice' (Flanders, 1970: 15) by 'exerting a major egalitarian influence on the British labour market' (Metcalf, Hansen and Charlwood, 2001: 74).

The potential for and efficacy of collective action that strengthens the bargaining position of the trade union and increases the degree of worker influence is determined by the associational power of labour (Wright, 2000) encompassing the density of trade union membership and propensity of the membership to participate in sanctions imposed on the firm (see also Offe and Wiesenthal, 1980). Associational power must also be mobilized by the trade union, whereby the trade union effectively defines the interest of the membership in contrast to the interests of management (Kelly, 1998: 25).

Reflective question

In what ways do the state and trade unions affect the degree of worker influence?

Management style

Management style has implications for the degree of worker influence. Purcell (1987) presents a range of management styles that might be charted along two dimensions: individualism and collectivism. The first refers to the way in which management deploys and develops the individual within the firm: whether the firm establishes strong internal labour markets and invests in employee development, or whether management views the employee as a cost or a commodity to be exploited (Purcell, 1987: 536–37). Collectivism, on the other hand, is synonymous with traditional industrial relations, focusing on whether or not management considers it right and appropriate for employees to participate in the decision-making processes of the firm. Purcell (1987) identifies three distinctive styles towards collectivism: unitary, adversarial and cooperative. The first holds that management are best placed to determine the nature of work and so representative participation is inappropriate and to be avoided. The second acknowledges that whereas employees have a right to participate in the decision-making processes of the firm, management relate to labour representatives not as collaborators in the interests of the firm but as adversaries whose interests are largely incongruent with the interests of management.

Labour-management partnership

Finally, cooperative collectivism is manifest in firms wherein management actively engages with labour representatives and this represents the ideal form of what has become known as *partnership* (Bacon and Samuel, 2016; Johnstone and Wilkinson, 2016). The Involvement and Partnership Association (IPA) is a not-for-profit organization whose advisory board includes members from the Confederation of Business Industry (representing employers) and the Trades Union Congress (representing trade unions and workers). The IPA sets out the underlying principles of partnership as:

- joint commitment to the success of the organization;
- joint recognition of each other's legitimate interests;
- joint commitment to employment security;
- joint focus on the quality of working life;
- joint commitment to operating in a transparent manner;
- joint commitment to add value to the arrangement (IPA, nd).

Partnership between management and trade unions became increasingly popular following the parliamentary election of New Labour in the UK in 1997. Advocates claim that partnership represents a 'revamped' version of pluralism (a recognition of different but legitimate interests of the partners) and an opportunity for enhanced worker influence as trade unions work in concert with management (see Ackers and Payne, 1998). Scholarly opinion has been mixed, however (see Heery, 2002; Roche and Geary, 2002), and research reveals similarly diverse outcomes (Samuel, 2014; Evans, Harvey and Turnbull, 2012a). Indeed, critics have argued that moderation on the part of trade unions (often associated with partnership) is potentially damaging to employee relations and the broader labour movement. Through moderation and collaboration with management towards achieving the goals of the firm rather than militancy, resistance and striving wholly to achieve the interests of its members, it is argued, the trade union loses its purpose (Kelly, 1998). Indeed, research has shown disaffection on the part of trade union members with their trade union following partnership (see for example Marks et al, 1998; Johnstone, Wilkinson and Ackers, 2004).

Globalization and employee relations

As discussed above, the state plays an influential role in employee relations and the role and orientation of the state towards employee relations is very different around the world (see Chapter 5). The context in which a firm is situated is critical for the nature of employee relations and the degree of influence of labour. For example, investment in training is effectively mandated by law in Germany and France, whereas no such training regulation exists in the UK (see Grugulis, 2016).

The liberalization of product and labour markets and the consequent increased international competition provides firms with greater choice in terms of where they are able to sell their product or service and where they are able to resource their operations, including the human resource. From the 1960s onwards, numerous multinational companies relocated parts of their operations in order to benefit from lower personnel costs (for example, see Gereffi, 2006), or have used the threat of relocation to weaken the degree of worker influence and extract concessions from labour, especially within inherently international operations such as civil aviation. Airlines have used outsourcing to reduce the cost of ancillary functions such as catering and ground handling (see Sull, 1999), and the threat of outsourcing has been used during collective bargaining negotiations with trade unions in order to gain concessions and reduce the cost of functions carried out in-house (Turnbull, Blyton and Harvey, 2004). More recently, the process of reshoring (Gray et al, 2013) has emerged, but the extent of such activity is limited, certainly within specific industries, such as automotive (Bailey and De Popris, 2014).

This process of capital seeking the most favourable conditions 'where labour standards are lowest and regulatory institutions least restrict management prerogatives' (Traxler and Woitech, 2000) is commonly referred to as 'regime shopping'. Multinational corporations have also sought 'spatial juridical fixes' (Lillie, 2010) whereby capital exploits the lack of clarity in national sovereignty in order to sustain seemingly illegitimate practices. By operating in the cracks between national systems of employment legislature, the multinational corporation thereby circumvents the power of the state and undermines the degree of worker influence (see Marginson, 2016). Both regime shopping and the spatial juridical fix are examples of the mobility of capital (Mundell, 1963) and reflect the options available to multinational corporations to choose the most conducive institutional setting and threaten the degree of worker influence. This new challenge to worker influence requires that the trade union 'scale shift' (Tarrow, 2005) and move beyond its traditional national locus of activity to operate at the transnational level, something trade unions are less adept at (Crouch, 2009).

CASE STUDY International civil aviation and employee relations

This section will explore employee relations within an industry that is inherently international. Civil aviation is critical in effecting and deeply affected by globalization, or in other words it is 'a cause and object of globalization' (Blyton et al, 2001: 448). Moreover, there are distinctive features of the industry that make employee relations different from other industries and crucial to the success of airlines. The case study will focus on the low-fares sector of the European and North American civil aviation industries, specifically featuring Ryanair, Norwegian Air International and Southwest Airlines. These airlines demonstrate the success of different employee relations strategies within the same industry and among airlines with broadly similar strategic orientations, ie offering low-cost flights. As the chapter shows, Norwegian Air International and Ryanair have been successful in following what Milkman (1998) refers to a *low road* to employee relations, marked by a low degree of worker influence, low levels of training and low wages. Southwest Airlines, on the other hand, offers a paradigm example of the *high road* to employee relations whereby the degree of work influence is high, as is investment in training, and wages at the airline are among the highest of employees in the US airline industry.

Civil aviation liberalization

The liberalization of the civil aviation product market and deregulation of the labour market in Europe that began in the 1980s provided airline management with the motive and opportunity to pursue innovative strategies and cut costs (Milkman, 1998). The liberalization of civil aviation, for example in the 1970s (United States) and 1980s (Europe), brought to an end the bi-lateral agreements between countries that restricted airline choice of base and destination.

Since liberalization, airlines possess even greater mobility of capital in the sense that the site of operations can be changed with relative ease in order to take advantage of benefits elsewhere. This poses a direct challenge to the degree of worker influence. For example, in July 2015, Ryanair decided to close its base at Billund airport in Denmark after a dispute with staff and their trade union, 3F, over pay and working conditions. In its explanation as to why it was closing the Danish base, the airline stated that the 'Danish model' of employment relations could not be applied to the airline industry (Crouch, 2015).

Why is employee relations important in civil aviation?

The civil aviation industry directly employs around 9.9 million people worldwide, a further 11.9 million indirectly and supports around 63 million jobs worldwide (Aviation Benefits Beyond Borders, nd). Many of those employed directly, such as cabin crew and ground staff, are front-line service-sector workers dealing with customers (passengers). The productivity of staff – the rate at which they work – is important for all airlines, and especially so for low-fares airlines, while the performance of staff (aesthetic labour and, more importantly, emotional labour) is likewise important for all airlines, and especially so for legacy or full-service airlines. A distinctive feature of the management of front-line service workers is the control imposed by the customer (Bélanger and Edwards, 2013; Korczynski et al, 2000). Recent high-profile incidents from the US civil aviation industry reveal the way in which customer surveillance of staff can have a significant impact on the airline. Take for instance the case of Dr David Dao, who in April 2017 was filmed being dragged from a United Airlines flight by security staff (Stanglin, 2017) or the case of the member of Delta Air Lines staff who was filmed 'slapping' a mobile phone from the hand of a 13-year-old passenger in July 2016 (Bazaraa, 2017).

Employee relations is further complicated by certain factors that are peculiar to civil aviation.

Cyclical demand for air transport

To begin with, demand for air transportation (expressed as revenue passenger kilometres, RPKs) is *cyclical* in that it follows fluctuations in economic growth (expressed by Gross Domestic Product, GDP), with demand increasing or decreasing as GDP grows or contracts, but at a much faster rate. The cyclical nature of air transport demand often leads to conflict between labour and management because the expectations of either are 'out of sync' with respect to current and future market conditions. A downturn in demand usually leads to greater cost control and reduced spend often impacting the employment relationship, with employees expected to make concessions such as accepting a pay freeze or pay cuts or the suspension of allowances such as staff travel (see Turnbull and Harvey, 2001; Harvey and Turnbull, 2009). However, increased demand rarely results in the immediate reinstatement of pay and benefits conceded in the downturn as managers are typically cautious, anticipating the next downturn in an increasingly competitive environment (Doganis, 2006: 137–38). For the employee, however, who is dealing with an increasing number of passengers and perceives the airline to be in rude (financial) health, there is an understandable expectation of improvements in terms and conditions.

Perishable nature of the airline service

Employee relations are also affected by the perishable nature of what the airline sells; airlines cannot stockpile seats on cancelled flights for use on another occasion. Therefore, flight cancellations have an immediate and direct impact on an airline's performance and so industrial action by employees can be extremely costly. Strike action by pilots has an immediate effect because the aircraft cannot take off without a pilot (Harvey, 2007) and so sanctions imposed by pilots employed by Lufthansa and Air France in 2014 cost the airlines an estimated €174 million and €500 million respectively. The threat of a strike action alone can lead to a loss of revenue as passengers transfer to other airlines (see Harvey, 2007: 113). Disgruntled airline staff are bad for customer service, for instance if they withhold their emotional labour or go on 'smile strike' (Fuller and Smith, 1991), while disruptive staff are disastrous for the bottom line. Therefore, the consent and compliance of the workforce are paramount. In addition, labour costs remain a sizeable proportion of an airline's operating costs, representing the single largest operation cost for US airlines (Stalnaker, Usman and Taylor, 2016). Labour costs are also one of the few costs that airline management can adjust, unlike (quasi-)fixed costs such as landing charges. Thus, airline cost-cutting initiatives invariably focus on labour costs (see Harvey and Turnbull, 2009).

Importance of employee performance

Finally, employee performance and the competitive advantage of airlines are intrinsically linked. In the decade to May 2014, European low-fares airlines grew at an average of 14 per cent per annum whereas legacy airlines grew by only 1 per cent per annum (Harvey and Turnbull, 2014: 13). The dominant European low-fares airlines, such as Ryanair, easyJet and Norwegian, have been exceptionally successful as a direct result of employee relations strategies that demand greater productivity from their staff but at a reduced cost, leading to both a cost gap and a productivity gap between the low-fares airlines and legacy airlines. Data on labour costs as a percentage of revenue reveals the labour 'cost gap' between legacy and low-fares airlines with Ryanair and easyJet at 9.5 and 12.4 per cent respectively compared with Lufthansa and the IAG group at 22.8 and 23.5 per cent respectively (see Harvey and Turnbull, 2014: 18). Data from airline financial statements for 2012 compiled by the CAPA Centre for Aviation illustrates the sheer scale of the 'performance gap'; the operating profit per employee at Ryanair (€80,943) was more than 10 times that of British Airways (€8,030). Consequently, legacy airlines have redoubled their efforts to replicate elements of the low-cost model and these gaps are narrowing (see Harvey and Turnbull, 2017). Recent low-cost subsidiary ventures by Lufthansa (Germanwings) and KLM-Air France (Transavia) have been successful, especially in terms of reducing labour costs within the airline. Alternatively, legacy airlines have been pioneered a two-tier workforce. British Airways, for example, introduced the Mixed Fleet, a workforce hired on inferior terms and conditions of employment compared to those of their colleagues. Time will tell whether its new venture, Level, offering low-fare transatlantic flights will be successful.

Reflective question

What conditions unique to civil aviation make employee relations more problematic and why?

Degree of worker influence at low-fares airlines

The low-fares airlines have also limited the degree of influence of their workers using strategies that range from *oppressive individualism* at Ryanair, ie the use of coercive measures to avoid trade unions (O'Sullivan and Gunnigle, 2009; see also Harvey and Turnbull, 2014; 2015) and *legislative circumvention* at Norwegian (discussed below), to *obstructive accommodation* marked by 'delaying tactics, prevarication, stalling, and at times outright hostility' at easyJet (Harvey and Turnbull, 2012b: 33).

European low-fares airlines are now able to *adopt* and *adapt* the maritime practice of flags of convenience and crews of convenience as a way of redefining the employment relationship, strengthening the position of management and leading to greater imbalance in the asymmetry of power. Ryanair have for some time claimed that as all cabin crew work for an Irish company – the aircraft where cabin crew work represents Irish territory – they are subject to Irish labour law (often leading to inferior terms and conditions to those they might expect if they were classified as a worker of the nation in which they are based) (see Harvey and Turnbull, 2012b). However, the clearest example of the crew of convenience strategy is Norwegian Air International, a subsidiary of Norwegian Air Shuttle, which is seeking to exploit the new market opportunities created through the negotiation of open skies agreements with non-EU countries, most notably the United States.

Norwegian Air International

Founded in 1993, the Norwegian Air Group is the third-largest low-fares airline in Europe and sixth-largest in the world, flying around 30 million passengers in 2016 (Norwegian Air, nd). Around half its flights are now between 'foreign' countries, neither taking off nor landing in Norway. In order to completely break all ties between labour, location and (operating) licence, the airline's new subsidiary, Norwegian Air International, has acquired an Irish Air Operator's Certificate (AOC). Bjorn Kjos, CEO of the Norwegian Air Group, has argued that the Irish AOC simply permits the airline greater flexibility in terms of its route network and benefits due to Ireland's adoption of the Cape Town Convention that also increases finance and credit options (Silva, 2016). However, Irish registration has been seen by others as a 'convenient flag' enabling Norwegian Air International to escape from national (Nordic) class compromises and exploit the EU–US Open Skies Agreement (Zander, 2014). Trade unions have pointed out that Norwegian Air International's international base strategy is estimated to save around 50 per cent on salary costs, enabling the appointment of flight and cabin crew from Singapore and Thailand respectively. Cabin crew at the airline are paid as little as NOK 3,000 per month (around €370) which is below the minimum wage in Norway and many other parts of Europe (Airport Watch, 2014).

Reflective questions

1   How do low-fares airlines achieve a competitive advantage through their staff?

2   What are the potential consequences of employee relations strategies such as those used by the European low-fares airlines?

The high road to employee relations at Southwest Airlines

In stark contrast to the low-road approach to employee relations at European low-fares airlines discussed above is the high-road approach to employee relations at Southwest Airlines (SWA). All low-fares airlines have to a greater or lesser extent replicated the original low-cost operating model developed by SWA. However, none have adopted the airline's employee relations strategy, despite the fact that the company's people strategy is at the heart of its sustained competitive advantage. SWA is now the largest US domestic carrier, with a market share in February 2017 of just under 30 per cent compared to around 18 per cent held by the next largest, American Airlines. It has recorded 40 years of consecutive profitability, carrying more than 100 million passengers in 2016 and with a net income of $372 million for the first quarter of 2017 (SWA, 2017).

Southwest Airlines: FUN-loving and good to work for

This success has been achieved in no small part due to the 'FUN-loving attitude' of its 54,000 staff who are keen to demonstrate their 'servant's heart' to provide passengers with a novel flight experience (the three values promoted by Southwest Airlines are the servant's heart, warrior spirit and FUN-loving attitude (SWA, nd)). The employee relations strategy as expressed by founder and former CEO, Herb Kelleher, is encapsulated in the statement: 'You put your employees first. If you truly treat your employees that way, they will treat your customers well, your customers will come back, and that's what makes your shareholders happy' (quoted by McDermott et al, 2013: 306). Treating staff well includes industry-leading pay and benefits. SWA is one of the highest-paying airlines in America and frequently appears in the list of 'best 100 US companies to work for' (Bamber et al, 2009: 4–5; Freiberg and Freiberg, 1996; Gittell, Von Nordenflycht and Kochan, 2004) making it a very attractive organization in which to pursue a career in aviation. In 2016, it paid around $620 million in profit sharing to its 49,000 employees (Ahles, 2016). In 2015, SWA recorded over 800,000 hours of safety and security training with over 34 hours per employee for flight and cabin crew, almost 38 hours per employee for ground staff and more than 53 hours per employee for maintenance workers (2015 Southwest Airlines One Report: 38).

Degree of worker influence at Southwest Airlines

The employee relations strategy at SWA is significantly different from that of its US civil aviation competitors (Bamber et al, 2009; Gollan and Lewin, 2013; Moen, 2016) and indeed its European low-fares airlines counterparts. Whereas Delta Air Lines operate a robust direct employee involvement and voice policy, the partnership at this airline is with the employees as individuals rather than as a collective (Kaufman, 2013). Around 83 per cent of SWA employees are members of a trade union. The airline currently negotiates with six trade unions and the relationship between management and its trade unions has been among the best in US civil aviation industry (Gittell, Von Nordenflycht and Kochan, 2004).

More recently, these relationships have been detrimentally affected by the success of the airline and its ongoing efforts to remain competitive as a low-tariff operator (as opposed to low-cost because its investment in people for example certainly does not reflect a cost leadership approach). Protracted disputes with the Transport Workers Union, which began in 2011, and the high-profile dispute with Southwest Airline Pilots Association (SWAPA), which began in 2012 and recently culminated in the threat of legal action against the airline to prevent the airline from operating the new Boeing 737 Max aircraft until an agreement has been signed. The pilot dispute is largely predicated upon the recent and growing success of the airline, which returned profits of $421 million (2012), $754 million (2013), $1.1 billion (2014) and $2.2 billion (2015) (CAPA, 2016). However, these disputes should be understood in light of what has been presented above and the fact that employee benefits at the airline increased over the three years between 2013 and 2015 by 6, 8 and 17.5 per cent respectively (CAPA, 2016). Labour costs as a percentage of operating cost have doubled, rising from 20 per cent in 2009 to more than 40 per cent in 2015, when labour costs were $6.4 billion of a total operating cost of $15.7 billion (CAPA, 2016). Moreover, senior management remain committed to dialogue and negotiation with SWAPA. As CEO Gary Kelly put it: 'All of this has to be addressed at the negotiating table, and with an eye towards rewarding our people, and compensating them handsomely, but doing so in a way where we maintain industry-leading productivity and efficiency so that we can sustain our low cost structure' (CAPA, 2016).

Reflective question

In what ways and to what extent is the Southwest Airlines employee relations strategy i) different from and ii) better than the strategies of European low-fares airlines?

Conclusions

The purpose of this chapter has been to introduce the concept of international employee relations. In so doing, the chapter has explained a variety of concepts, namely:

- the gig economy;
- human capital (and its four dimensions);

- the labour process;
- the indeterminacy of labour power;
- the disruptive capacity of labour power (and its structural and associational dimensions);
- the asymmetry of power in employee relations;
- frames of reference for understanding the firm and structured antagonism;
- the role of the state and of trade unions;
- degree of worker influence;
- management style and partnership; and
- globalization and employee relations.

The chapter also includes an extended case study that reviews employee relations at low-fares airlines in Europe and the United States. The case study compares the employee relations at Ryanair and Norwegian Air International – the European airlines – and the US pioneer of low fares, Southwest Airlines. These airlines have been very successful with very different approaches to employee relations, for example an adversarial management style marked by a low degree of worker influence at the European low-fares airlines contrasted with a cooperative management style (or partnership) and a high degree of worker influence at Southwest Airlines. It is hoped that this chapter has conveyed the fundamental importance of employee relations even within the contemporary workplace of the gig economy.

Key learning points

- Employee relations is a term that encompasses all aspects of the relationship between worker and the firm, broadly encompassed within two dimensions: market relations and managerial relations.

- Employee relations is fundamental to the success of the firm as it influences the ways in which and extent to which workers utilize their human capital.

- These dimensions are determined by negotiation between the worker and management wherein there is an asymmetry of power and management are ascendant.

- Whereas an asymmetry of power exists, workers are able to draw on power resources to challenge management.

Further reading suggestions

Bamber, G J, Lansbury, R D and Wailes, N (2015) *International and Comparative Employment Relations: National regulation, global changes*, Sage, Thousand Oaks

Bernaciak, M (2012) Social dumping: political catchphrase or threat to labour standards? *Working Paper 2012.06*, European Trade Union Institute, Brussels

Blyton, P et al (1998) *Contesting Globalisation: Airline restructuring, labour flexibility and trade union strategies*, International Transport Workers' Federation, London

Hall, P A and Soskice, D (2001) *Varieties of Capitalism: The institutional foundations of comparative advantage*, Oxford University Press, Oxford

Harvey, G and Turnbull, P (2010) On the go: piloting high road employment practices in the low-cost airline industry, *International Journal of Human Resource Management*, **21** (2), pp. 230–41

Many of the concepts covered with shameful brevity in this chapter are explained in:

Heery, E and Noon, M (2008) *A Dictionary of Human Resource Management*, Oxford University Press, Oxford

References

Ackers, P and Payne, J (1998) British trade unions and social partnership: rhetoric, reality and strategy, *International Journal of Human Resource Management*, **9** (3), pp. 529–50

Ahles, A (2016) Southwest Airlines to pay $620 million in profit-sharing to employees, *Star Telegram*, 11 February

Airport Watch (2014) Norwegian Airlines – with transatlantic Gatwick plans – under fire from unions for employing Thai staff on lower pay [online] http://www.airportwatch.org.uk/2014/02/19763/

Aviation Benefits Beyond Borders (nd) Employment [online] https://aviationbenefits.org/economic-growth/employment

Bacon, N and Samuel, P (2016) Social partnership and political devolution in the national health service: emergence, operation and outcomes, *Work, Employment and Society*, **31** (1), pp. 123–41

Bailey, D and De Popris, L (2014) Manufacturing reshoring and its limits: The UK automotive case, *Cambridge Journal of Regions, Economy and Society*, **7** (3), pp. 379–95

Bamber, G J et al (2009) *Up in the Air: How airlines can improve performance by engaging their employees*, Cornell University Press, Ithaca, NY

Bamber, G J, Lansbury, R D, and Wailes, N (eds) (2011) *International and Comparative Employment Relations*, Sage

Batstone, E (1988) The frontier of control, *Employment in Britain*, ed D Gallie, Blackwell, Oxford

Bazaraa, D (2017) Delta Air Lines employee 'slaps phone out of 13-year-old's hand' as he filmed 'chaos of flight delay', *Mirror*, 4 May

Behling, F and Harvey, M (2015) The evolution of false self-employment in the British construction industry: a neo-Polanyian account of labour market formation, *Work, Employment & Society*, **29** (6), pp. 969–88

Bélanger, J and Edwards, P (2013) The nature of front-line service work: distinctive features and continuity in the employment relationship, *Work, Employment and Society*, **27** (3), pp. 433–50

Blyton, P and Turnbull, P (2004) *The Dynamics of Employee Relations*, Palgrave, Basingstoke

Blyton, P et al (2001) Globalization and trade union strategy: industrial restructuring and human resource management in the international civil aviation industry, *International Journal of Human Resource Management*, **12** (3), pp. 445–63

Bolton, S C and Boyd, C (2003) Trolley dolly or skilled emotion manager? moving on from Hochschild's managed heart, *Work, Employment and Society*, **17** (2), pp. 289–308

Bourdieu, P (1984) *Distinction: A social critique of the judgement of taste*, Routledge, London

Bourdieu, P and Wacquant, L J (1992) *An Invitation to Reflexive Sociology*, University of Chicago Press

Boxall, P (2014) The future of employment relations from the perspective of human resource management, *Journal of Industrial Relations*, **56** (4), pp. 578–93

Braverman, H (1974) *Labor and Monopoly Capital: The degradation of work in the twentieth century*, Monthly Review Press, New York

Burawoy, M and Wright, E O (1990) Coercion and consent in contested exchange, *Politics and Society*, **18** (20), pp. 251–66

Burt, R S (2001) The social capital of structural holes, in *New Directions in Economic Sociology*, eds M F Guillen et al, Russell Sage Foundation, New York

CAPA (2016) Southwest Airlines pilot discontent as the union pushed to be paid for industry leading productivity [online] https://

centreforaviation.com/insights/analysis/southwest-airlines-pilot-discontent-as-the-union-pushes-to-be-paid-for-industry-leading-productivity-284738

Crouch, C (2009) collective bargaining and transnational corporations in the global economy, *International Journal of Labour Research*, **1** (2), pp. 43–60

Crouch, D (2015) Ryanair closes Denmark operation to head off union row, *Guardian*, 17 July

Davis, H (2015) False self-employment, in *Stretching the Sociological Imagination: Essays in honour of John Eldridge*, eds M Dawson et al, Palgrave Macmillan

Doganis, R (2006) *The Airline Business*, Routledge, London

Donaghey, J et al (2014) From employment relations to consumption relations: balancing labor governance in global supply chains, *Human Resource Management*, **53** (2), pp. 229–52

Dubois, P (1979) *Sabotage in Industry*, Pelican, Middlesex

Edwards, P K (1990) Understanding conflict in the labour process: the logic and autonomy of struggle, in *Labour Process Theory*, eds D Knights and H Wilmott, Palgrave Macmillan, Basingstoke

Edwards, P K (2003) *Industrial Relations: Theory and practice*, 2nd edn, Blackwell, Oxford

Evans, C, Harvey, G and Turnbull, P (2012) When partnerships don't 'match-up': an evaluation of labour–management partnerships in the automotive components and civil aviation industries, *Human Resource Management Journal*, **22** (1), pp. 60–75

Farnham, D and Pimlott, J (1995) *Understanding Industrial Relations*, Cassell, London

Flanders, A (1970) Trade unions in the sixties, in *Management and Unions*, ed A Flanders, Faber and Faber, London

Fox, A (1974) *Beyond Contract: Work, power and trust relations*, Faber and Faber, London

Frege, C and Kelly, J (2013) *Comparative Employment Relations in The Global Economy*, Routledge, London

Freiberg, K and Freiberg, J (1996) *NUTS! Southwest Airlines' crazy recipe for business and personal success*, Broadway Books, New York

Friedman, G (2014) Workers without employers: shadow corporations and the rise of the gig economy, *Review of Keynesian Economics*, **2** (2), pp. 171–88

Fuller, L and Smith, V (1991) Consumers' reports: management by customers in a changing economy, *Work, Employment and Society*, **5** (1), pp. 1–16

Gereffi, G (2006) *The New Offshoring of Jobs and Global Development*, International Labour Organization

Gittell, J H, Von Nordenflycht, A and Kochan, T (2004) Mutual gains or zero sum? labor relations and firm performance in the airline industry, *Industrial & Labor Relations Review*, 57 (2), pp. 163–80

Godard, J (2014) The psychologization of employment relations? *Human Resource Management Journal*, 24 (1), pp. 1–18

Gollan, P J and Lewin, D (2013) Employee representation in non-union firms: an overview, *Industrial Relations: A Journal of Economy and Society*, 52 (1), pp. 173–93

Gratton, L and Ghoshal, S (2003) Managing personal human capital: new ethos for the 'volunteer' employee, *European Management Journal*, 21 (1), pp. 1–10

Gray, J V et al (2013) The reshoring phenomenon: what supply chain academics ought to know and should do, *Journal of Supply Chain Management*, 49 (2), pp. 27–33

Grugulis, I (2016) Training and development, in *Contemporary Human Resource Management*, eds A Wilkinson, T Redman and T Dundon, Pearson, Harlow

Harvey, G (2007) *Management in the Airline Industry*, Routledge, London

Harvey, G and Turnbull, P (2009) *The Impact of the Financial Crisis on Labour in the Civil Aviation Industry*, International Labour Office, Geneva

Harvey, G and Turnbull, P (2012a) Power in the skies: pilot commitment and trade union power in the civil aviation industry, *Advances in Industrial and Labor Relations*, 20, pp. 51–74

Harvey, G and Turnbull, P (2012b) *The Development of the Low-Cost Model in the European Civil Aviation Industry*, European Transport Workers' Federation, Brussels

Harvey, G and Turnbull, P (2014) *Evolution of the Labour Market in the Airline Industry Due to the Development of the Low Fares Airlines (LFAs)*, European Transport Workers' Federation, Brussels

Harvey, G and Turnbull, P (2015) Can labor arrest the 'sky pirates'? Transnational trade unionism in the European civil aviation industry, *Labor History*, 56 (3), pp. 308–26

Harvey, G and Turnbull, P (2017) Human resource management and the low-cost model, in *The Routledge Companion to Air Transport Management*, eds A Graham and N Halpern, Routledge, London

Harvey, G, Vachhani, S J and Williams, K (2014) Working out: aesthetic labour, affect and the fitness industry personal trainer, *Leisure Studies*, 33 (5), pp. 454–70

Heery, E (1993) Industrial relations and the customer, *Industrial Relations Journal*, **24** (4), pp. 284–95

Heery, E (2002) Partnership versus organising: alternative futures for British trade unionism, *Industrial Relations Journal*, **33** (1), pp. 20–35

Hochschild, A R (1983) *The Managed Heart: Commercialization of human feeling*, University of California Press, Berkeley

IPA (nd) Partnership in the workplace [online] http://www.ipa-involve.com/partnership-in-the-workplace/

Johnstone, S and Wilkinson, A (2016) *Developing Positive Employment Relations: International experiences of labour management partnership*, Palgrave, Basingstoke

Johnstone, S Wilkinson, A and Ackers, P (2004) Partnership paradoxes: a case study of an energy company, *Employee Relations*, **26** (4), pp. 353–76

Kaufman, B (2013) Keeping the commitment model in the air during turbulent times: employee involvement at Delta Air Lines, *Industrial Relations: A Journal of Economy and Society*, **52** (1), pp. 343–77

Kelly, J (1998) *Rethinking Industrial Relations*, Routledge, London

Korczynski, M (2002) *Human Resource Management in Service Work*, Palgrave, Basingstoke

Lillie, N (2010) Bringing the offshore ashore: transnational production, industrial relations and the reconfiguration of sovereignty, *International Studies Quarterly*, **54** (3), pp. 683–704

Marchington, M and Suter, J (2013) Where informality really matters: patterns of employee involvement and participation (EIP) in a non-union firm, *Industrial Relations: A Journal of Economy and Society*, **52** (1), pp. 284–313

Marchington, M et al (1992). *New Developments in Employee Involvement* (No. 2), Employment Department, London

Marginson, P (2016) Governing work and employment relations in an internationalized economy: the institutional challenge, *Industrial and Labor Relations Review*, **69** (5), pp. 1033–55

Marks, A et al (1998) The politics of partnership? innovation in employment relations in the Scottish spirits industry, *British Journal of Industrial Relations*, **36** (2), pp. 209–26

Martin, R (1992) *Bargaining Power*, Clarendon Press, Oxford

McDermott, A M et al (2013) Promoting effective psychological contracts through leadership: the missing link between HR strategy and performance', *Human Resource Management*, **52**, pp. 289–310

Metcalf, D, Hansen, K and Charlwood, A (2001) Unions and the sword of justice: unions and pay systems, pay inequality, pay discrimination and low pay, *National Institute Economic Review*, **176** (1), pp. 61–75

Milkman, R (1998) The new American workplace: high road or low road? In *Workplaces of the Future*, eds P Thompson and C Warhurst, Palgrave, Basingstoke

Moen, E (2016) Succeeding in international competition by making use of home-country institutions, *Critical Perspectives on International Business*, **12** (1), pp. 83–99

Mundell, R A (1963) Capital mobility and stabilization policy under fixed and flexible exchange rates, *Canadian Journal of Economics and Political Science/Revue Canadienne De Economiques Et Science Politique*, **29** (4), pp. 475–85

Norwegian Air (nd) Our story [online] https://www.norwegian.com/uk/about/our-story/

O'Sullivan, M and Gunnigle, P (2009) 'Bearing all the hallmarks of oppression': union avoidance in Europe's largest low-cost airline, *Labor Studies Journal*, **34**, pp. 252–70

Offe, C and Wiesenthal, H (1980) Two logics of collective action: theoretical notes on social class and organizational form, *Political Power and Social Theory*, **1** (1), pp. 67–115

Polanyi, M (1962) Tacit knowing: its bearing on some problems of philosophy, *Review of Modern Physics*, **34** (4), pp. 601–16

Purcell, J (1987) Mapping management styles in employee relations, *Journal of Management Studies*, **24** (5), pp. 533–48

Ramsay, H (1977) Cycles of control: worker participation in sociological and historical perspective, *Sociology*, **11** (3), pp. 481–506

Roche, W K and Geary, J F (2002) Advocates, critics and union involvement in workplace partnership: Irish airports, *British Journal of Industrial Relations*, **40** (4), pp. 659–88

Samuel, P J (2014) *Financial Services Partnerships: Labour–management dynamics*, Routledge, London

Silva, V (2016) From inauguration to arbitration: Norwegian Air International's brief, entangled history', *Apex Aero* [online] https://Apex.Aero/2016/08/09/Inauguration-Arbitration-Norwegian-Air-International-History

Smith, C (2006) The double indeterminacy of labour power: labour effort and labour mobility, *Work, Employment and Society*, **20** (2), pp. 389–402

Southwest Airlines (nd) Culture [online] https://www.southwest.com/html/about-southwest/careers/culture.html

Southwest Airlines (2015) 2015 One Report [online] http://investors.southwest.com/financials/company-reports/one-reports

Southwest Airlines (2017) Company overview [online] http://www.southwestairlinesinvestorrelations.com/our-company/company-overview

Stalnaker, T, Usman, K and Taylor, A (2016) Airline economic analysis, *Oliver Wyman* [online] http://www.oliverwyman.com/content/dam/oliver-wyman/global/en/2016/jan/oliver-wyman-airline-economic-analysis-2015-2016.pdf

Stanglin, D (2017) United Airlines reaches settlement with passenger violently dragged off flight, *USA Today*, 27 April

Sull, D (1999) Case study: easyJet's $500 million gamble, *European Management Journal*, **17** (1), pp. 20–38

Tarrow, S (2005) *The New Transnational Activism*, Cambridge University Press, Cambridge

Thompson, P (1989) *The Nature of Work*, 2nd edn, Macmillan, London

Traxler, F and Woitech, B (2000) Transnational investment and national labour market regimes: a case of regime shopping, *European Journal of Industrial Relations*, **6** (2), pp. 141–59

Turnbull, P, Blyton, P and Harvey, G (2004) Cleared for take-off? Management–labour partnership in the European civil aviation industry, *European Journal of Industrial Relations*, **10** (3), pp. 287–307

Turnbull, P and Harvey, G (2001) The impact of 11 September on the civil aviation industry: social and labour effects, *International Labour Office Working Paper No. 182*, Geneva, December

Walton, R E (1985) From control to commitment in the workplace, *Harvard Business Review*, **63** (2), pp. 76–84

Warhurst, C and Nickson, D (2009) 'Who's got the look?' Emotional, aesthetic and sexualized labour in interactive services, *Gender, Work And* Organization, **16** (3), pp. 385–404

Witz, A M, Warhurst, C and Nickson, D P. (2003) The labour of aesthetics and the aesthetics of organisation, *Organization*, **10** (1), pp. 33–54

Wright, E O (2000) Working-class power, capitalist-class interests, and class compromise, *American Journal of Sociology*, **105** (4), pp. 957–1002

Zander, C (2014) Norwegian Air may buy another carrier if denied U.S. permit, *Wall Street Journal*, 12 March

12
Work organization and job design across national contexts

DANIEL WINTERSBERGER AND JORGE MUNIZ JR

Learning outcomes

At the end of this chapter, you should be able to:

- understand different paradigms of work and production organization;

- understand the cultural and institutional embeddedness of differences in work organization and job design across different national contexts;

- link factors of organizational design and structure such as diffusion of responsibility, knowledge sharing, hierarchy and degree of centralization to some of the cultural factors discussed in Chapter 2;

- appreciate the implications of different management approaches to work organization and job design for different modes of production and service delivery.

Introduction

In this chapter we examine cross-national differences in patterns of work organization, job design and operations management. Although previous chapters have shown that employment in manufacturing has been in steady decline in advanced industrial economies (for example, less than 20 per cent of US and UK employment is today found in manufacturing), forms of work organization and operations management discussed in this chapter are also relevant for service occupations. This chapter will highlight that despite the homogenizing forces of globalization, substantial differences still exist between nations in terms of how production systems are organized. This is of major significance for those looking to understand HRM from an international perspective, as these cross-national differences are intricately linked with cultural and institutional factors, as discussed in Chapters 2 and 5 respectively, as well as some of the functional areas of international HRM, such as differences in national training and development infrastructure and workforce skills development, discussed in Chapter 10. It is therefore important for multinational companies to understand the different production models that emerge from different cultural and institutional factors.

Traditionally, production management models are categorized either into the technical or the social dimension (Emery, 1959). The technical dimension refers to production organization and processes, including the physical arrangement of equipment and the flow of material that results in the end product (which can include goods and services). The social dimension in turn refers to work organization and human resources aspects. However, people's behaviour at work often depends on the way in which work and production are organized (Emery, 1959). This chapter therefore spans the boundary between technical and social issues firstly by looking at influential models of production organization (technical dimension) and secondly by discussing the implications of these models for HRM and employment relations (social dimensions) and, more importantly, the applicability of these models in different cultural and institutional contexts.

When organizations adapt their work organization and production systems to the external environment (eg the educational system in the country and types of skills available among the workforce) then they are more likely to have what we discussed in Chapter 5 as a 'comparative institutional advantage' (Streeck, 1991; Hall and Soskice 2001; Ferner, Almond and Colling, 2005) insofar as organizations from particular countries derive advantages over competitors in other countries in certain fields. As discussed in Chapter 10, the service sector thrives to a greater extent in liberal market economies (LMEs) such as the UK and the US relative to coordinated market economies (CMEs) such as Germany and Japan. This is because a larger proportion of young people in CMEs tend to opt for university education, hence acquiring high-level general skills. In CMEs, in contrast, a relatively larger proportion of young people opt for vocational education and training (VET) in the form of apprenticeships (see Chapter 10 for a more detailed discussion of these), hence acquiring higher levels of firm-specific skills and tacit knowledge in fairly niche areas. As a result, manufacturing sectors such as automotive are contemporarily stronger in CMEs and account for a higher proportion of employment. Moreover, as revealed in the comparative case study on biscuit manufacturing covered in Chapter 10, the type of operations in manufacturing sectors in different countries will differ in accordance with factors such as the type of skills within the workforce as well as models of employment.

Work organization over time and across continents

In Chapter 9 (International reward), we looked at Taylorism, or 'scientific management' (Taylor, 1911) and the associated 'piece-rate system' (today know as performance-based pay or payment by results) as one of the earliest contributions to determining employee reward based quite simply on quantity of output. In this chapter we focus on Frederick Taylor's principles of scientific management more from the perspective of what work sociologists refer to as 'work organization' (Grint, 2005) and psychologists often refer to as 'job design' (Parker and Wall, 1996). In other words, this chapter is interested more generally in the way in which production facilities are organized and how the people that do the work are managed. Taylorism, hereafter referred to as scientific management (SM), may be a dated approach to work organization, but as we shall explore further in this chapter, is still highly influential in contemporary work organizations both in manufacturing and services.

One of the key principles of scientific management is a **separation of conception from execution**. Frederick Taylor called for a distinction between those that plan the work and those that actually carry out the tasks. Through what he referred to as the 'division of labour', he aimed to ensure that managers can fully focus on developing and optimizing the production processes to ensure maximum efficiency. Consistent with 'Theory X' (McGregor, 1960) of motivation, Taylor assumed that workers had an inherent apathy towards work and needed to be told what to do. Taylor did not envisage any overlap between managerial and non-managerial functions due to a perceived inability among those carrying out simple manual tasks to engage in more complex conceptual work on production systems. With reference to the mundane task of handling iron, Taylor stated the following:

> This work is so crude and elementary in its nature that the writer firmly believes that it would be possible to train an intelligent gorilla so as to become a more efficient pig-iron handler than any man can be. Yet it will be shown that the science of handling pig iron is so great and amounts to so much that it is impossible for the man who is best suited to this type of work to understand the principles of this science, or even to work in accordance with these principles without the aid of a man better educated than he is. And the further illustrations to be given will make it clear that in almost all of the mechanic arts the science which underlies each workman's act is so great and amounts to so much that the workman who is best suited actually to do the work is incapable (either through lack of education or through insufficient mental capacity) of understanding this science (Taylor, 1911: 40).

Another reason why Taylor sought a strict separation between those who think and those who work was that he viewed workers who have too much knowledge about the production process as a threat to efficiency. This he attributed to a phenomenon he compared to 'soldiering' whereby workers, well aware of the implications of working faster, deliberately restrict their output in order to deny management the knowledge of how the production process could be made more efficient. Taylor sought to overcome systematic soldiering on the side of workers through his infamous 'time and motion studies' through which he aimed to derive the most efficient way to carry out small elements of the production process and to record the time it takes to carry out these tasks. As a result, Taylor was able to stipulate minimum output levels for workers, leaving limited scope for soldiering. This approach was complemented by a pay system that was based on worker output (the 'piece rate' system) and thus penalized those who were working too slowly. Moreover, through 'task fragmentation' (Parker and Wall, 1996) Taylor sought to break down tasks into as many sub-tasks as possible as a means to ensure that they could be performed by virtually anyone with minimal training. This in turn enhanced managerial bargaining power as workers only had knowledge of simple, repetitive sub-tasks, so had relatively limited discretion to disrupt operations and to organize themselves to resist work intensification.

From Taylorism to Fordism: the moving assembly line

While Taylor's principles of scientific management are preoccupied with the standardized and efficient handling and manufacturing of sub-parts for a wider production process, his work paid little attention to the actual assembly of products. Henry Ford adapted the principles of scientific management for the production process of cars in the Ford Motor Company, but extended these ideas. By introducing the moving assembly line, Ford ensured that the pace of work for assembly of the final product could now be easily set by management. By mechanically moving the cars between highly specialized (but unskilled) workers, Ford ensured that complex products could be mass produced in a highly efficient manner using a relatively unskilled workforce with limited bargaining power. The latter emanates from the fact that workers on the moving assembly line, by virtue of their relatively narrowly defined jobs, had limited scope to resist management prerogative as they (as unskilled workers) were fairly easily replaceable as individual workers acting as the proverbial 'cog in the machine'.

From a managerial perspective, there are several benefits to Fordist principles of production and assembly. As mentioned earlier, it allows the assembly of products in a very efficient manner, hence allowing companies to benefit from economies of scale. Once the production mechanism has been set up, standardized output can be produced very efficiently with minimal adaptation. In other words, such modes of work organization are particularly suited for mass production. Second, it cheapens labour costs by virtue of 'deskilling' (Braverman, 1974) jobs to the extent that they can be done by unskilled (hence cheaper) and more replaceable (hence compliant) workers. Of course, such production systems also significantly reduced pressures on employers to invest in workforce training, leading to significant cost-cutting potential.

There are of course also several potential downsides to some of the aforementioned strengths of Fordism. The greater potential to derive economies of scale from standardized production systems is to some extent outweighed by the inevitable sluggishness of such systems in adapting to changing circumstances such as input or raw materials as well as changes on the demand side. As competitors began emulating the principles of the moving assembly line, competition for Ford increased insofar as there was increasing pressure not only to compete on the basis of cost (which competitors, emulating Fordist production mechanisms, could easily match), but also on the basis of customization and quality enhancement (Porter, 1980) as more sustainable sources of differentiation. While firms implementing moving assembly line production principles did to some extent benefit from economies of scale, the rigidity of the highly standardized production process became a disadvantage when it was necessary to adapt to changing demands in the market and pressures towards customization. Another key challenge of Fordism is associated with one of its apparent strengths. By drawing primarily on an unskilled workforce, an organization emulating Fordist principles is potentially more vulnerable to disruptions and errors in the production process. With limited workforce skill and opportunity for discretion available in such rigorously standardized systems, there is inevitably limited scope for workers to solve production issues or improvise when technological glitches happen.

Within Fordist production and assembly systems, there are high degrees of interdependence whereby one component is likely to serve as the input for another product assembly but also is likely to be dependent on another input. In other words, when one area of the assembly line delivers an erroneous product, the sequential nature of interdependence means that the entire operation is likely to be halted. In order to mitigate this risk, it has long been quite common for firms operating under Fordist production principles to produce 'buffer' inventory, so that any errors in production would be compensated (Krafcik, 1988). Unfortunately, the diseconomies of such modes of operation become a serious constraint when more customized production is required. Moreover, the resulting time lag (for example the consequence of having to adapt machinery and systems to new production batches) may significantly impede the ability of a firm to respond in a timely and adequate manner to changing market and customer demands.

As the diseconomies of overly standardized production systems relative to the increasing customer demands for tailored and customized products increased (Dupuy, 1999), those designing production systems to some extent attempted to mitigate these disadvantages by using fairly inexpensive, interchangeable parts in the production process (Womack, Jones and Roos, 1990) in order to become more quickly adaptable to changing customer demands. However, such adaptations to the production process to some extent watered down Taylor's key principle that work should be fragmented and standardized. As a production process requiring frequent adaptation requires higher levels of worker skills and tacit knowledge, modern forms of Fordist production to some extent appear to offer potential opportunities for revival of craft production (more on these principles later) where highly skilled workers have fairly high levels of autonomy and broader job descriptions than under Taylorism.

Nonetheless, we still today find examples of principles of scientific management and Fordism, mainly in labour-intensive service and manufacturing sectors. The following section provides some examples of standardization and assembly line principles in services.

The production line approach to service

So far in this chapter we have examined work organization and job design only within manufacturing contexts. This is a limited level of analysis, for as discussed in previous chapters, the service sector now comprises the majority of employment in virtually all advanced industrial and most emerging economies (OECD, 2015). While it may seem counterintuitive that Taylorism and Fordism can be applied to service contexts (after all, service workers tend to deal with people rather than inanimate products, therefore making the work less amenable to standardization) the last four decades have seen an increased standardization of service sector work as a result of advances in IT and artificial intelligence.

At the customer interface, Taylorism is often reflected in a managerial standardization of worker interactions with customers. In the American fast-food industry, for example, Leidner (1993) has observed a tendency within large restaurant chains such as McDonald's to 'script' worker interactions with customers by not only telling them what to say and when to say it, but also providing detailed specifications of the method and order for assembling the tangible product (the meal). Following Leidner's formative work on the routinization of service work in fast-food and insurance companies, call centres have more recently come to be viewed as exemplar of a 'production line approach to service' (Levitt, 1972) due to their notoriety for being particularly low-skill, standardized and tightly controlled working environments (Russell, 2008). Owing to the prevalence of standardization and surveillance, call centres have over the past two decades been widely associated with dysphemisms such as 'electronic panopticon' (Bain and Taylor, 2000), 'assembly line in the head' (Taylor and Bain, 1999), 'new sweatshops' (Fernie and Metcalf, 1998: 2), and even 'dark satanic mills' (Fernie and Metcalf, 1996: 2). Similarly, standardization in a range of other sectors including fast food has led to some arguing that some of these jobs in services have become virtually 'idiot proof' (Royle, 2004: 56). A unifying feature of various studies on work organization in interactive service work is that deskilling has been substantial due to the combination of an advent of technology, increased division of labour and the subsequent facilitation of closer control and monitoring of employee behaviour (Braverman, 1974: 256; Taylor and Bain, 1999).

CASE STUDY Scientific management in the global fast-food industry

The multinational fast-food industry is often used as an example of contemporary manifestations of bureaucratic, Taylorite forms of work organization (Ritzer, 1998; Royle and Towers, 2004). Firstly, the work is highly standardized. The 'production' process is clearly separated between product assembly (kitchen) on the one hand and product delivery to the customer on the other. Virtually all aspects of the work are highly standardized and fairly identical products are produced around the globe through a process closely resembling assembly line work. Pictograms break the assembly of products such as burgers down into rigorously planned and tested sub-tasks (the scientifically derived most efficient way in perfect scientific management style). As many as 19 carefully planned and calculated steps are required to prepare and bag a portion of French fries (Royle and Towers, 2004: 55), and lights and buzzers tell workers what to do, making the work virtually 'idiot proof' (Royle and Towers, 2004: 55) and separating conception from execution as called for by Taylor's scientific management (Taylor, 1911). To avoid resistance, the way the production process, tools and machinery are designed allows workers limited discretion to carry out tasks in any other way or sequence than what has been specified by management. At the customer interface, standardization is similarly rigorous. For example, electronic point of sale (EPOS) systems take all discretion from the checkout operatives. A touch screen where the different menu options can simply be selected can be learnt in as little as a day, and the sales figures for each operator are automatically calculated (Royle, 2004).

Reflective questions

1 To what extent does the McDonald's restaurant resemble some of the principles of scientific management discussed earlier in the chapter?

2 Why do you think it is particularly important for multinational fast-food restaurants to 'separate conception from execution'?

3 Can you think of any other service sectors which may resemble some of the key principles of scientific management?

4 With reference to some of the dysfunctions of scientific management and Fordism discussed earlier, can you think of any disadvantages of this approach, particularly when applied to interactive service work?

The limits of scientific management in interactive service work

The case study above is exemplary of a 'production line approach to service' (Levitt, 1972). However, service delivery has been substantially reorganized in recent years due to the widespread finding that Taylorism reaches its limits in interactive service work (ie where workers deal with people rather than inanimate objects). To understand the recent changes to how service work is organized, we need to understand what makes service work distinctive. First, we need to acknowledge that in *interactive* service work, production and consumption generally take place simultaneously (see for example Korczynski, 2002: 6). This has the consequence that the customer is often a participant in the process of 'production' (Bowen and Schneider, 1988), and is therefore *inseparable* from the process of production. The managerial implication of this is that it becomes impossible to perform any form of 'quality monitoring' prior to the delivery of the service (Schneider, White and Paul, 1998). Customer (dis)satisfaction with service quality (ie the nature of the interaction) is therefore easily influenced by individual employees. The front-line employee therefore *repeatedly* recreates the company image through his or her demeanour, often with a high volume of customers, such as in civil aviation where check-in staff and cabin crew may interact directly with thousands of passengers each day (Carlzon, 1987). It has been argued that customer (dis)satisfaction is determined in such brief 'moments of truth' (Carlzon, 1988: 25), which may last as little as a few seconds, but leave lasting impacts on customer assessments of service quality. Customer satisfaction is a key determinant of repeat business, which, particularly in the service industry, is presented as vital for business survival and prosperity (Berry and Parasuraman, 1992; Zeithaml and Bitner, 1996; Gazzoli, Hancer and Park, 2010: 56; Heskett and Schlesinger, 1994: 164).

A second key consequence of the simultaneous production and consumption of services is that, due to an inability on the side of firms to pre-produce 'buffer-inventories', many services are perishable (Korczynski, 2002: 5). Unlike in manufacturing, where a firm can stockpile inventory during quiet periods in order to cope with later demand peaks, this cannot be done in the majority of service settings, where a company needs to respond flexibly to fluctuating customer demand (Herzenberg, Alic and Wial, 1998: 22; Korczynski, 2002: 5). This is reflected in the way in which a large number of firms implement strategies aimed at ensuring flexibility in their responses to different customer demands. The civil aviation industry, for example, is a particularly pro-cyclical industry, with strong seasonal demand fluctuations (Doganis, 2006). It is therefore a crucial determinant of success for airlines to remain responsive to these changing demand patterns (Monteiro and Macdonald, 1996).

A third consequence of simultaneous production and consumption is that the direct interaction with the customer cedes interactive service workers, regardless of the extent to which management attempt to standardize and codify the service delivery, substantial discretion on the manner in which they engage with customers (Heskett and Schlesinger, 1994; Bain and Taylor, 2000; Callaghan and Thompson, 2001). In this context, we can envisage the existence of a 'satisfaction mirror' which is a euphemism for the intuitively appealing notion that customer treatment by staff reflects the way staff feel treated by management (Heskett and Schlesinger, 1997).

In manufacturing contexts, it has been well documented that alienated workers often direct their anger in the form of dysfunctional behaviours at those factors that are at least partially responsible for their subdual and dehumanization; for example, sabotage of machines has been one commonly documented form of 'misbehaviour' (Ackroyd and Thompson, 1999: 38). In services, however, the simultaneous production and consumption allows alienated employees to direct these dysfunctional behaviours directly at the customers (Schlesinger and Heskett, 1991: 74). Even within 'service factories' (Schmenner, 1991), where standardization has been taken to the logical extreme, as in the aforementioned case of call centres (Taylor and Bain, 1999), and fast food (Leidner, 1993), there arguably remains ample scope for employee resistance. For example, scripts can be ridiculed (eg used inappropriately) by employees (Leidner, 1993). Similarly, Van Maanen (1999), in his account of Disneyland workers, found that there is substantial scope, for example, for ride operatives to resist managerially imposed behaviour rules. Van Maanen's study has also exemplified, with the example of the notorious 'seatbelt slap', that in interactive service work it is often the customer rather than management against which alienated and disgruntled employees 'lash out'.

As service organizations only have a 'flimsy and permeable boundary between themselves and their customers' (Schneider and Bowen, 1993: 40), it might therefore be argued that labour's indeterminacy weighs heavier in interactive service work than in other sectors, for as 'no matter how much scripting there is ... the individual employee still decides whether to be

helpful to customers or to be plainly rude in a way that alienates them'
(Boxall and Purcell, 2011: 27).

The limitations of standardization in manufacturing

Throughout the late 1970s, firms in advanced industrial economies began to
identify some of the dysfunctions of implementing Taylorism and excessive
standardization, and by the early 1980s, strong interest developed in 'new
forms of work organization'. In their highly influential book *The Second
Industrial Divide*, professors Piore and Sabel (1984) argued that Taylorism
and Fordism were reaching their limits in mature economies and a radi-
cal rethink was needed about the way in which production processes are
designed and work is organized. Accordingly, mass markets for highly standardized goods were to be a thing of the past as product markets become
more competitive and firms therefore need to focus on non-cost forms of
comparative advantage. This, they argued, was particularly important for
firms operating in countries with high labour costs.

Instead of the Taylorite principles of standardization and division of
labour that long dominated manufacturing, Piore and Sabel argued that the
opposite was needed for firms in advanced industrial economies to become
competitive again. By advocating a new form of work organization they
termed 'flexible specialization', they called for a defragmentation of jobs
and a move away from standardization towards giving workers greater
discretion in their work. This approach, they argued, called for replacing
unskilled workers with skilled machine operatives and engineers and a more
flexible organization of the work, allowing worker discretion and the use of
their creative potential which in turn was argued to facilitate innovation.

Piore and Sabel's call for flexible specialization did not occur in a vacuum.
Profound changes in the global division of labour arguably underpin the
perceived need for this shift. It is not a coincidence that this call came at a
time when emerging industrial economies, particularly low-wage countries
in Southern and Eastern Asia as well as Latin America, rapidly expanded
production of standardized goods – at a far cheaper price than 'mature'
economies. Manufacturing firms in advanced industrial economies increasingly found themselves having to refocus on production strategies where
high labour rates would not put them at such a disadvantage. Pressures
from countries with lower labour costs were compounded by changes in
demand in home countries whereby in mature markets, a proliferation of
competitors meant that goods and service providers had to provide more
customized and high-quality goods in order to remain competitive. In
Michael Porter's terms, the new imperative was differentiation by quality
enhancement rather than cost leadership.

Without changes to the technological context, the aforementioned shift
in production principles would have been difficult to achieve. Faster IT
processing times and increased mechanization of production have meant
that firms are increasingly able to respond to changing customer demands.

The greater flexibility and shorter machine down time associated with changes to production batches have also meant that economies of scale for mass production are easier to achieve not only for existing large-scale mass producers, but also new entrants into the market (Sorge, Noorderhaven and Koen, 2015: 260).

The aforementioned changes do not necessarily spell the end of low-skill, standardized mass production in advanced industrial economies. What they do mean, though, is that there is increasing diversification in systems of industrial design and work organization in those economies. Sorge, Noorderhaven and Koen (2015: 260) categorize work systems along two continua: first, by level of 'differentiation of output' (ranging from cost leadership to differentiation through quality) and second, by 'volume of output' (ranging from small to large). Today it is only those firms that produce large volumes of output alongside a cost leadership approach that operate by Fordist mass-production principles, while low volume and/or differentiation through quality and customization calls for diversified quality production and craft production (Sorge, Noorderhaven and Koen, 2015: 261).

The impact of flexible specialization on HRM

So what does this shift towards customization and quality mean for labour utilization? First and foremost, flexible specialization (Piore and Sabel, 1984), by drawing on more complex technology, requires a skilled workforce. Firms pursuing flexible specialization to some extent had to eschew two of Taylor's key principles (task fragmentation and division of labour) and organize the work so that skilled workers were able to work in a functionally flexible manner in order to make the transition between different batches of production smoother. Within such working environments, worker discretionary effort and tacit knowledge become more important. While Taylorism and Fordism aimed to make the workforce *disposable* (by making it 'idiot proof' through task fragmentation and division of labour), flexible specialization requires a workforce that is *dependable*.

As a result of these demands, it is not surprising that the 'human relations' school of job design gained strength in advanced industrial economies throughout much of the late 1970s and early 1980s. Rather than task fragmentation, 'job enrichment' (Hackman et al, 1975) became the key imperative in manufacturing environments throughout much of the last four decades. These developments are associated not only with changing production systems (requiring higher worker skill and discretionary effort), but also with increasing pressures on managers to 'humanize' work by reducing monotony, physical exertion, and by making work more 'intrinsically' satisfying. This was also against the backdrop of high employment rates, whereby workers could pick and choose between companies to work for.

In France, for example, the three decades up until the 1970s were characterized by virtually full employment, allowing not only workers to be more picky but also trade unions to assert their prerogative in order to achieve improvements for workers in the areas of job design and work organization (Sorge, Noorderhaven and Koen, 2015: 262). In Germany, the 'work humanization programme' starting in the 1970s, funded by government and conducted in partnership with trade unions and employers' associations was one of the key catalysts for widespread job redesign in its burgeoning manufacturing sector. But what does 'work humanization' actually entail? Hackman and Oldham (1976) propose that to re-humanize work requires making it more interesting and meaningful. Specifically, they propose five core job dimensions which employers need to address to make the work more meaningful:

1 Skill variety – defined by Hackman and Oldham as 'The degree to which a job requires a variety of different activities in carrying out the work, which involve the use of a number of different skills and talents of the person.'

2 Task identity – 'The degree to which the job requires completion of a "whole" and identifiable piece of work; that is, doing a job from beginning to end with a visible outcome.' This dimension aims to meet employee needs for 'closure' (Parker and Wall, 1996) – eg their involvement in the full production process, rather than just a narrow part of the assembly.

3 Task significance – this dimension is about the extent to which a worker perceives that what he or she does on a day-to-day basis is meaningful to themselves but potentially also to others in society.

4 Autonomy – this dimension is about the extent to which employees feel that they are being given freedom on the job to use their own method of working and their discretion when it comes to problem solving.

5 Feedback – the last dimension is about the extent to which workers receive timely feedback about the quality of their work and what might be needed to improve it. One of the key principles of performance management systems is that frequent feedback is provided to employees regarding their strengths and weaknesses and how to improve. A system that only measures, rewards and punishes without providing meaningful feedback to employees in turn would be perceived as weak.

(Based on Hackman and Oldham, 1976: 257).

CASE STUDY Job redesign and the Swedish model of production

The Swedish car manufacturer Volvo was perhaps one of the first of the large European manufacturers to drive forward humanist reforms in its work organization. Similar to the cases of Germany and France, the economic context in the 1970s when Volvo spearheaded trials with job redesign at its famous manufacturing plant in Uddevalla, Sweden, was favourable towards experimenting with attempts to make work more interesting. There was virtually full employment at the time, and there was great societal and governmental interest in and concern about adverse consequences from standardized, repetitive work under Fordism, including physical ailments such as repetitive strain injuries (Sorge, Noorderhaven and Koen, 2015: 262). Part of the pioneering job redesign initiatives involved an increased emphasis on teamworking and longer work cycles with higher degrees of autonomy and functional flexibility for workers. It was at the Uddevalla plant that teams were responsible for the production of entire cars rather than separate components, hence meeting worker need for 'closure' of their tasks, and increasing perceived meaningfulness of these tasks (Sandberg, 1995). Evidence suggest that job redesign at the Uddevala plant effectively solved several issues accounting for the then-prevalent 'assembly line blues' (Dowling, 1973), including a reduction in repetitive strain injuries, increased worker job satisfaction as a result of lower degrees of repetitiveness, and more perceived purpose and meaning in the work done (Sandberg, 1995).

Reflective question

Recap again on Hackman and Oldham's (1976) 'job characteristics model'. In what ways and to what extent have Volvo's job redesign initiatives met some of the core job dimensions posited by Hackman and Oldham?

Despite the largely positive findings associated with the Uddevalla initiatives, the 'Swedish model' has not become fully established practice in manufacturing. With Sweden joining the EU, geographical flexibility increased for manufacturing firms who were now in a better position to offshore their production facilities into countries with lower labour costs, mainly in Eastern Europe. Although Ikea is often used as an example of positive workplace relations and good job design leading to high-quality outcomes, much of its furniture is assembled in Eastern Europe in mass-production facilities that resemble more closely Taylorism and Fordism than flexible specialization (Sorge, Noorderhaven and Koen, 2015: 263). This is perhaps not surprising, given that Ikea goods are fairly standardized (hence low customization) and produced in very large quantities.

This is not to argue, however, that flexible specialization has not been influential since the 1970s in advanced industrial economies with high labour costs. However, it is a question of context and company competitive strategy (high volume versus low volume and cost leadership versus differentiation) which impact on the extent to which manufacturing firms lean more towards standardization (scientific management and Fordism) or customization and quality enhancement (flexible specialization) that determines their approach to work organization and job design.

In the next section, we look at another influential model of work organization: the Toyota production system.

CASE STUDY   Towards 'lean' thinking: the Toyota production system

The founding of the Toyota Motor Company dates back to 1918, when the entrepreneur Sakichi Toyoda established his spinning and weaving business based on his advanced automatic loom. He sold the patents to the Platts Brothers in 1929 for £100,000, and these funds provided the foundation for his son, Kiichiro, to realize his vision of manufacturing automobiles (Holweg, 2007). Krafcik (1988) coined the term 'lean' to describe the Toyota Production System (TPS), which captures the essence of the far less resource-hungry TPS compared with typical western production systems. Lean was made popular by Womack, Jones and Roos (1990) and their study evidenced a huge performance gap between Japanese and western car producers.

> Lean is a management practice with a measurable set of principles
> and tools that looks for continuous improvement in agreement with the
> organizational goals.

Perhaps one of the earliest proponents of 'lean' production systems was Toyota engineer Taiichi Ohno. Following a visit to one of Ford's manufacturing plants in the United States, Ohno was convinced that this model of production would be likely to fail for Toyota in Japan due to several challenges. First, Toyota initially primarily served domestic Japanese demand, which was very small compared to the scale served by Ford. Moreover, the Japanese market demanded a wide range of vehicles (Sorge, Noorderhaven and Koen, 2015: 263). One of the key constraints was that, while they needed to serve all segments (from luxury to agricultural vehicles), they additionally had to diversify the model range to incorporate smaller cars to meet the rather crowded conditions in megacities such as Tokyo. Another key constraint that stopped Toyota from implementing pure Taylorism or Fordism was the relatively higher bargaining power of Japanese workers. Typical for a 'coordinated market economy' (Hall and Soskice, 2001 – see also Chapter 5), labour legislation was significantly tighter in Japan than the legal constraints faced by Ford in the United States. Moreover, at Toyota, enterprise unions (as discussed in Chapter 5) broke down any divisions between blue- and white-collar workers, leading to substantial inter-group solidarity amongst the workforce, hence undermining potential management attempts at implementing a 'division of labour' between conception and execution in scientific management style. This is because such a division of labour is unlikely to be received well by a cohesive workforce with strong enterprise unions. A further constraint imposed by the Japanese context was the inability of firms to access the same kind of low-wage, 'peripheral' labour as their counterparts in Europe and North America. Part of what fuelled the industrial revolution in the United States was a steady supply of migrant labour (mostly from Europe) willing to work for low wages and under poor working conditions. It is perhaps not a coincidence that some of Frederick Taylor's anecdotes in *Principles of Scientific Management* refer to a person called 'Schmidt', a recent immigrant from Europe. The Japanese workforce, in contrast, was more homogeneous and less marginalized and, coupled with strong enterprise unions that ceded them substantial degrees of 'associational' bargaining power (Wright, 2000), had a lot of 'strength in numbers'.

The 14 Management Principles of Toyota

1 *Base your decisions on a long-term philosophy* – do the right thing for the company and their customers, stakeholders, employees, and society as a whole.

2 *Create continuous flow* to mitigate waste in the service/product value stream. Value is related to aspects that impact consumer needs satisfaction.

3 *Use pull systems to avoid overproduction* – relates to production aligned with customer demand and avoiding buffers.

4 *Level out the workload* – eliminate unevenness in labour and/or machines to support a smooth supply for upstream processes and suppliers.

5 *Stop and fix the problem* – it is better to stop production and solve the problem at the root cause than to continue production at the risk of creating more defects.

6 *Work with standards* – each employee must follow standard operating procedures to guide his/her work.

7 *Make problems visual* – process should be supported by the 5S system.*

8 *Use only reliable tested technology.*

9 *Grow your leaders internally* – focus on creating people who have deep knowledge of the work and are engaged with Toyota principles; it is also expected that leaders are able to share knowledge with other employees (*senseis*).

10 *Develop exceptional people and teams* empowered to participate in continuous improvements.

11 *Respect your network partners* – focus on the long term and create common goals with partners.

12 *Go see for yourself* the problems on the shop floor (*gemba*) to help you understand the context and to make the best decisions.

13 *Make decisions slowly by consensus and implement rapidly.*

14 *Use reflection and continuous improvement to become a learning organization.*

(Adapted from Liker, 2004)
*5S:

- Sort – eliminate whatever is not needed.
- Straighten – organize whatever remains.
- Shine – clean the work area.
- Standardize – schedule regular cleaning and maintenance.
- Sustain – make 5S a way of life.

American Society of Quality (2017).

Although Toyota have been very open and transparent about their practices, few companies have had success in implementing their principles in a sustainable way. While many organizations have tried to implement specific lean techniques, few have managed to fully replicate the TPS as a system. The most important point of lean is the pursuit of increased production efficiency by consistently and completely eliminating waste related to people, process, products and machines. Spear and Bowen (1999) indicate that the front-line workers make the improvements to their own jobs and their supervisors provide direction and coach them. Toyota employees are educated systematically to look for and eliminate wastage such as overproduction of inventory or products which are then rejected on the basis of there being no demand for them or them not meeting the requisite quality standards, which is one of seven categories of unproductive manufacturing practices identified by Taiichi Ohno. When a problem appears, workers are encouraged to discover their root causes, discuss actions to eliminate these causes, implement actions and review work instructions so that the problem does not recur. More recently, Liker (2004) indicates underutilized talent as an additional waste. Companies that fail to recognize or utilize people's talents, skills or special knowledge are not only missing the benefit of these resources, but the underutilized employees are likely to become dissatisfied and may begin to perform poorly or leave the organization. This waste of talent happens when management is not responsive, does not assign tasks appropriately or does not train properly, which brings the focus back to factors related to work organization and job design. Such factors include organization objectives, the structure of the organization, communication channels across departments and levels in the organization, opportunities for training, and a reward system that effectively links incentives to performance. Objectives represent a measurable way to relate the work of the group to the achievement of results, indicating progress, establishing priorities and justifying the claim for material and time resources to be used in problem solving and improvement projects.

Clearly, among the various work organization models, the Swedish (Uddevalla – see earlier in this chapter) model of work organization in production and the Japanese model (Toyota) share some similarities, but Table 12.1 below also highlights some differences between the Uddevalla model and the TPS discussed in this section.

Table 12.1 Models of work organization

Swedish – Uddevala	Japanese – Toyota
Semi-skilled workers with high levels of vocational training	Semi-skilled workers enter the firm at a young age with limited training, though receive substantial training on the job

(continued)

Table 12.1 *(Continued)*

Swedish – Uddevala	Japanese – Toyota
Holistic tasks with long work cycles of more than one hour. Often teams produce entire products from separate parts to full assembly	Highly repetitive work; cycle times around one minute on the assembly lines
High partial autonomy for teams due to carrying out entire work processes	Limited autonomy for teams
De-hierarchization with elected speaker and self-regulation of group affairs	Strong hierarchical structures, group leader appointed by management, no group self-regulation

Adapted from Sandberg (1995)

Reflective questions

1 To what extent do you believe that the TPS is applicable to your own socio-cultural context?

2 Which of the aforementioned systems (Uddevalla vs TPS) do you find more appealing from an employee perspective?

CASE STUDY Transferring lean management to Toyota plants in Brazil

Brazil is one of the 10 largest car manufacturers in the world, with over 2 million vehicles produced in 2016 (OICA, 2017), and the automotive industry therefore represents a significant Brazilian economic sector. The major global automotive brands are located in Southern Brazil – including Ford, GM, VW, Toyota, Hyundai, FIAT, Land Rover, Nissan, PSA Citroën (including Peugeot), Cherry, Honda, Scania, MAN and Mercedes Benz VW AUDI, Renault, Nissan, BMW, Volvo and Agrale. More recently, plants have also been set up in the north-east by companies such as Ford, Jeep, JAC and Troller.

The Brazilian automotive industry has undergone a significant transformation in relations with suppliers, relocating production activities, engineering and product development, work and production organization in recent years, and there is evidence that firms are beginning to implement some of the Toyota production system principles, although with varying success.

The growth of the Toyota Production System principles in Brazil raises issues about their applicability within a distinctive cultural context that is very different to Japan. Success in sustaining lean production principles is determined to a large extent by the hybridization (Liker, Fruin and Adler, 1999) of where it is being implemented. In other words, the implementation of lean principles may require different strategies which to some extent adapt to the local culture of the host country.

The first overseas Toyota plant was established in Brazil in 1958. The Toyota companies located in Brazil enjoy a good public reputation, as they are seen to place great emphasis on focusing on customer needs, the engagement of suppliers, and, importantly, worker health and safety at plant level. All Toyota plants in Brazil also have a reputation for looking after general worker welfare at a high level.

This case analyses one car assembler and three suppliers from the Toyota Motor Company located in Brazil. Supplier C (tier 2) provides auto parts to Suppliers A and B (tier 1), which produce components and provide them to the car assemblers as illustrated in the Figure 12.1.

Figure 12.1   Toyota Brazilian plants relationship

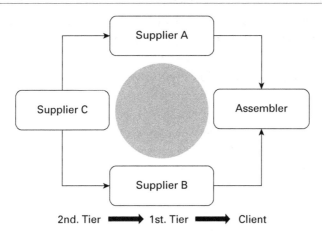

This case explains the daily activities in Toyota's Brazilian plants and by doing so focuses primarily on factors related to work organization (objectives, organizational structure, communication, training as well as issues around incentives). However, we also examine the role of relevant factors associated with the production system itself, including problem-solving methods and standard operating procedures.

Working days at Toyota plants are rigidly structured. A typical day begins with five minutes of light exercise which is compulsory for everyone, including executives, support staff and workers. This event is followed by a morning meeting (*Tiorey*) to discuss the key events that occurred the day before and to plan for the current day.

After the morning meeting the operators check the production process, ie they check the devices involved in production as well as the set-up model and error-proofing devices. All these items are pre-checked following an orientation checklist, and it becomes a record given by the line leader. Some of these items are still checked by the production supervisor. These practices aim to ensure discipline of tasks at the start of the shift and control of the production process.

The shift of production, illustrated in Figure 12.2, is divided into eight production cycles. After each cycle the operators exchange processes and every two cycles the workers stop for a 10-minute coffee break. It is understood that the exchange process means, most of the time, changing work to another production process and not just a job change.

After the second coffee break there is a meeting called *Yuichi*, similar to *Tiorey*. The workers discuss any problems they faced during the day. *Tiorey* addresses all matters relating to the working day (visits, reports, events) and the day before. *Yuchi* addresses problems that are occurring on the same day. The cycles of shifts are completed (final) with clean tasks (5S) and closing of production reports. The shift in charge is responsible for leaving very good conditions for the next. Daily meetings such as Tiorey and Yuchi play an important role to facilitate internal communication and support a better flow of information through the shifts of all plants. Both events seek to allow top-down and bottom-up communication between the workers and support areas. Through encouraging communication, the Toyota subsidiary seeks to improve the exchange of information based on verbal communication and regular meetings, which is grounded in the principle of *Hourensou*, which is the combination of three Japanese words: *Houkoku* (Report), *Renraku* (Contact), and *Soudan* (Discussion).

Figure 12.2   Activities of a typical day in a Toyota plant

Labour Gym	*Tiorey*	Pre check	Cycle 1	Cycle 2	Coffee	Cycle 3	Cycle 4
Lunch (1st shift)/Dinner (2nd shift)							
Labour Gym	Cycle 5	Cycle 6	Coffee break	*Yuich*	Cycle 7	Cycle 8	Final

Enriched groups within these plants seek continuous improvements in their operational performance with the aim of increasing quality levels and reducing production cycle time (internal objectives). New business is targeted to sustain their operations in Brazil (external objectives), which means increasing return on investment and market share.

In terms of organizational structure, Toyota subsidiaries aim at having only four hierarchical levels in the plants (director, supervisor, line leader and workers). This facilitates communication and information flow and it is supported by the presence of support staff on the shop floor.

Training focuses on the development of technical skills in the areas of product quality, production techniques, safety, cost saving, and the maintenance of machines. Suggestions and best-practice programmes are listed in order to engage workers to develop solutions on a regular basis. Incentives such as travel, shirts, small bonuses, English courses, and lunches for the family are used to stimulate workers' suggestions.

Training aims at worker specialization. There is substantial exchange with Japan, which provides workers with an opportunity to develop professional experience in production processes associated with TPS. All plants aim to reduce their dependency on the headquarters in Japan by sending their employees there to learn the TPS techniques and to effectively implement them in Brazil.

By creating an environment that facilitates worker knowledge sharing (for example through *kaizen*, which entails continuous improvement meetings) the organization sustains the principles of the TPS (Muniz et al, 2010; Nakano, Muniz Jr and Dias Batista Jr, 2013). Spear and Bowen (1999) indicated that Toyota's managers use a teaching and learning approach that allows their workers to discover the rules as a consequence of solving problems, for example by asking a series of questions:

- How do you do this work?
- How do you know you are doing this work correctly?
- How do you know that the outcome is free of defects?
- What do you do if you have a problem?

The integration of new employees entails specific training in quality and production. It is expected that the new operator makes parts with zero defects as soon as possible. Generally, new recruits in the Brazilian Toyota subsidiary have little or no previous industry experience, and this is in part a policy that is consciously driven by management, as inexperienced workers are likely to be more amenable to learning the TPS from scratch. While executive staff including plant managers and supervisors tend to be of Japanese descent, many plants already have local staff in management positions.

The findings have indicated strong similarity in the daily work of the plants consistent with the Japanese headquarters orientation and the lean manufacturing literature, and there appears to be a strong discipline to sustain the principles of TPS.

Based on J Muniz Jr et al (2013)

Reflective questions

1 What sort of cultural challenges might organizations encounter when trying to implement and sustain the Toyota Production System?

2 Which management actions may incentivize worker engagement in continuous improvement?

Conclusions

In this chapter we have examined different models of work organization and job design across different eras and cultural and institutional contexts. We have traced the development of production organization in manufacturing from the roots of scientific management and Fordism during the heyday of the industrial revolution in the UK and US, but have also looked at the issues associated with the implementation of such forms of work organization in the service occupations and the extent to which they have transformed people's working lives. Beginning with the human relations movement, we then charted the development of job redesign initiatives as organizations in advanced industrial economies increasingly found themselves having to compete more on the basis of quality and customization than on cost. To chart these changes, we focused on the automotive industry, first looking at Volvo's job redesign initiatives at their plant in Uddevalla, Sweden, and then comparing and contrasting their job redesign (job enrichment, teamwork, worker autonomy) measures with perhaps one of the most influential work organization paradigms over the last four decades, namely lean production based on the Toyota Production System (TPS). Finally, we critically evaluated the extent to which these principles, firmly rooted in Japanese cultural values (collectivism, long-term orientation – see chapter 2) and institutional factors (such as long-term employment and enterprise unionism – see chapter 5) are applicable to distinctive national contexts with reference to a case study of Toyota subsidiaries in Brazil.

Key learning points

- History has shown us that what is considered the 'best' form of organizing work is contingent on many contextual factors, including the extent to which firms:
  - prioritize either standardization or customization;
  - operate in knowledge- or labour-intensive industries: the former constitutes a more favourable context for standardization and Fordism whereas the latter calls for greater worker autonomy and discretion;
  - pursue cost leadership (standardization) or quality enhancement (customization) as their key source of competitive advantage;
  - operate within countries with high or low labour costs.
- Models of production and work organization (such as Taylorism, Fordism and 'Lean') are embedded to a great extent in the aforementioned contextual factors, but also in specific cultural and institutional factors. Any attempt to implement some of their principles in a piecemeal manner is therefore likely to fail.

References

Ackroyd, S and Thompson, P (1999) *Organizational Misbehaviour*, Sage Publications

American Society of Quality (2017) 5S tutorial [online] http://asq.org/learn-about-quality/lean/overview/five-s-tutorial.html

Bain, P and Taylor, P (2000) Entrapped by the 'electronic panopticon'? Worker resistance in the call centre, *New Technology, Work and Employment*, **15** (1), pp. 2–18

Berry, L L and Parasuraman, A (1992) Prescriptions for a service quality revolution in America, *Organizational Dynamics*, **20** (4), pp. 5–15

Bowen, D E and Schneider, B (1988) Services marketing and management implications for organizational behavior, *Research in Organizational Behavior*, **10**, pp. 43–80

Boxall, P and Purcell, J (2011) *Strategy and Human Resource Management*, Palgrave Macmillan

Braverman, H (1974) *Labor and Monopoly Capital: The degradation of work in the twentieth century*, Monthly Review Press, New York

Callaghan, G and Thompson, P (2001) Edwards revisited: technical control and call centres, *Economic and Industrial Democracy*, **22** (1), pp. 13–37

Carlzon, J (1987) *Moments of Truth*, Ballinger, Cambridge, MA

Doganis, R (2006) *The Airline Business*, Routledge

Dowling, W F (1973) Job redesign on the assembly line: farewell to blue collar blues? *Organization Dynamics*, **2**, pp. 51–67

Dupuy, F (1999) *The Customer's Victory*, Palgrave Macmillan UK, pp. 36–51

Emery, F (1959) *Characteristics of Socio-Technical Systems*, Tavistock Institute, London, Document no. 527

Ferner, A, Almond, P and Colling, T (2005) Institutional theory and the cross-national transfer of employment policy: the case of 'workforce diversity' in US multinationals, *Journal of International Business Studies*, **36** (3), pp. 304–21

Fernie, S and Metcalf, D (1998) *(Not) Hanging on the Telephone: Payment systems in the new sweatshops*, Centre for Economic Performance, London School of Economics and Political Science

Gazzoli, G, Hancer, M and Park, Y (2010) The role and effect of job satisfaction and empowerment on customers' perception of service quality: a study in the restaurant industry, *Journal of Hospitality & Tourism Research*, **34** (1), pp. 56–77

Grint, K (2005) *The Sociology of Work*, Polity Press

Hackman, J R and Oldham, G R (1976). Motivation through the design of work: test of a theory, *Organizational Behavior and Human Performance*, **16** (2), pp. 250–79

Hackman, J R et al (1975) A new strategy for job enrichment, *California Management Review*, **17** (4), pp. 57–71

Hall, P A and Soskice, D W, eds (2001) *Varieties of Capitalism: The institutional foundations of comparative advantage*, Oxford University Press, Oxford

Herzenberg, S A, Alic, J A and Wial, H (1998) Toward a learning economy, *Issues in Science and Technology*, **15** (2), pp. 55–62

Heskett, J L and Schlesinger, L A (1994) Putting the service-profit chain to work, *Harvard Business Review*, **72** (2), pp. 164–74

Holweg, M (2007) The genealogy of lean production, *Journal of Operations Management*, **25** (2), pp. 420–37

Korczynski, M (2002) *Human Resource Management in Service Work*, Palgrave, London

Krafcik, J F (1988) Triumph of the lean production system, *MIT Sloan Management Review*, **30** (1), p 41

Leidner, R (1993) *Fast Food, Fast Talk: Service work and the routinization of everyday life*, University of California Press

Levitt, T (1972) Production-line approach to service, *Harvard Business Review*, **50** (5), pp. 41–52

Liker, J K (2004) *The Toyota Way*, Esensi

Liker, J K, Fruin, W M and Adler, P S, eds (1999) *Remade in America: Transplanting and transforming Japanese management systems*, Oxford University Press on Demand

McGregor, D (1960) Theory X and Theory Y, *Organization Theory*, pp. 358–74

Monteiro, L and Macdonald, S (1996) From efficiency to flexibility: the strategic use of information in the airline industry, *The Journal of Strategic Information Systems*, **5** (3), pp. 169–88

Muniz Jr, J et al (2013) Lean management practice: Toyota Brazilian plants case, in *POMS*, Production and Operations Management Society, Denver

Muniz Jr, J, Dias Batista Jr, E and Loureiro, G (2010) Knowledge-based integrated production management model, *Journal of Knowledge Management*, **14** (6), pp. 858–71

Nakano, D, Muniz Jr, J and Dias Batista Jr, E (2013) Engaging environments: tacit knowledge sharing on the shop floor, *Journal of Knowledge Management*, **17** (2), pp. 290–306

OECD (2015) Employment by activity [online] https://data.oecd.org/emp/employment-by-activity.htm

OICA (Organization Internationale des Constructeurs d'Automobiles) (2017) Production Statistics [online] http://oica.net/category/production-statistics/ [accessed 13 May 2017]

Parker, S K and Wall, T D (1996) Job design and modern manufacturing, in *Psychology at Work*, ed P B Warr, Penguin, New York, pp. 333–59

Piore, M and Sabel, C (1984) *The Second Industrial Divide*, Basic Books

Porter, M E (1980) *Competitive strategy: Techniques for analysing industries and competitors*, Simon and Schuster

Ritzer, G (1998) *The McDonaldization Thesis: Explorations and extensions*, Sage Publications

Royle, T (2004) *Working for McDonald's in Europe: The unequal struggle*, Routledge, London

Royle, T and Towers, B, eds (2004) *Labour Relations in the Global Fast-Food Industry*, Routledge

Russell, B (2008) Call centres: a decade of research, *International journal of management reviews*, **10** (3), pp. 195–219

Sandberg, A (1995) *Enriching Production: Perspectives on Volvo's Uddevalla plant as an alternative to lean production*, Avebury

Schlesinger L A and Heskett, J L (1991) The service-driven service company, *Harvard Business Review*, **69** (5), pp. 71–81

Schmenner, R W (1991) International factory productivity gains, *Journal of Operations Management*, **10** (2), pp. 229–54

Schneider, B and Bowen, D E (1993) The service organization: human resources management is crucial, *Organizational Dynamics*, **21** (4), pp. 39–52

Schneider, B, White, S S and Paul, M C (1998) Linking service climate and customer perceptions of service quality: tests of a causal model, *Journal of Applied Psychology*, **83** (2), p. 150

Sasser, W E, Schlesinger, L A, and Heskett, J L (1997) *The Service Profit Chain*, Simon and Schuster

Sorge, A, Noorderhaven, N and Koen, C (2015) *Comparative International Management*, Routledge

Spear, S and Bowen, H K (1999) Decoding the DNA of the Toyota production system, *Harvard Business Review*, **77**, pp. 96–108

Streeck, W (1991) On the institutional conditions of diversified quality production. *Beyond Keynesianism*, eds W Streeck and E Matzner, Edward Elgar Publishing, pp. 21–61

Taylor, F W (1911) *The Principles of Scientific Management*, Harper

Taylor, P and Bain, P (1999) 'An assembly line in the head': work and employee relations in the call centre, *Industrial Relations Journal*, 30 (2), pp. 101–17

Van Maanen, J (1999) *The Smile Factory: Work at Disneyland*, South-Western College Publishing

Womack, J P, Jones, D T and Roos, D (1990) *The Machine that Changed the World*, Simon and Schuster

Wright, E O (2000) Working-class power, capitalist-class interests, and class compromise, *American Journal of Sociology*, **105** (4), pp. 957–1002

Zeithaml, V A and Bitner, M J (1996) *Services Marketing*, McGraw-Hill Education, *New York*

13
Conclusions: change or continuance in national systems of HRM?

Learning outcomes

At the end of this chapter, you should be able to:

- understand the process and underlying forces of globalization and their homogenizing impact on national systems of HRM;

- understand key global trends (offshoring and reshoring) in response to globalization and their impact on work in emerging and advanced industrial economies;

- understand the potential scenarios which emerge with the advent of mechanization, especially with regards to job destruction and the creation of new jobs;

- link several of the preceding chapters both in the context of IHRM and its functional areas (such as reward, employee voice and training) together.

Introduction

In Chapter 5 (The institutional context of IHRM), we discussed the role of institutional factors in shaping and perpetuating different HRM practices in different countries. Drawing predominantly on the 'varieties of capitalism'

(VoC) framework (Hall and Soskice, 2001), we paid particular attention to differences between liberal market economies (LMEs) and coordinated market economies (CMEs) and the way in which 'institutional complementarity' (Amable, 2000; Hall and Soskice, 2003) shapes company decisions on how to approach the functional areas of IHRM examined in Chapters 7–12, including employee voice, training and development, and reward. Put simply, institutional complementarity is the idea that one institutional factor (such as the law) facilitates or eases the functioning of another institutional factor (eg common practice on training and development). In Chapter 5 we acknowledged that institutions can be very hard, formal and binding. For example, most would argue that the legal context (eg minimum standards for training provision in organizations or rules on corporate governance) poses a very hard, non-pliable institutional constraint for firms insofar as they can be punished for breaking the law. As discussed in more depth in Chapter 10, training levies (traditionally a stronger feature in CMEs) tend to punish firms that are reluctant training providers and incentivize firms to provide better-quality training. The 'hard' institution of legally enforced minimum standards for training provision, in turn, is complementary to a softer institutional factor, namely the tendency amongst firms in CMEs to offer more high-quality apprenticeships due to reduced fears of competitors taking away their trained workers.

The VoC framework, by focusing on two 'ideal types' of market economy, may have an intuitive appeal in part due to its simplicity. However, as recognized in more detail in Chapter 5, it does not fully grasp the increasing complexity of the dynamic interplay of institutional factors within countries as well as the increasing influence of globalization. The examples of Japan and Germany are a case in point. On the one hand, they are both categorized as CMEs and appear to be polar opposites (eg in terms of corporate governance, employee voice and company policy on employee retention) to LMEs such as the US and UK (which do share many similarities with one another, although to varying extents). However, Germany and Japan are also quite different to one another in many areas. For example, while collective bargaining tends to take place at industry level in Germany (where works councils tend to represent worker interests at senior management level), enterprise unions engage directly in collective bargaining with management in Japan.

As outlined in more depth in Chapter 12, various models of work organization and job design have been diffused across different cultural and institutional contexts over time. Starting with the principles of scientific management (Taylor, 1911) and Fordism across manufacturing contexts (and later service contexts) throughout much of the 20th century, the last two decades of the last century saw a growing interest in job redesign towards less standardized modes of production and service delivery. While the global 'West' (mainly the UK and US) diffused Fordist principles eastwards in the first seven decades of the 20th century, the West's increasing interest in customization and lean manufacturing meant that Japanese management principles started to be diffused from East to West in recent decades. However, to argue that all nations are cyclically gravitating to different models of production and work organization would be overly simplistic.

Different trajectories between emerging and advanced industrial economies

An overarching theme of all of the chapters in this book is an increasing interdependence of national economies. However, some political developments (such as Donald Trump's 'America First' policy of protectionism, and the gains of the Eurosceptic and globalization-sceptic far right in general elections in Europe) seem to show large degrees of popular disenfranchisement with some of the consequences of globalization in advanced industrial economies. These consequences include, among other factors, the increasingly deregulated labour markets where competition from emerging economies with lower labour costs and more flexible labour markets have led to a deterioration of terms and conditions in mature economies. In the UK context, for example, 'real' (ie inflation-adjusted) average earnings have more or less stagnated since 2011, with falling wages in real terms being reported in 2017 as the weak pound following Brexit drives up the prices of imported goods (and hence the consumer price index) to levels with which wages fail to keep pace (ONS, 2017). With mechanization at an advanced level, some mature economies such as the UK have seen a similar 'stagnation' in terms of worker productivity measured as gross domestic product (GDP) per hour worked. At the same time, economies in the global South such as Chile have seen staggering productivity increases of as much as 10 per cent year on year over the past five years or so (OECD, 2017). In response to these different trajectories and dynamisms, with a strong split between rapidly emerging economies such as India on the one hand, and stagnating mature economies such as the UK on the other, we can see why globalization is a key factor to take into consideration when considering the contemporary relevance of the different models of capitalism (Chapter 5) and work organization (Chapter 12) discussed in this book. While Taylorism and Fordism brought huge productivity gains to the UK and US during the industrial revolution, the emulation of these methods in emerging economies (such as China) has led to a rapid equalization of worker output across the globe. By responding through lean techniques, inspired by the Toyota production system and the Swedish (Uddevalla) model of work organization (Chapter 12), advanced industrial economies with higher labour costs somewhat buffered their workforce against low-cost completion from emerging economies. However, as such techniques are also increasingly emulated by emerging economies such as China's automotive industry (Zhang, 2008), the productivity gap will close.

Flexibilization of labour markets

In response to these pressures, some advanced industrial economies have chosen to 'flexibilize' their labour markets. Many of the English-speaking countries have over the past decade implemented legal reforms that make it easier for employers to employ staff on casual contracts. One example in the UK is the 'zero-hours contract'. As the name suggests, this is an employment contract within which the employer guarantees the employee no fixed number of hours of work. Such reforms make it easier for employers to hire people when they need them, while still making them disposable during times when they are not needed. The implementation of measures focused on the flexibilization of labour markets is perhaps one key reason why the UK has one of the lowest unemployment rates (4.4 per cent) in the European Union (Eurostat, 2017).

From offshoring to 'reshoring' of jobs in mature economies

Much attention was paid in the 1990s and onwards to a trend called 'offshoring'. This entails the movement of generally low-skill jobs to countries with lower labour costs. However, attention now seems to be focusing more on reshoring (Gray et al, 2013). Contrary to offshoring, this trend actually involves the return of low-skill jobs from countries with (formerly) lower labour costs back to the original high-labour-cost country from which they were initially offshored. General Electric, for example, has recently reshored a significant proportion (several hundred jobs) of its appliance manufacturing activities – previously offshored to China and Mexico – back to the United States as a means to more swiftly and efficiently meet domestic demand for its products (Gray et al, 2013), but also in response to rapidly rising wages (hence labour costs) in China and Mexico and the increasing erosion of the cost advantage of outsourcing due to stagnating labour costs in the United States since the recession of 2008 (Crooks, 2013). The reasons outlined for reshoring are manifold. First, the cost of shipping is one of the key motifs for keeping production close to where products are bought. This particularly becomes an issue when the oil price rises, as the cost of shipping increases significantly with these fuel costs. Second, production supply chains spanning different countries or even continents (as in the case of companies such as General Electric and Apple) are not as nimble (due to long shipping times) as when products are solely domestically designed, produced and assembled. Finally, there is the issue of the shrinking labour cost advantage already alluded to in the aforementioned case of General Electric. To quantify this, the labour cost advantage of manufacturing in China as opposed to the United States has more than halved from the Unites States being nearly five times more expensive in terms of labour costs to only a little over two times, with this gap rapidly closing in response to wage inflation being up to 10 times higher in China than in the United States in recent years (Crooks, 2013).

The trend towards reshoring is not surprising given protectionist economic policies in countries such as the United States. Consistent with Trump's slogan of 'America first', the head of the Trade Council of the White House (David Navarro) announced that the repatriation of international supply chains is one of the 'key priorities' of the administration (Donnan, 2017). It is estimated that around half a million jobs have been 're'created in the United States as a result of reshoring since 2008. Similarly, in the UK, it is estimated that some 200,000 jobs could be 'brought back' over the next decade or so (Powley, 2014). Growth of employment is expected to be particularly pronounced in low-wage sectors such as textiles which have previously been offshored to countries with lower labour costs and are now coming back to the UK as labour costs stagnate.

It seems, therefore, that the global division of labour (between labour-intensive and knowledge-intensive work) may become a weaker phenomenon over the coming decades, as wages in emerging economies catch up while those in mature economies stagnate. Another trend that is likely to profoundly shape IHRM activity in the future is the advent of mechanization in various sectors. With artificial intelligence improving rapidly, mechanization has the potential to replace many unskilled jobs. A study by PricewaterhouseCoopers (PWC) in the UK concluded that some 30 per cent of jobs are at risk of mechanization by 2030 (PWC, 2017), highlighting fairly repetitive low-skill jobs in retail and manufacturing as well as transport (taxi drivers) as most at risk of automation. Meanwhile, for emerging economies such as India or China, it is estimated that as many as one in four current jobs could be under threat of automation by 2025 (*Economic Times India*, 2016), as a large proportion of the workforce are still carrying out jobs which have in the global West already been mechanized.

Daunting as the prospect of widespread job losses following mechanization may sound, care needs to be taken not to draw rushed conclusions from such figures. For one thing, the destruction of the superfluous is nothing new in world economic history. As outlined in Chapter 10, most advanced economies have gone through the same trajectory over the past 120 years or so. In the beginning, most people worked in agriculture until jobs were lost to mechanization (eg when ploughing and harvesting became no longer purely manual tasks). Then the majority of people worked in manufacturing until mechanization and the subsequent efficiency gains through the deployment of Fordist principles of production (hence mechanization) meant that the most routine and repetitive jobs could be replaced with machines. This was actually one of the key goals of Frederick Taylor in his *Principles of Scientific Management* (1911). More recently, in the service occupations, mechanization initially only served to 'deskill' jobs (see for example Braverman, 1974). For example, in the previous chapter we looked at the 'production line approach to service' (Levitt, 1972) as an influential paradigm throughout the 1970s and beyond. Increasingly, however, it is likely that mechanization not only de-skills but actually replaces jobs. Cases in point are self-service check-in kiosks at airports or self-service checkouts in supermarkets, as commonly adopted by large retailers in the UK. As you will note from the aforementioned trajectory, jobs that were lost were soon replaced with other jobs in new sectors that emerged. With self-driving cars, a realistic prospect over the next decade or two, the job of a taxi driver may well all but cease to exist, but new jobs (eg in caring occupations) will emerge. Whether or not the skills of taxi driving or manufacturing are congruent with the requirements (eg emotional skills) of the caring professions is another question.

Globalization and the future of IHRM

In the preceding section we looked at how globalization and its homogenizing forces lead to the global diffusion of technology and modes of work organization, and that such modes of work organization, while traditionally emanating from the global West, are also more recently moving in the other direction. Some would even argue that HRM itself is based to a large extent on Japanese management principles such as teamworking and direct communication (Boxall and Purcell, 2011). We also looked at the extent to which globalization facilitated offshoring as firms sought to move labour-intensive operations such as production and assembly of products and also labour-intensive service work such as entire call centres to countries with lower labour costs. However, we also looked at the more recent phenomenon of 'reshoring' as labour costs in emerging economies increase rapidly while wages in mature economies stagnate.

What does all this mean for IHRM? For one thing, the world is in a process of rapid economic rebalancing between emerging and advanced industrial economies. HRM practitioners in multinationals therefore need to be acutely aware of the potential downsides of offshoring and the potential benefits derived from keeping operations close to the market which they serve. As the wage gap between 'core' (ie high-wage countries) and 'periphery' (low-wage countries where labour but not knowledge-intensive tasks have traditionally been offshored) narrows (and probably eventually closes), the cost of outsourcing significantly increases.

Labour costs (mostly associated with labour rates as well as taxes and additional benefits as discussed in more depth in Chapter 9) are, however, only one variable an organization needs to consider when determining where to most cost-effectively carry out operations. Workforce skill levels (as examined in more depth in Chapter 10) are another key factor which is likely to shape the way in which organizations make use of the increasing freedom of movement of capital associated with globalization. For example, it is unlikely that a firm will relocate very specialized niche manufacturing activities (requiring middle-range vocational skills) to countries and regions where a low proportion of the labour force has vocational qualifications (eg gained through an apprenticeship).

Moreover, wages are just one factor with a potential impact on labour costs; other factors such as employment law (specifically, how employer or employee friendly it is), covering key aspects of the employment contract such as the relative ease with which employers can hire and fire their workforce are often considered by organizations when making decisions as to which countries to operate in. And while the trend of offshoring appears to be recently being counterbalanced by reshoring, we need to acknowledge another trend that is increasingly facilitated through globalization, namely that of 'flags of convenience' (see for example Lillie, 2004). Commonly observed in shipping but increasingly also in civil aviation (Blyton et al, 2001), flags of convenience involve companies 'shopping around' for favourable legal contexts for employment terms and conditions. Take for example the case of international shipping and the different nationalities you are likely to find represented onboard individual vessels. Officers are likely to come from the country of the owners, while crew might be from the Philippines, and the ship may sail under the flag of a third country, often Panama, Liberia or Greece (Sorge, Noorderhaven and Koen, 2015: 405). The reasons why shipping companies opt for flags of convenience are clear when examined from the perspective of their operations and employment relations. Take for example the case of US shipping companies. For one thing, legislation on health and safety and quality of work is significantly stricter in the United States than in many of the emerging economies such as Panama. Second, US seafarers would earn US wages which, while stagnating in recent years (see preceding section), are still significantly higher than those paid to seafarers in many emerging economies. Finally, US seafarers are likely to be members of either the US National Maritime Union (NMU), or the Seafarers' International Union (SIU) (see for example Mendelsohn, 2014).

Similarly, in civil aviation, Norwegian Airlines is a case in point of the benefits derived from flags of convenience. Norwegian Airlines, now running under a holding company (Norwegian Air International), has effectively circumvented Norwegian policies on corporate taxation as well as employment legislation by using flags of convenience. First, the airline evades the Norwegian corporate tax rate of 27 per cent by registering operations in Ireland, where the current corporate tax rate stands at only 12.5 per cent (Mendelsohn, 2014: 153). Second, the carrier evades Norwegian employment law, which is considered more employee friendly (in terms of aspects such as rights of temporary workers, self-employment as well as rules on dismissal) than the Irish employment law (Mendelsohn, 2014). It may well not be a coincidence that Ryanair, the airline with a reputation for the most notoriously poor working conditions in Europe and a track record of hard union suppression tactics (such as the dismissal of pilots attempting to organize their colleagues), with some 40 per cent of their pilots temporarily or self-employed (Harvey and Turnbull, 2012), operates from Ireland. However, Norwegian Air International goes a step further in terms of staff recruitment. In order to avoid paying Norwegian salaries and the significant social security contributions associated with them, the airline has set up crew bases in Bangkok (Thailand) where they recruit flight crew and cabin crew for their inter-continental flights. Additionally, they have tasked an employment agency in Singapore with the recruitment of further flight and cabin crew (European Cockpit Association, 2017). Essentially, the airline flies under a Norwegian brand, under Irish corporate regulation, with temporary/agency staff under Thai or Singaporean employment law.

Under such changing competitive environments brought about by globalization, IHRM practitioners are confronted with additional complexities. While preceding chapters (eg Chapter 8) have focused on IHRM activity in terms of multinational companies and their staffing policies, particularly regarding expatriates, globalization and the increasing opportunities associated with legal loopholes through flags of convenience (as exemplified in the aforementioned case of Norwegian Air International) have made IHRM more complicated. For example, how does one deal with IHRM activity in an organization where hardly any of the staff are actually from the home country of the organization? Increasing awareness of employment law in other countries is required to navigate these complexities.

Convergence or divergence in national systems of HRM?

In this book we have looked at some of the key etic contributions that help our understanding of cultural differences between different countries. These included Hofstede's cultural dimensions and the World Values Survey (see Chapter 2). We then also examined how these cultural factors might interplay with institutional factors. As you may recall, Chapter 5 examined hard and soft institutions such as the law (hard) and common customs (soft, eg lifetime employment in Japan) and how these institutional factors may interplay with cultural factors mentioned earlier. To finalize this book we look ahead into the future and the extent to which recent events and likely future developments are likely to influence HRM and employment relations outcomes at national level.

A good starting point is the convergence–divergence debate (see for example Katz and Darbishire, 2000). This debate revolves around the extent to which employment relations contexts around the world are becoming more similar (convergence) or whether key cultural and institutional differences remain influential. The convergence perspective has been significantly more influential, and the most common assumption amongst IHRM and employment relations scholars has been that the world is gravitating towards a liberal model of HRM and employment relations (Bamber et al, 2016: 342). Although Chapter 5 highlighted several key distinctive institutional factors, for example in the German and Japanese contexts, some of these are being increasingly eroded. Trade union density in Germany, for example, has been in steady decline over the past two decades, and the majority of the working population are now not union members. On the other hand, they still fall under sectoral agreements (or in the worst case, the minimum wage introduced in 2015 – see Chapter 5) and enjoy significantly higher employment protection (eg protection from unfair dismissal) than their counterparts in the UK and US. However, declining trade union membership levels across the globe are a key overarching trend, and one which is likely to profoundly shape the future of IHRM activity both in emerging and advanced industrial economies. This is because declining trade union membership generally cedes increasing bargaining power to management and the HRM function becomes important in creating other (non-union) channels of communication between workers and management. Whether such non-union forms of employee voice can stand the test of time in terms of sustainability and effectiveness is another question. As highlighted in the VW case study in Chapter 5, the German system of co-determination, associated with employee representation through works council representatives at supervisory board level, is often associated with the successful German manufacturing sector, where job security leads to greater employee tacit knowledge and subsequently to better innovations. At the same time, the VW case study highlighted some of the potential downsides of the CME model including an emphasis on 'insider' governance where local government and employee interests collude.

Many of the cases discussed in this book have highlighted key national differences in patterns of corporate governance, HRM and employment relations. However, we also need to acknowledge the rapid changes and cultural convergence taking place as a result of globalization. The pressures of globalization, while leading to some degree of alignment in terms of culture and institutions, are refracted in different economies and, while the legal contexts of countries can change quickly, 'soft' institutions may persist. For example, in the case of Japan, lifetime employment (ie a lifetime job guarantee) may increasingly be a myth, but average employee job tenure is still significantly longer than in the US and UK (Bamber et al, 2015). In the German case, the system of co-determination has recently been under attack in response to the emissions cheating scandal at VW (see Chapter 5); however, the system is still seen by the majority of people in Germany as an integral part of a successful and sustainable industry with a greater emphasis on manufacturing than in liberal market economies (Bamber et al, 2015). So in summary, it might well be the case that convergence (things becoming more similar) is taking place in some areas (such as legal frameworks and wages) while many distinctive features persist in different national contexts.

Key learning points

- Although much of this book has connected IHRM activity with some of the consequences of globalization, more recent trends suggest a stronger degree of public and political resistance against globalization, particularly in advanced industrial economies.

- While outsourcing to low-wage countries has been a dominant mode of organizing value chains over the last two to three decades, the tide seems to be turning, with a growing trend in mature economies towards the reshoring of low-skill work.

- The trend towards reshoring can be attributed to stagnating labour costs in advanced industrial economies and rapid wage inflation in many emerging economies, particularly China.

References

Amable, B (2000) Institutional complementarity and diversity of social systems of innovation and production, *Review of International Political Economy*, **7** (4), pp. 645–87

Bamber, G J, Lansbury, R D and Wailes, N, eds (2016) *International and Comparative Employment Relations*, Sage Publications

Blyton, P et al (2001) Globalization and trade union strategy: industrial restructuring and human resource management in the international civil aviation industry, *International Journal of Human Resource Management*, **12** (3), pp. 445–63

Boxall, P and Purcell, J (2011). *Strategy and Human Resource Management*, Palgrave Macmillan

Braverman, H (1974) *Labor and Monopoly Capital: The degradation of work in the twentieth century*, Monthly Review Press, New York

Crooks, E (2013) US manufacturers reshoring from China, *Financial Times* [online] https://www.ft.com/content/e14d6cae-249d-11e3-8905-00144feab7de

Donnan, S (2017) US Trade Chief seeks to reshore supply chain, *Financial Times* [online] https://www.ft.com/content/8dc63502-e7c7-11e6-893c-082c54a7f539

Economic Times India (2016) Automation's impact will be grave: 1 out of 4 jobs to go [online] http://economictimes.indiatimes.com/jobs/by-2021-four-out-of-10-jobs-would-be-lost-to-automation-experts/articleshow/57836659.cms

European Cockpit Association (2017) US DOT reveals EUs inability to prevent flags of convenience in civil aviation [online] https://www.eurocockpit.be/news/us-dot-reveals-eus-inability-prevent-flags-convenience-aviation

Eurostat (2017) Unemployment Statistics [online] http://ec.europa.eu/euro-stat/statistics-explained/index.php/Unemployment_statistics

Gray, J V et al (2013) The reshoring phenomenon: what supply chain academics ought to know and should do, *Journal of Supply Chain Management*, **49** (2), pp. 27–33

Hall, P A and Soskice, D W (2001) *Varieties of Capitalism: The institutional foundations of comparative advantage*, Oxford University Press, Oxford

Hall, P A and Soskice, D (2003) Varieties of capitalism and institutional complementarities, in *Institutional Conflicts and Complementarities*, eds R J Franzee Jr, P Mooslechner and M Schürz, Springer US, pp. 43–76

Harvey, G and Turnbull, P (2012) *The Development of the Low-cost Model in the European Civil Aviation Industry*, European Transport Workers' Federation, Brussels

Katz, H C and Darbishire, O R (2000) *Converging Divergences: Worldwide changes in employment systems, Vol 32*, Cornell University Press

Levitt, T (1972) Production-line approach to service, *Harvard Business Review*, **50** (5), pp. 41–52

Lillie, N (2004) Global collective bargaining on flag of convenience shipping, *British Journal of Industrial Relations*, **42** (1), pp. 47–67

Mendelsohn, A I (2014) Flags of convenience: maritime and aviation, *Journal of Air Law and Commerce*, **79**, p. 151

OECD (2017) Productivity Statistics [online] http://www.oecd.org/std/productivity-stats/

ONS (2017) Inflation and price indices [online] https://www.ons.gov.uk/economy/inflationandpriceindices

Powley, T (2014) Reshoring could create 200,000 jobs over next decade, Financial Times [online] https://www.ft.com/content/057abd80-a92c-11e3-9b71-00144feab7de

PWC (2017) Will robots steal our jobs? [online] https://www.pwc.co.uk/economic-services/ukeo/pwcukeo-section-4-automation-march-2017-v2.pdf

Sorge, A, Noorderhaven, N.G and Koen, C I (2015) *Comparative International Management*, Routledge

Taylor, F (2011) *Principles of Scientific Management*, Harper and Brothers

Zhang, L (2008) Lean production and labor controls in the Chinese automobile industry in an age of globalization, *International Labor and Working-Class History*, **73** (1), pp. 24–44

INDEX

ability tests 134
adjustment 159–60, 162–63
affective organizational commitment 175, 211
affective training approach 157
affinity bias 138
Air France 230, 231
Air India 18–19
airline industry 178, 227, 230–31
    see also Air France; Air India; American Airlines; civil aviation industry; Delta Air Lines; easyJet; Norwegian Air International; Ryanair; Southwest Airlines; United Airlines
alienation, worker 85–86, 251–52
ambassadors 126
American Airlines 233
analytical job evaluation 180–82
analytics 127, 132, 133, 134, 180–82
anticipatory adjustment 160
Apple 5, 272
appraisals 138–39
apprenticeship levies 77, 210
apprenticeships 77, 83, 205, 207–08, 210–11, 212, 244, 270
aptitude tests 134
area studies see cognitive training approach
Argentina 25, 98, 104–05, 111
artefacts, cultural 14–15
ASEAN Free Trade Agreement 100
Asia 19, 20, 38, 40, 43–44, 71, 165, 176, 252
    see also ASEAN Free Trade Agreement; China; India; Japan; Singapore; Taiwan
assertiveness 21, 38–39
assessment centres 133, 134, 135
associational power 225
asymmetry of power 222–23, 231, 235
attribution training 157
Austria 19, 80, 81, 190, 207
autocratic leadership 18, 21, 37
automotive industry 81, 211, 227, 244, 260, 264, 271
    see also car production; Toyota; Toyota Production System (TPS); Volkswagen (VW); Volvo

autonomous work groups 71, 86, 87
autonomy 185, 188, 248, 254, 255, 260
    see also autonomous work groups

bank loans 78, 79, 204
behavioural leadership 31
bench strength 130, 139, 140, 141
benchmarking 176
best practice 3, 8, 71, 83, 84, 142
bias 17, 138
biscuit manufacturing 211–13
bonuses 85, 136, 184, 185, 190
brand
    employer 121, 124–26, 132
    talent 125, 132
Brazil 6, 183, 260–64
BRIC 6
    see also Brazil; China; India
British Airways 231
BT Group 187–89
buffer inventories 87–88, 247, 251
Business Principles (Telefonica) 107–08

ca'canny 222
capability 127
capacity 127
capitalism see varieties of capitalism (VoC)
car production 6
    see also automotive industry; Toyota; Toyota Production System (TPS); Volkswagen (VW); Volvo
career development planning 141, 142
CBI 83, 176
Cepetel 111
charismatic leadership 38
Chile 271
China 5, 6, 271, 272, 273, 278
    leadership styles 38, 40
    reward systems 183, 190, 191–92
civil aviation industry 5–7, 227, 228–34, 250, 251, 275–76
    see also Air India; airline industry; easyJet; United Airlines
CLS (core labour standards) 99–100
CMEs (coordinated market economies) 75–76, 78–83, 89, 206, 214–15, 244, 270

co-determination 80, 89–91, 92, 277
codes of conduct 102
cognitive training approach 155–56
collective bargaining 77, 80, 81, 82, 84, 92, 109, 111, 227, 270
collectivism 20, 37–38, 82, 164, 189–90, 226
collectivism-individualism 20, 189–90
comfort zones 128
communication, cross-cultural 52–69, 154
Communications Workers Union 111
communicative behaviours 55, 57, 58, 61, 154
commuting 177, 187
company funding 76, 78
comparative HRM 8
compensation 141, 179–80
    see also bonuses; cost of living (allowances); market relations; minimum wage; pay management (setting); performance-based pay; wage setting
competencies 127, 133, 153
competency frameworks 127
Confederation of British Industry 83, 176
confirmation bias 138
conflict management 223
confucian dynamism 18, 22, 39–40
contingency theory 31–32
continuance organization commitment 175, 211
Convention 87 (ILO) 104–05
convergence-divergence debate 29, 32, 56, 59, 63, 83, 276–77
coordinated market economies (CMEs) 75–76, 78–83, 89, 206, 214–15, 244, 270
Copenhagen 176
core competencies 127
core industrial production 5
core labour standards (CLS) 99–100
corporate governance 76, 79, 89–91, 277
corporate social responsibility (CSR) 102, 104, 107, 109
corporate websites 132
cost of living 175–77, 187, 192
cost of living allowances 177, 187
cost of living survey (EIU) 175–76
cross-cultural adjustment 159–60
cross-cultural communication 52–69
cross-cultural leadership 35–44
cross-cultural management 9, 53, 153
cross-cultural training 58–62, 152–58, 162–65, 166
CSR (corporate social responsibility) 102, 104, 107, 109

CTrip 191–92
cultural artefacts 14–15
cultural bias 17
cultural (cultural sensitivity) training 40, 57, 154, 157
cultural (general) adjustment 160, 162–63
culture 13–28, 35, 44–45, 124, 276
    and leadership 29–51
    and reward 189–91
    see also cultural (cultural sensitivity) training; cultural (general) adjustment; culture shock
culture shock 58, 159
'culture's consequences' study (Hofstede) 18–23
customer brand 125
customer satisfaction 124, 250
CWU 111
cyclical demand 229–30, 251

Declaration of Fundamental Principles and Rights at Work (ILO) 99–100
deficit view of training 203–05
Delta Air Lines 229, 233
Denmark 19, 206, 229
    see also Copenhagen
deregulation 6–7, 32, 228–29, 271
deskilling 85, 247, 249, 273
Deutsche Bank 187
diagnosing talent requirements 127–29
Disneyland 251
distributive equity 180
divergence-convergence debate 29, 32, 56, 63, 83, 276–77
diversity training 40, 57
division of labour 5, 245–46, 252, 253, 257, 273
dual training system 206

e-recruitment 132
easyJet 174, 230, 231
Egypt 37, 39
electronic point of sale systems 249
emerging economies (markets) 3, 5, 6, 16, 53, 83, 98, 201, 271, 273
    legislation 275
    manufacturing 252
    reward systems 173, 174, 183, 274, 278
    see also peripheral industrial production
emic approach (culture) 15–16, 17
emissions scandal (VW) 90–91
emotion capital 220, 221
employee relations 76, 77, 218–42
    see also collective bargaining
employees 126, 136, 263

engagement of 32, 124, 125–26, 140,
141, 185–86, 263
performance 127, 139, 177–78, 179,
184, 191–92, 230–31
and representation 80, 83, 89, 90, 92,
101
retention of (turnover) 79, 87, 88, 124,
173, 187
see also employee relations; expatriates;
workers
employer brand 121, 124–26, 132
employment *see* employment legislation;
self-employment; zero-hours
contracts
employment legislation 98, 208, 224,
274–75
employment protection legislation 208
Employment Relations Act (1999) 224
engagement factors 185–86
see also employee engagement
enterprise unionism *81*, 82, 83, 257,
264, 270
entry level recruitment 129, 179
EPOS systems 249
equity, in compensation 179–80
equity-based finance 78
ethnocentrism 63–64, 71, 148–49
etic approach (culture) 16, 17, 18–25, 26
European Works Councils (EWCs) 80, *81*,
89, 90, 101
exclusive talent management 128–29
executive development 34
see also leadership development
executive pay 190–91
expatriates 52–53, 54, 55–67, 147, 148,
150–66
expectation management 63, 164
experiential training approach 156–57
explicit cultural manifestations 14–15
explicit knowledge 220
external agencies 133
external validity 16
extrinsic rewards (motivation) 179,
185–86, 188

fact-orientation training *see* cognitive
training approach
fashion sector 41–44
fast-fashion industry 43–44
fast-food industry 72, 248, 249
see also McDonald's
feedback, performance 34, 138, 141, 254
femininity-masculinity 21–22
field experiences 156
financial institutions 98, 130
see also Deutsche Bank
five-factor model personality tests 135

flags of convenience 275–76
flexible specialization 252–56, 272
flexible working practices 23, 187–89,
191–92
forced distribution performance
appraisals 139
Ford, Henry (Fordism) 183, 246–48, 252,
253, 255, 265, 270, 271
foreign direct investment 152
formal rules 224
Foxconn 5
France 43, 80, 83, 211, 213, 227, 254, 255
free market approach 74, 75, 77
free riding 76, 78, 79, 206
free trade agreements 100
future orientation 39

Gap 43–44
genchi genbutsu 87
gender 21–22, 38
gender egalitarianism 38
general (cultural) adjustment 160,
162–63
General Electric 139, 272
general skills 77, 205, 208, 209, 214, 244
Generation Y 126
geocentric staffing 149, *150*
Germany 7, 74, 78–81, 83, 254
employee relations 72, 73, 77, 90, 91,
190, 270, 276–77
skills development 202, 203, 205, 206,
207, 208, 211, 213, 227
see also Volkswagen (VW)
Ghana 60–66, 160–65
gig economy 219, 235
Global Compact (UN) 101, 107
global labour governance 97–116
global leadership and organizational
behaviour (GLOBE) 36–40
global recruitment strategy 152
Global Reporting Initiative (GRI) 102, 107
Global Union Federations (GUFs) 103,
104, 105–06, 108
globalization 5–7, 26, 29–30, 32, 53, 113,
164–65, 227–28, 271, 274–76
goal setting 141
Google *125*, 126, 129, 177, 182–83
governance
corporate 76, 79, 89–91, 277
labour 97–116
governments 5–7, 77, 206, 208–13, 224–25
Greece 36, 275
group-building training methods 155
group interviews 134
groupthink 138
Guidelines for Multinational Enterprises
(OECD) 101

halo and horns effect 138
hands-on training methods 155
hard institutions 72–74
Hay Group total reward framework *186*
HCCOs (human capital-centric
    organizations) 124
HCNs 148, 149, *150*, 152, 161
Herzberg, Frederick 184–85
hierarchy of needs (Maslow) 179,
    184–85
high humane orientation 40
high margin service work 202
high performance orientation 40
high power distance (PD) 18–19, 37
high skill service work 201
high uncertainty avoidance (UA) 19–20
high volume service work 202
Hitachi 178
home working (homeshoring) 187–89,
    191–92
horizontal coordination 40
host-country nationals (HCNs) 148, 149,
    150, 152, 161
hot desking 187
hourensou 87
human capital 33, 124, 220–21, 222
human capital-centric organizations
    (HCCOs) 124
humane leadership 39
humane orientation 40
Hunt, Jeremy 182
hygiene factors 184–85

iceberg metaphor, culture 14–15
'ideal types' of varieties of capitalism
    76–82
ideographic view, culture 25
IFAs (international framework
    agreements) 98, 103–04, 107–12
IG Metall 80, 81, 90, 91
Ikea 255
ILO 97, *98*, 99–100, 104–05
immersion 156–57
implicit cultural manifestations *14*, 15
implicit leadership theory (ILT) 32–33
in-country adjustment 160
in-group collectivism 37–38
India 6, 22, 193, 201, 271, 273
individual interviews 134
individualism 20, 189–90, 226, 231
industrialized economies (mature
    markets) 5, 6, 22, 24, 252, 271,
    272–74
informal rules 223–24

information giving *see* cognitive training
    approach
information-acquiring approach to cross-
    cultural training of expatriates
    155–56
inside perspective *see* emic approach
institutional complementarity 73, 78
institutional factors 70–96, 104, 189–91
institutions, defined 72–74, 82
instructions 65
intellectual capital 220
inter-cultural workshops 157
interactive service work 250–52
internal benchmarking 176
international framework agreements
    (IFAs) 98, 103–04, 107–12
International Labour Organization
    (ILO) 97, *98*, 99–100, 104–05
international recruitment strategy 152
internationalization 4–7
Internship, The 126
interpretivism 16
interviews *133*, 134, 137
intrinsic reward (motivation) 179, 185–86
    see also non-monetary reward
inventories, buffer 87–88, 247, 251
investment 152
Involvement and Partnership Association
    (IPA) 226
Ireland 19, 39, 98, 111, 232, 275
Israel 39

Japan 26, 71, 72, 74, 81–88, 178, 190,
    202–03, 208, 277
    see also enterprise unionism
job advertisements 136
job analysis 130
job descriptions 130
job design 34, 245, 253, 254, 255
    see also job redesign; work organization
job enrichment 253
job evaluation 180–82
job previews 132
job redesign 254–55, 264, 270
just in time production (JIT production) 85,
    86, 88

knowledge 5, 200, 207, 208, 212, 220
knowledge-intensive activities 5

labour costs 230–31, 274
labour governance 97–116
labour-management partnership 226–27
labour market restructuring 183, 200–08

labour power 222–23
labour process 221
labour standards 99–100
language 55, 56–58, 63
language training 59–60, 67, 158,
        163, 165
Latin America 38, 104, 108–09
leader development 33
leadership 29–51
        autocratic 18, *21*
leadership development 33–35, 41–42
leadership theory 30–33, 36–40
lean manufacturing 85, 86, 88, 256–64,
        271
learn by doing 156–57
legislation 104–05
        employment 98, 208, 224, 274–75
liberal market economies (LMEs) 74, 75,
        76–80, 83, 203–05, 209–10, 214,
        244, 270
lifetime employment 82, 277
living cost allowance 177, 187
London (weighting allowance) 176–77, 187
long-term versus short-term orientation 22
low-fares airlines 230–34
low humane orientation 40
low-margin service work 202
low performance orientation 40
low power distance (small power
        distance) 19, 37
low-skill service work 201
low uncertainty avoidance (UA) 20
low volume service work 202
        see also easyJet; Norwegian Air
        International; Ryanair; Southwest
        Airlines
Lufthansa 230, 231

McDonald's 72, 200, 248
McKinsey-GE nine-box grid 139–40
macro level IHRM 7–8, 72
management boards 80, 89–90
management style 226–27
        see also conflict management; cross-
        cultural management; managerial
        relations
managerial relations 219
manufacturing sector 81, 85, 183, 200–03,
        207, 208–09, 211–13, 243–45,
        251–53
        see also lean manufacturing
market mechanisms 75
        see also free market approach
market rates (pay) 175
market relations 219
masculinity-femininity 21–22

Maslow, Abraham 179, 184–85
mature markets (industrialized
        economies) 5, 6, 22, 24, 252, 271,
        272–74
May, Theresa 83
mechanization 273–74
MERCOSUR 100
meso level IHRM 8, 72
micro level IHRM 9
minimum wage 72, 73, 77, 80, 83
motivation theories 179, 184–85
moving assembly lines 246–49
multi-domestic / national recruitment
        strategy 152
multi-stakeholder initiatives 102–03
multiculturism 54–55, 164–65

NAFTA 100
National Health Service job
        evaluation 180–82
National Instruments 140–42
Nationwide Building Society 177
nature versus nuture 24–25
nenko system 72, 190
neo-liberalism 74, 76, 77
Netherlands 7, 22, 41, 79, 211, 213
new employee integration 263
new leadership theories 32
NHS job evaluation 180–82
nomothetic approach *see* etic approach
non-analytical job evaluation 180
non-governmental organizations
        (NGOs) *98*, 102–03
non-market mechanisms 75
non-monetary reward 173, 182–85
        see also intrinsic reward (motivation)
non-verbal expressions (language) 55, 58
normative organizational commitment 20,
        175, 188
North America 39, 53, 86, 189, 228, 257
        see also United States (US)
North Atlantic Free Trade Agreement 100
North Korea 37, 76
Norwegian Air International 193, 228, 231,
        232, 275–76

OECD *98*, 101, 205
offshoring 5, 105, 272
Ohno, Taiichi 256
O'Leary, Michael 204
open skies agreements 7
organizational commitment 20, 175, 188,
        211, 224
organizational culture 124
        see also human capital-centric
        organizations (HCCOs)

organizational structure 34–35, 105, 124, 160
Osborne, George 210
O2 Ireland 111
outside perspective *see* etic approach
outsourcing 5, 227

Panasonic 178
panel interviews 134
parent-country nationals (PCNs) 148, 149, *150*, 151, 161–62
participative leadership 38, 40
paternalism 18–19, 40
patient capital 78, 79
pay management (setting) 173–79, 190–91
    see also bonuses; compensation; cost of living (allowances); market relations; minimum wage; performance-based pay; sectoral-level pay bargaining; wage setting
pay ratios 190–91
PD (power distance) 18–19, 37, 190
Peck, Art 43–44
People Platform (National Instruments) 140–41
performance 127, 139, 177–78, 179, 184, 191–92, 230–31
performance appraisals 138–39
performance-based pay 183–85, 190
    see also piece-rate system (output-based system)
performance feedback 34, 138, 141, 254
performance management 138–40, 254
performance orientation 39–40
performance reviews 141
peripheral industrial production 5, 257
    see also emerging economies
person specifications 130–31
personality questionnaires *133*, 134–35
Peru 110
Peter Principle 128
phone interviews 134
physical capital 220
piece-rate system (output-based system) 85, 179, 183–84, 245–46
planning talent requirements 127–29
pluralist frame of reference 223
poaching 78, 79, 204, 206, 214
points-based job evaluation 180–82
Poland 25
political context 105–06
polycentric staffing 148, *149*
Portugal 20, 36
positivism 16–17
power 178, 182, 222–23, 225, 231, 235
power distance (PD) 18–19, 37, 190

presentation training methods 155
private sector 102–03
procedural equity 180
'product to market' business transformation initiatives 44
production management 244
protectionism 271, 273
psychological adjustment 159
psychometric testing 134–35
public bond market finance 78
public opinion 225
Puerto Rico 104

quality 85, 86–88

rational-secular societies 23
Reagan, Ronald 7, 74, 225
recruitment 129–38, 148, 151–52, 179
reference checks 137
referrals, employee 136
regime shopping 227, 228
regiocentric staffing 149, *150*, 161–62
relational adjustment 160
research, leadership 35
reshoring 227, 272–74, 275, 278
retention (turnover) 79, 87, 88, 124, 173, 187
'Rethinking Education' (EC) 210
reward 172–98
    see also bonuses; compensation; cost of living (allowances); market relations; pay management (setting)
risk aversion 20
rules 223–24
Ryanair 204, 228, 229, 230, 231

San Francisco 177
satisfaction mirror 251
Scandinavia 38
    see also Denmark; Norwegian Air International; Sweden
scientific management 85–86, 179, 183–84, 245–46, 248–52, 257, 273
SCOs 124
sectoral-level pay bargaining 80, *81*
selection, employee 129–38
self-employment 219
self-expression values 23–24
self-reporting 16, 17, 135, 205
semi-structured interviews 134
seniority (pay) 178–79, 190
sensitivity training 40, 157
service sector 201–02, 205, 208, 215, 248–52
shareholders 76, 79, 80, 89, 90, 108, 204, 206, 233

shipping sector 275
short-term versus long-term orientation 22
shortlisting candidates 132
Siemens 207
Singapore 175, 176, 201, 210
skill equilibria 200, 209
skill variety 254
skills (development) 34, 77, 199–217, 253, 244, 254, 274
    see also apprenticeships; deskilling
Skullcandy 135–37
small power distance (low power distance) 19, 37
Social Accountability 8000 102-03
Social and Labour Commission 100
social capital 33, 34, 221
social media 126, 132
social production management 244
societal collectivism 37
socio-cultural adjustment 159
soft institutions 72–74
soft skills 202, 205, 208
soldiering 85, 246
South Korea 6, 202, 203, 208
Southern Europe 38
Southwest Airlines 174, 228, 232–34
spatial juridical fixes 227–28
staffing 146–71
status quo bias 138
steel production 6
strategic relevance (pay) 177–78, 182
strategy
    organizational 124
    recruitment 151–52
stretch assignments 128
strike action 222, 230
structural power 178, 182, 222
structure-centric organizations 124
structured antagonism 223–24
structured interviews 134
Sub-Saharan business culture 55
subconscious beliefs (underlying beliefs) 14, 15
succession planning 139–40
supervisory boards 80, 89–90, 91, 277
survival values 23, 24
Sweden 23–24, 38, 77, 79, 254–55, 260, 271

tacit knowledge 207, 208, 212, 220
Taiwan 208–09
talent, defined 121–22
talent anchor concept 122–35
talent brand 125, 132
talent management 119–45
'talent on demand' framework 130

talent reviews 140
talentship evolution 127
task identity 254
task significance 254
Tata Steel 177
Taylor, Frederick (Taylorism) 85–86, 179, 183–84, 245–46, 248–52, 257, 270, 273
TCNs 148, 149, 150, 151, 161–62
team leaders 87
teams 39, 54–55, 65
    see also autonomous work groups
technical production management 244
telecommuting 187–89
Telefonica International Framework Agreement 98, 107–12
tertiary education sector 205
testing 133, 134–35
Thatcher, Margaret 7, 74, 225
third-country nationals (TCNs) 148, 149, 150, 151, 161–62
time and motion studies 246
time management 63, 164
tiorey 262
top 10 global companies (to work for) 125
total quality management 85, 86–88
total reward 185–86, 192–93
Toyota 178
Toyota Production System (TPS) 85, 86–88, 256–64
trade, and labour standards 100
trade barriers 5
Trade Union Act (2016) 224–25
traditional HRM activities 120
traditional societies 23
training 34, 77–79, 83, 92, 199–217, 227, 263
    cross-cultural 58–62, 152–58, 162–66
    cultural sensitivity 40, 57
    language 59–60, 67, 158, 163, 165
    see also apprenticeships; executive development; leadership development programmes
trait approach, leadership studies 31
transactional leadership 32
transfer of training 205
transferable skills 200
transformational leadership (TFL) 32, 34
transnational recruitment strategy 152
Truchard, Dr James (Dr T) 140
Trump, Donald 271, 273
Turkey 39
turnover (retention) 79, 87, 88, 124, 173, 187

2008 financial crisis 24
two-tier board structure 80, 89–90

uncertainty avoidance (UA) 19–20, 36–37
underlying beliefs (subconscious beliefs)
    14, 15
UNI 108–10
Unilever 192–93
unions (trades unions) 72, 97, *98*, 112, 206,
    224–28
    Argentina 104–05, 111
    France 254
    Germany 73, 80, 81, 90, 91, 276–77
    Ireland 111
    Japan 81, 82, 83
    Peru 110
    US 77, 80, 233–34
    see also collective bargaining; enterprise
        unionism; Global Union Federations
        (GUFs)
unitary frame of reference 223
United Airlines 126, 229
United Kingdom (UK) 7, 22, 72, 77, 83,
    271–73, 277
    employee relations 224–25, 227
    reward systems 173, 183, 190
    skills development 200–03, 205, 208,
        209–10, 211–13
United Nations (UN) *98*, 101, 176
    Global Compact 101, 107
United States (US) 7, 37, 39, 72, 73, 83,
    154, 271, 272–73, 277
    employee relations 76–77, 80, 229,
        233–34
    reward systems 173, 177–78, 182,
        190–91
    shipping sector 275
    skills development 201, 202–03, 205, 208
    US-Cambodian Free Trade
        Agreement 100
    US-Jordan Free Trade Agreement 100
    see also North America
unstructured interviews 134

values *14*, 15, 23–24, 57
varieties of capitalism (VoC) 74–83, 200,
    208, 269–70
video interviews 134
visionary leadership 39
vocational training 206, 207–13
Volkswagen (VW) 76, 89–91, 277
voluntarism 77–79, 203
Volvo 254–55, *260*

wage setting 77, 124, 173
    see also minimum wage
Walmart 73
websites 132
weighting allowances 177, 187
work adjustment 160
work behaviours (cross-cultural) 164
work humanization 254
work organization 243–68
    see also Ford, Henry (Fordism);
        scientific management; Taylor,
        Frederick (Taylorism); total quality
        management; Toyota Production
        System (TPS)
work-life balance 23–24
work to rule 224
worker influence 224–25,
    231–34
workers 222, 224–25, 231–34
    alienation of 85–86, 251–52
    see also employees; expatriates
works councils 80, *81*, 89, 90,
    101
workshops 157
World Trade Organization (WTO)
    100
World Values Survey 23–24

Yahoo 189
yuchi 262

Zara 43
zero-hours contracts 272